JUNG AND EDUCATION

Elements of an Archetypal Pedagogy

Clifford Mayes

Rowman & Littlefield Education
Lanham, Maryland • Toronto • Oxford
2005

KH

Published in the United States of America
by Rowman & Litttlefield Education
An imprint of The Rowman & Littlefield Publishing Group, Inc.
4501 Forbes Boulevard, Suite 200, Lanham, Maryland 20706
www.rowmaneducation.com

PO Box 317
Oxford
OX2 9RU, UK

British Library Cataloguing in Publication Information Available

Library of Congress Cataloging-in-Publication Data
Mayes, Clifford.
  Jung and education : elements of an archetypal pedagogy /
Clifford Mayes.
       p. cm.
  Includes bibliographical references and index.
  ISBN 1-57886-254-X (pbk. : alk. paper)
  1. Jung, C. G. (Carl Gustav), 1875–1961. 2. Educational
psychology. 3. Archetype (Psychology) I. Title.
  LB775.J85M39 2005
  370.15—dc22

                                           2005000087

∞™ The paper used in this publication meets the minimum requirements of
American National Standard for Information Sciences—Permanence of Paper
for Printed Library Materials, ANSI/NISO Z39.48-1992.
Manufactured in the United States of America.

9/19/06

TABLE OF CONTENTS

FOREWORD

Although Jung published only three papers specifically on education in his *Collected Works*, namely "Child Development and Education," "Analytical Psychology and Education," and "The Significance of the Unconscious in Individual Education," all in volume 17, one might say that education of the soul was a chief preoccupation of his lifelong attention to the psyche. He clearly enunciated his belief that even in psychotherapy, the work of catharsis (emotional cleansing) was to be followed by education or intellectual understanding of the individual's psyche. He also warned against what he called the *furor paedagogicus*, the emotional possession that tries to solve every problem or cure all ills by means of the educational process. But he said the same thing about the *furor therapeuticus* as well. Balance, or integration of the opposites resulting in wholeness, was his constant refrain.

Despite Jung's central interest in education, there has been, to my knowledge, no single book that has discussed what Jungian psychology can contribute to the educational process—until, that is, the lively, graceful, and informative work at hand by Professor Clifford Mayes. He has done this with remarkable erudition, along with feeling and a practical sense of what is relevant and useful in Jung's work for the educational endeavor.

He accomplishes this feat by first presenting a concise and accurate review of the elements of Jungian psychology, even including areas where there is considerable discussion and conflict within the professional field itself. Professor Mayes comes by this honestly, having had a Jungian analysis himself (a requirement for all Jungian analysts) and by keeping up, amazingly, with the literature of almost every aspect of the field itself. He combines a lively and deeply committed connection to the archetypal depths, along with an understanding of the "developmental" branch of Jungian scholarship and therapy, which focuses on infancy and childhood, along with other depth psychological perspectives.[1] The latter interest, he has pointed out, is particularly important for the educator, who perforce needs to be informed on such matters.

Professor Mayes also takes up, for example, the rather abstruse issue of whether or not Jung was "religious," concluding that he was and that Jung was "one, who in the midst of the dogmatic materialism of the late nineteenth and early twentieth centuries—and in the face of considerable opposition dared to introduce, examine, and honor spirituality in the study of the human psyche. For that alone we owe him an enormous debt of gratitude." Professor Mayes is surely right, and one wonders why anyone who has read Jung's *Memories, Dreams, Reflections* could think otherwise. The answer is that Jung had an empirical, scientific attitude along with spirituality based on his own experience of the divine. That is how he could legitimately suggest the empirical concept of the Self, the divine image in the human soul.

The second half of the book, "Elements of an Archetypal Pedagogy," more fully reveals Professor Mayes's originality, the product of many years of reflection and teaching. His "ten pillars" of a Jungian approach to curriculum and instruction begin with a central attitude: Because of the archetypal nature of the teacher/student relationship, there is a certain sanctity to this work and therefore overly stressing technical proficiency or abstract intellectualism should be avoided. Professor Mayes strongly states his case against the corporatization of schooling, merely turning out "worker-citizens" who contribute to the global economy, forgetting the needs of the soul, individuality, and wholeness. This is surely a desideratum, but is it not apparent that the technological approach seems to be a practical necessity of the working class, while the longed-for wholeness/individuality approach is a luxury granted to wealthier citizens who can afford private education? Think of the New England prep academies and their more Socratic approach versus the technical schools advertised on television in urban centers. I wonder what Professor Mayes or Jung would suggest to bring that wholeness to students despite the barriers of class and custom?

The second and third pillars suggest that subject matter in the classroom should be mined for archetypal themes and that the intuitive function be nurtured, something rather difficult for an extraverted and sensate society oriented toward facts and techniques. His fourth pillar, allowing students to "fail" productively and with support, resulting in deeper moral and intellectual growth, is indeed revolutionary and would be truly splendid if accomplished by sensitive and informed teachers. The same can be said for Professor Mayes's fifth pillar, which suggests that teachers need to be aware of transference dynamics, something he takes up fully, knowledgeably, and helpfully later on. The sixth and seventh pillars, asking that the child be addressed holistically and be helped to explore and affirm the culture in which he or she lives and also be empowered to build on that, is surely less controversial. But the last pillar—and most important from my point of view—is the need for teachers to experience a sense of calling, what we used to call "vocation," that would enable them to practice on the basis of archetypal energy and enhance their growth as well as that of their students. This is, for me, the main aspect of being a Jungian psychotherapist: helping clients connect to their inner authority, the Self, and discover their own "vocation" in life, in a spiritual and practical sense. If teachers could do this too, in their own way, it would be a blessing indeed.

In the chapter on the foundations of a Jungian approach to curriculum and instruction, Professor Mayes usefully quotes Jung's suggestion that the educator, in order to understand the mentality of his or her students, should pay attention to the findings of analytical psychology but should not, as unfortunately sometimes happens, unload this information on the child. This happens, alas, when diagnostic categories are employed inappropriately. As Professor Mayes warns, although teaching has a therapeutic aspect, the teacher needs to remember that he or she is not a therapist.

Chapter 7, "Reflecting on the Archetypes of Teaching," is indeed a gem and presents, in a most helpful way, Professor Mayes's own story of his classroom experiences and the wisdom gained thereby. If this were a book review rather than a foreword, I would surely recount some of this but luckily, since the book is in the hand of the reader, this is simply a hint of what lies ahead. The same can be said for the recounting of synchronistic events that occur in the classroom, via dreams and events. This must be exciting stuff for Professor Mayes's students and a wonderful example of how the living depths can be meaningfully experienced thereby.

As noted above, Professor Mayes notes that "the most fundamental implication of Jungian psychology for education is that there is a certain sanctity in the teacher-student relationship." If that fact is acknowledged and accepted, then good things will certainly flow from it in terms of classroom practice. If the reader needs any further indication of why I recommend this book, I can say that I am passing it along to two teachers in my practice—one a senior professor of education and the other, tellingly, my daughter, an excellent teacher who relies considerably on the philosophy of Rudolf Steiner (the schooling of my grandson), a viewpoint that Professor Mayes also values.

J. Marvin Spiegelman
Los Angeles
October 2004

NOTE

1. "Depth psychology" refers to any approach to perception, cognition, and emotion that acknowledges the existence of subconscious and unconscious processes. The depth psychologies assert that these processes often influence an individual's conscious thoughts and actions.

ACKNOWLEDGMENTS

In a sense, I started writing this book in 1970 when, as a sophomore at the University of California at Irvine, I picked up my first book by Carl Jung—a dog-eared, passionately underlined copy of *Man and His Symbols* that my girlfriend was reading. Since that time, Jung has been an integral part of my intellectual and spiritual journey. In the three succeeding decades I have spent in academe, there have been many scholarly writers whom I have liked very much and even a few whom I have loved. However, the only one to whom I turn again and again because his work never grows old but always seems, amazingly, to be able to offer new treasures of insight and unexplored terrains for exploration is C. G. Jung. To him I owe an enormous personal and professional debt, which I hope this book in some small measure discharges.

I am also grateful to have been so ably mentored in the archetypal analysis of literature in graduate school at the University of Oregon in the late 1970s by my beloved professor and great formalist literary critic, the late W. J. Handy. Now, these many years later, I continue to be blessed by the privilege of associating with friends and colleagues who have helped me develop as a student of Jungian theory. Foremost among these is Dr. J. Marvin Spiegelman—a Jungian analyst who, in my view, is one of the most intellectually significant and spiritually courageous neo-Jungians writing and practicing today. He has graciously shared his time and wisdom with me over the last several years since I first heard him speak at the C. G. Jung Institute in Los Angeles, after having just read his groundbreaking work *Psychotherapy as a Mutual Process*. Since that time, his body of writings has shed considerable light for me on Jung's foundational ideas while, at the same time, extending those ideas in bold new ways. My research into synchronicity in the classroom really began the evening I first heard Marvin speak at the Jung Institute, and my work on transferential dynamics in the classroom has been much enriched by conversations with him.

I lovingly give thanks to my colleagues at Brigham Young University for their support. Professor Joe Matthews is the consummate educational scholar/practitioner. His ability to synthesize theory and praxis is a model that the rest of us in our department are always trying to emulate. I have turned to him many times over the years in order to try to achieve a similar blend of the paradigmatic and practical in my own work. About Professor Robert Bullough, the director of the BYU Center for the Improvement of Teacher Education and Schooling in the McKay School of Education, I can only say that he thinks more broadly and deeply about educational issues than any scholar I have ever personally known. Despite an impossibly busy schedule, he always seems to find time to read my manuscripts and offer a perfect mix of kind encouragement and straight-talking critique that makes my work better. Professor Vance Randall, the chair of the Department of Educational Leadership and Foundations, in which I work, is, in addition to his widely acknowledged importance as a scholar of U.S. educational policy, a dear friend and supportive leader who brings a large measure of grace and goodness to our department-family. I am also grateful to Professor Ellen Williams for her enthusiastic responses and valuable insights regarding my previous books. I have frequently drawn on her inexhaustible energy and ready wisdom in writing this present book.

I am indebted to Professor Robert Carson, chairman of the Department of Education at Montana State University, Bozeman, for sharing with me over the years his elegant vision of the integrated curriculum. It has been exciting and educative for me to observe the evolution of his *Ourstory* approach to curriculum—one that is culturally, historically, and ideologically compelling and encompassing.

I owe much to Professor Robert Boostrom, coauthor of *Thinking: The Foundation of Critical and Creative Learning in the Classroom* and the U.S. editor of the *Journal of Curriculum Studies*, who has supported and guided me in my work on Jung and education when others were not willing to take a chance on a topic that did not fit easily into mainstream academic discourse. I am also grateful to my research assistants, Katherine Pratt and Laura Von Arx, for their unfailing kindness and competence.

Some of my most valuable help has come from outside academia. Gene "Mortalman" Gillespie—my dear friend since we were boys in Tucson, Arizona, and an artist of vision and integrity—has always challenged me to go more deeply, see more clearly, and speak more honestly, continuing to do so in reading and commenting on various drafts of this book. Victoria Hanley took valuable time out of her own busy schedule as an author of young adult fiction to edit the final draft of this study, which now reads more gracefully because of her deft touch.

All of these people have played important roles in my intellectual and spiritual growth, and they have certainly helped me do the best I can in writing this book. Whatever inadequacies and errors remain in this present study, despite these good people's best efforts, are entirely my own doing and responsibility.

I am inexpressibly thankful for my children Josh, Lizzy, and Dana for simply being who they are—ethical, loving, gifted, and exciting young people whom I am honored to know and whom I will always love, here and hereafter. My wife, Dr. Pam Mayes, a Jungian-oriented therapist, is simply the smartest and wisest person whom I have ever known. In virtually every respect, she is my superior. Yet, owing to her tender heart, she never makes me feel that way, never fails to support me with inexhaustible compassion, and even allows me to believe (usually erroneously) that I have arrived at some insight that she had never thought of before!

Above all I shall ever be grateful for a loving Father in Heaven. Despite my many blatant inadequacies, He never gives up on me but always sends me just what I need, just when I need it, and yet almost always in a manner and form that I would have least expected. It is *from* Him, I believe, that all that is good fundamentally comes, and it is *to* Him that all that is good ultimately points.

PERMISSIONS

Various scholarly journals have also allowed me to explore and express my ideas about Jung and education over the last several years, and to their editors and reviewers I am sincerely grateful for having both encouraged and critiqued my work so amiably and constructively. Hence, much of chapter 7 first appeared in 2003, as an article entitled "Foundations of an Archetypal Pedagogy" in *Psychological Perspectives: A Semiannual Journal of Jungian Thought of the C. G. Jung Institute of Los Angeles*. Chapter 8, which deals with transference in educational settings, is based on a longer study of mine that was published in 2002, as "Personal and Archetypal Aspects of Transference and Counter-transference in the Classroom" in *Encounter: Education for Meaning and Social Justice*. Finally, chapter 9 is based on "The Teacher as an Archetype of Spirit," which appeared in 2002, in the *Journal of Curriculum Studies*.

INTRODUCTION: WHY JUNG?

In the last decade or so, there has been a marked increase in educational research and practice regarding the work of the Swiss psychiatrist Carl G. Jung. I believe that there are several reasons for this heightened interest.

First, Jung was perhaps the first major psychologist of the twentieth century to take ethical and spiritual issues seriously—as being important in their own right and essential to psychological health, which consisted, he believed, in bringing all of the rich and varied aspects of the psyche into harmonious interaction. His psychology was, as he said, "holistic." As such, it laid crucial psychological groundwork for not only the modern holistic education movement but also many of the educational theories and practices that have attempted over the last eighty years or so to resist the ongoing federal agenda of both conservative and liberal administrations of turning schools into training centers for obedient "worker-citizens," cogs in the transnational corporate machine. According to Jung, the ultimate goal of psychic functioning is to discover oneself personally, politically, and culturally as an integrated being who lives in the light of a commitment to a transcendent truth. Thus, Jung launched what has now come to be known as the "transpersonal psychology" movement, which, never ignoring personal psychodynamics, fundamentally stresses the individual's transpersonal commitments and how they can be key in providing wholeness to a psyche at odds with itself.

For Jung, these commitments did not need to be tied to a specific doctrine or set of practices. Jung's own psychospiritual explorations were quite unique. Although he was affected by a wide range of cultural and religious perspectives of both the West and East, he did not sign on to any particular dogma or party affiliation. And this brings us to the second reason for Jung's appeal to a growing number of scholars and teachers. He provides a way to explore psychospiritual issues in a very inviting fashion—one which is able to engage in conversation with individuals from other spiritual perspectives and traditions so that everyone involved might be edified and expanded psychologically, politically, and spiritually. Jungian psychology offers a way to frame our educational questions, interests, and practices so that we can learn from each other's deepest beliefs without either imposing or negating our own beliefs in the process, whether those beliefs are "formal" or "informal." Jungian terms and techniques provide a way to carry on fruitful and friendly psychospiritual dialogue in a multicultural, postmodern environment.

A third reason for the heightened interest in Jung is an outgrowth of the first and second. Jungian concepts offer ways to engage with our students, and help them engage with each other, about ethical and spiritual matters in legally and institutionally acceptable ways. Similarly, they allow us to *engage with ourselves*—through deeply introspective processes—about the powerful psychospiritual dynamics that have shaped our decision to become educators and school leaders, that influence how we practice our craft, and that can be mined for clues about how to become even more pedagogically effective and spiritually satisfied in what we do. In a day and age when political agendas for educational "reform" are making it increasingly difficult for us to maintain our sense of ethical and spiritual purpose as teachers, we need to be able to renew our sense of "calling." Jungian psychology offers many ways to do just that, as this book attempts to demonstrate.

Despite the growing interest in Jungian psychology's enormous potential to enrich educational theory and practice, and despite a few interesting articles along these lines recently, there has as yet been no book-length study of Jung that caters especially to educators. I mean for this book to fill that void and offer examples of and suggestions for further scholarship and practice along Jungian lines. There are several reasons for my doing so.

First, my work over the last six years has been acknowledged to be on the leading edge of Jungian educational research. Second, in addition to being a professor of the history of education in an educational leadership graduate program, I am also a Jungian-oriented counselor, so I understand how Jungian ideas and techniques for psychospiritual discovery and recovery play out concretely in a wide variety of contexts and for many different purposes—including educational ones. And finally, as a teacher of educational history, I am interested in the social precedents and ramifications of Jungian psychology, a topic that has become of some interest in the Jungian literature generally over the last several decades.

The reader will note that the book is divided into two major parts. Part I is an introduction to the psychology of C. G. Jung. In clear terms and with many examples, the most central concepts in Jungian psychology are explained. This is important because, in my view, too much of the work on Jung and education that *does* exist evidences only a very incomplete and sometimes even incorrect understanding of Jung, picking and choosing from among his many, often difficult concepts in a way that is theoretically and pedagogically shallow. If we seriously want to muster the greatness of Jungian psychology for educational topics and practices, we need to *understand* that psychology in the first place.

By the end of part I, the reader should have a good grasp of such pivotal Jungian notions as archetypes and archetypal images, persona, shadow, *enantiodromia*, anima and animus, the transcendent function, synchronicity, the Self, and the collective unconscious. He or she will also know the rudiments of Jungian typology, Jung's view on a therapeutic phenomenon with many educational implications called *the transference/countertransference*, his pioneering model of psychosocial development, and some of the most relevant political aspects of Jungian theory.

Part II applies these and other ideas from Jung's writings to a wide variety of educational issues. I begin by examining the archetypal nature of the student–teacher relationship and how it is endangered by both liberal and conservative federal agendas to make education dance to the tune of business. I go on to detail a Jungian approach to the theory of the curriculum. Next, I turn to the use of Jungian terms and techniques to provide examples of how they can be used to help the teacher deepen his understanding of himself, his "calling," and his classroom practice— and in the process help his students discover themselves more profoundly in relationship to the teacher, the curriculum, and each other. To help readers engage in these kinds of reflective processes and practices, I have provided topics for group discussion, individual reflection, and research at the end of each chapter in part II.

After that, I discuss how Jung's envisaging of the therapeutic dynamic between analyst and analysand can help teachers clarify and enhance their relationships with their students. Finally, I examine various images of teachers that have emerged in the last several decades in the literature regarding the educator's sense of calling and purpose, concluding that they fall into four major archetypal categories—the teacher as a philosopher, the teacher as a federal prophet of democracy, the teacher as a Zen master, and the teacher as a priest. The study winds up with a review of the ground covered as well as suggestions for further theoretical and practical explorations.

In order to avoid sexist pronoun usage, I have employed the male pronouns as the general ones in chapters 1, 3, 5, 6, and 9, and the female pronouns in chapters 2, 4, 7, 8, and 10. I believe this is fair and avoids the frequent stylistic dilemmas caused by the rhetorically unwieldy "he or she" and "he/she." Furthermore, I follow the convention in Jungian scholarship of referring to Jung's writings by indicating which of the volumes from the more than twenty volumes of his *Collected Works* (*CW*) and which numbered paragraph or paragraphs within that volume (i.e., *par.* or *pars.*) contain the reference. Thus, the reference *CW* 10, par. 145 refers to paragraph 145 in the tenth volume of the *Collected Works*.

So without further ado, let us begin our journey into the exciting territory of Jungian psychology and its educational applications.

I

ELEMENTS OF
JUNGIAN PSYCHOLOGY

❶

PERSONA, SHADOW, AND ARCHETYPE

THE FREUD-JUNG YEARS

Many of the most important roots of Jungian psychology, or *analytical psychology* as it is also known, are in Freudian psychology—or *psychoanalysis*. The similarity between the terms *analytical psychology* and *psychoanalysis* is not a coincidence, for Jung's prominence as a psychiatrist, researcher, and theoretician began through his association with Sigmund Freud. Their professional collaboration, beginning so auspiciously in 1907, when Jung was thirty-two years old, ended acrimoniously a mere six years later with the publication of Jung's work *Psychology of the Unconscious*. This book, although indebted to Freud's pioneering explorations into the regions beyond ego consciousness, took that journey much farther, into much deeper psychospiritual realms than Freud, the nineteenth-century Darwinian rationalist, wished. The personal and professional rupture between Freud and Jung was traumatic for both men, interrupting as it did their self-styled father–son relationship. Early in that relationship, Freud had called Jung his "crown prince." Freud felt that it was the brilliant young doctor from Zurich, Carl Jung, who would carry the dogmas and practices of psychoanalysis into the promised land of not only medical and philosophical acceptance but dominance.

Freud's successor, then, would not be one of his many fellow Jewish associates in Vienna. It would be a Swiss disciple whose father had been a Protestant country minister. Some have speculated that Freud's enthusiasm about Jung may have had something to do with the hope that Jung's presence would lend psychoanalysis a certain air of gentile respectability. This is something that Freud may well have wanted, given the fact that certain members of the psychiatric establishment may have dismissed him, his largely Jewish followers, and his peculiar new theories—replete with mysterious language, heterodox practices, and an emphasis on fertility and blood—as a strictly Jewish affair, even a sort of Kabalistic mysticism disguised as medical psychology (Stevens 1999). Of course, talk of infantile sexuality, incest, patricide, perversion, and darkly repressed psychic further marginalized Freud in the eyes of some member of the polite academic elite.[1]

How much such considerations might have played into Freud's professional "adoption" of Jung, we can never know, but one thing is clear: In Jung, Freud immediately recognized a kindred spirit whose passion and potential, and whose breadth of learning and depth of insight, exceeded even the most talented of his other gifted disciples. Unfortunately for both men—and for the history of twentieth-century psychology—this alliance would not last long. The problem lay in Freud's insistence that sexual instincts were the foundation of all psychic functions and dysfunctions—a notion with which Jung was never quite comfortable, even during the height of his association with Freud (CW 4).

Actually, this critique of Freud—which has become a popular tool for caricaturing and dismissing the man and his theories—is not completely fair. As early as 1912, Freud had admitted the possibility that there were "various points in favor of the hypothesis of a primordial differentiation between sexual instincts and other instincts, ego instincts" (1914/1957, 106). What sexual instincts are was fairly easy for Freud's readers to understand. However, the nature and function of these hypothesized "ego-instincts" was less obvious, which is probably one reason that Freud focused on the former instead of the latter. In addition to physical self-preservation, ego-instincts were presumably responsible for the formation and maintenance of personal identity and existence, an *ego*, whose specific yet always shifting range of memories, perspectives, dispositions, and capacities comprised *conscious awareness*. Indeed, as Freud's research evolved, he would spend an increasing amount of time focusing upon the psychology of the conscious ego and its structural issues.

It was the ego, Freud said, that allowed one not only a personal identity but also a social one, for the ego was precisely that "psychic organ" that enabled an individual to realistically perceive and successfully negotiate the natural and social worlds in which he must exist. As such, the ego worked in the service of what Freud called *the reality principle*. Just as no two snowflakes are ever exactly alike, neither were any two egos. These differences made up the individual's unique *personality*. However, as Marx (1952/1978) had written just fifty years earlier in *The Eighteenth Brumaire of Louis Bonaparte*, "Men make their own history, but they do not make it just as they please" (595). In other words, the birth and growth of the ego was not only *constrained* by society and its many formal and informal rules and regulations but, in a real sense, existed to *serve* them.

Neurosis was the failure of the ego to mediate the ongoing battle between one's animalistic desires—what Freud called *the pleasure principle*—and his social roles. Typically, the ego dealt with these essentially antisocial desires by banishing them from conscious awareness. The *subconscious* was simply the repository of these exiled instincts, a kind of psychic junkyard—and it represented the price that the human animal had to pay in order to enjoy the benefits of living in society. According to Freud, the contents and complexities of the subconscious would inevitably grow both in number and intensity as the child—at birth a mass of raw drives and undifferentiated desires—became increasingly socialized.

The problem for the individual in all of this, said Freud, was that the exiled energy of our animal natures would simply not go quietly and obediently into subconscious oblivion. As is true with any dammed-up energy, these banished impulses were constantly clamoring for release, for conscious recognition and physical satisfaction—and all the more so as they had been so violently negated by the ego, whose job now was to act as a negotiator between biological instinct and socioethical conventions so as to avoid a *return of the repressed*. Freud called those internalized conventions *the superego*, claiming in his later work *The Ego and the Id* (1923) that the superego was a mostly subconscious entity in the individual's psychic makeup.

The overall picture that finally emerged in the Freudian model was of a three-layered psyche: the id (which was amoral and even immoral), the ego (which strove to follow *mores* and thus to be "moral"), and the superego (which was hypermoral, hypercritical, and the unconscious source of depression and masochism). Given the fact that both id *and* superego functioned mostly outside of the range of conscious awareness, Freud observed that "the normal man is not only far more immoral than he believes but also far more moral than he has any idea of" (1923/1957, 230). All of these tensions—between the ego and the id, the id and superego, and the ego and the superego—would often result in either *repression* or *sublimation*. Repression was the organism's attempt to keep the pounding passions of the libido entirely out of its circle of awareness so that it would cause no harm to its reality functioning. This was rarely successful because repressed energy would ultimately press to the surface as the unpleasant symptoms of a *reaction formation*.

A generally more successful strategy was *sublimation*, in which the organism strategically allowed forbidden energy to express itself in a much reduced, highly symbolic, and therefore socially acceptable form. Instead of playing with its own feces, the child would learn to shape figures in clay and might ultimately become an architect or sculptor. Instead of withdrawing into an autistic world of complete self-absorption in fantasy, the healthy child would learn to construct mental models and images and might become a scholar or poet. And instead of sexually uniting with his mother—who was, after all, the literal matrix out of which the child's physical being had emerged and whose full breast and gentle caresses had flooded his earliest perceptions and sensations—the young boy would learn to direct that love to a sublimated mother, a wife, and thereby symbolically express his primal passions in a socially cohesive and literally generative manner.

Freud pessimistically concluded that we are all more or less caught in an ultimately irresolvable tension between biological instincts and social institutions, and this will always be so, for we are all animals with passions that simply must be forcibly cornered and corralled with symbols and sublimations if we are to find ways to live and work together. There is simply no way out of this conundrum. Freud agreed with Thomas Hobbes in his treatise *Leviathan* that man, in his natural state, could only live a life that was "nasty, brutish and short." We survive both individually and collectively only through the protection that society offers, but this will always require some measure of painful repression and sublimation.

The depth of Freud's despair at our incurably paradoxical condition deepened as he aged. In 1923, for instance, he somberly portrayed the ego as "a poor creature owing service to three masters and consequently menaced by three several dangers: from the external world, from the libido of the id, and from the severity of the superego" (1923/1957, 232). And when (as too often happened) the individual could no longer manage to balance the call of the animal within him with the demands of the society outside of him, then psychologically and even physically painful and debilitating symptoms would start rearing their ugly visages from the roiling blackness of the subconscious.

The function of *psychotherapy*, said Freud, was to identify, analyze, and treat the subconscious source of the symptom by bringing the repressed desire or memory to conscious awareness and allowing the patient to express (or *cathect*) it within the safe confines of the consulting room and in the presence of the doctor. This new awareness, coupled with release and relief, would hopefully effect a cure—if indeed a cure was possible: of *that* there was never any guarantee. Ideally, however, the therapeutic process would either eliminate the source of the tension and the bothersome presence of the symptom, or—what was much more typical—at least bring it under sufficient control for the individual to be able to return to the normal state of *functional neurosis*, not the state of *pathological neurosis* in which the patient—unable to contain the inevitable and tragic tug-and-pull between desire and duty—became and remained a problem for his family, friends, associates, and society.

It would be a mistake to conclude, as many superficial readers of Freud do, that he somehow spun this radically new model of the psyche in the comfort of his own study and out of the depths of his own imagination. Far from it. To be sure, any psychological theory will bear the imprint of its creator, but this does not necessarily discredit the theory. Indeed, one would have to suspect *any* theory about the depths of the psyche if that theory was not formed—or at least confirmed—by the psychologist's looking deeply into his own psyche.

It is clear that Freud's theory developed incrementally—based upon his daily clinical practice in Victorian Vienna and upon the great body of research into the unconscious and its sexual nature that preceded Freud by at least a century (Ellenberger 1970). We must recall that Freud's patients—many of them women—were consistently coming to his consulting room with problems whose origins clearly lay (so it seemed to Freud) in repressed sexuality.

It is probably also true that some of the women who found their way to Freud's consulting room had experienced some sort of sexual abuse as children, which they had repressed. Uncovering these memories in the course of treatment, Freud at first acknowledged their authenticity but later concluded that they probably represented an "incest fantasy" on the female patients' part regarding their fathers. As erroneous as this latter conclusion probably was in most of the women whom Freud was treating, it is nevertheless the case that he was the first doctor to attempt to explain what we now know to be a vicious and widespread practice.

In the last phase of his writing and practice, Freud would expand the notion of *libido* considerably, calling it *Eros* and depicting it as a sort of generalized life-instinct (still deeply involved with sexuality, of course, but not completely reducible to it) that was constantly doing battle with a death-instinct that he called *Thanatos*—or the desire of every creature to return to an undifferentiated state of eternal rest in the primal ground of being. In this war, death must inevitably triumph for it always has the last word. "The goal of all life is death. . . . The inanimate was there before the animate" (1920/1957, 160). But Freud would not fully articulate these broader hypotheses until 1920, in his famous work *Beyond the Pleasure Principle*—in other words, long after Jung had parted ways with him.

In Freud's work during the Freud-Jung years, however, such as *Three Essays on the Theory of Sexuality* (1909/1975) and *The Interpretation of Dreams* (1900/1965), the old master's emphasis *was* almost entirely sexual. In his *General Introduction to Psycho-analysis,* for instance, Freud (1915–1917/1970) proclaimed during his famous nineteenth lecture to American medical students at Clark University on "The General Theory of the Neuroses" that whenever a psychotherapist gets to the root of a patient's symptoms, the cause of the dysfunction is always the same.

> What we found in these two examples [that had just been discussed] we should find in every case submitted to analysis. Every time we should be

led by analysis to the sexual experiences and desires of the patient, and every time we should have to affirm that the symptom served the same purpose. This purpose shows itself to be the gratification of sexual wishes; the symptoms serve the purpose of sexual gratification for the patient; they are a substitute for satisfactions he does not obtain in reality. (308)

So single-minded was Freud about the sexual etiology of both healthy and pathological psychic functioning that he told Jung that the hypothesis must become, as he put it, a "dogma."[2] Jung remarks in his autobiography *Memories, Dreams, and Reflections* (1963) that it was probably at that moment that he was finally convinced that he would soon have to break with Freud, for Jung believed no mere theory should ever be above critique, modification, or even rejection if the evidence warranted it—especially a theory he had never fully subscribed to anyway.

This is not to say that Jung denied the psychological importance of sexuality. It is merely that he saw sexuality as only one of many factors and impulses that power and direct psychic functioning. Jung frequently praised Freud during the remaining fifty years of his own medical and academic work (a courtesy that Freud never chose to return to Jung), insisting that Freud had offered a powerful model of the psyche that was useful as far as it went. The problem was that it just did not go far enough. He accorded the same sincere but qualified praise to Freud's other great disciple, Alfred Adler, who saw the will-to-power as the fundamental human drive, and the ability to establish a sound social identity as the fundamental psychological and moral imperative. That both theories were valid, Jung never denied. Indeed, he asserted that:

both theories fit the neurotic mentality so neatly that every case of neurosis can be explained by both theories at once. This highly remarkable fact, which any unprejudiced observer is bound to corroborate, can only rest on the circumstance that Freud's "infantile eroticism" and Adler's "power drive" are one and the same thing, regardless of the clash of opinion between the two schools. It is simply a fragment of uncontrolled, and at first uncontrollable, primordial instinct. (*CW* 7, par. 256)

Freud's sexual hypothesis and Adler's power hypothesis—although both "a faithful picture of real facts that force themselves upon our observation"—were incomplete. This was the case, Jung argued, because reducing the many mysterious aspects of psyche to "nothing but" one animalistic drive or other, or even an assemblage of them, was both simplistic and counter-intuitive (*CW* 15, par. 68). The reduction of human experience to merely biological mechanics could never yield a picture of the psyche that was whole, satisfying, and healing. Such an approach was as intellectually indefensible as it was morally belittling.

But Jung's objections were not merely academic. They were also medical. It was becoming increasingly clear to Jung in both his clinical practice and scholarly investigations that the appetite for sex and power were themselves ultimately just dynamic "fragments" that emerged from an even deeper layer of psychic functioning—a "primordial" layer (as Jung was fond of putting it) that formed the ancient, irreducible ground of the human psyche. But what was this ancient ground of the psyche? What were its elements and how did it work?

FROM THE PERSONAL SUBCONSCIOUS
TO THE COLLECTIVE UNCONSCIOUS

It was as a young resident psychiatrist at the Burghölzli Clinic in Switzerland that Jung got his first *mature* glimpses (as a child he had certain experiences and dreams that presaged his later insights) into this primordial realm of psychic functioning whose nature and dynamics he would spend the rest of his life attempting to explore and map.

Jung recounts a story of a young man in his thirties whom he was treating at the Burghölzli Clinic. A schizophrenic and megalomaniac, the patient thought that he was Christ. Jung's account of this man is worth citing at length since it exemplifies the kind of clinical experience that led him away from—or rather, *beyond*—Freud:

> One day I came across [the young patient], blinking through the window up at the sun, and moving his head from side to side in a curious manner. He took me by the arm and said he wanted to show me something. He said that I must look at the sun with eyes half shut, and then I could see the sun's phallus. If I moved my head from side to side the sun-phallus would move too, and that was the origin of the wind. I made this observation about 1906. In the course of the year 1910, when I was engrossed

in mythological studies, a book of Dietrich's came into my hands. It was part of the so-called Paris magic papyrus and was thought to be a liturgy of the Mithraic cult. It consisted of a series of instructions, invocations and visions. One of these visions is described in the following words: "And likewise the so-called tube, the origin of the ministering wind. For you will see hanging down from the disc of the sun something that looks like a tube. And towards the regions westward it is as though there were an infinite east wind. But if the other wind should prevail towards the regions of the east, you will in like manner see the vision veering in that direction."(CW 8, pars. 317–19)

Jung noted at the time that "the parallelism of the two visions cannot be disputed." Could this weird correspondence between a schizophrenic hallucination and an ancient creation myth be due to the fact that this relatively uneducated young man had heard or read this very obscure Mithraic fable somewhere and was now producing it from the depths of his subconscious? Although unlikely, this possibility could not be ruled out. Furthermore, it was no great stretch for Jung to discern the Freudian elements in the dream (the phallic sun) as well as its Adlerian ones (the patient was a megalomaniac). Jung suspected that there was more to it than that, however—believing that these sexual/power elements were examples of those "fragments" that emerged from an even deeper layer of psychic functioning—that "primordial" layer that Jung believed to be the ultimate ground of the human psyche (CW 7, par. 199).

Confirmation of this hunch was provided by the fact that Jung, who was adept at various ancient languages and a competent scholar of ancient mythologies, now started to see these correspondences between individual psychic contents and mythic patterns creeping up all over the place in both the patients in his bustling clinic and the old volumes spread out over his sequestered study. In the dreams, fantasies, and hallucinations of his patients, many of whom were humble Swiss villagers, Jung began to observe, record, and analyze what would ultimately amount to scores of thousands of instances of close correspondences to ancient images, motifs, and narratives.[3]

Of course, he was aware that these parallelisms between individual psychic contents and culturo-religious narratives did not mean that his patients' fantasies were *necessarily* religious (although some of them might be) any more than it meant that all religions are just fantasies (as Freud, the great anti-religionist, had summarily declared in *The Future of an Illusion* and *Totem and Taboo*). It did suggest, however, that there was a very deep psychosocial well from which individuals of all sorts, and cultures of all times and all places, drew in order to produce the images, themes, and stories that expressed their ways of seeing and being in the world both. "This discovery," declared Jung,

> means another step forward in our understanding: the recognition, that is, of two layers in the unconscious. We have to distinguish between a personal unconscious and an *impersonal* or *transpersonal unconscious*. We speak of the latter also as the *collective unconscious*, because it is detached from anything personal and is common to all men, since its contents can be found everywhere, which is naturally not the case with the personal contents. The personal unconscious contains lost memories, painful ideas that are repressed . . . , subliminal perceptions that were not strong enough to reach consciousness, and finally, contents that are not yet ripe for consciousness. . . . The primordial images [of the collective unconscious], however, are the most ancient and the most universal "thought-forms" of humanity. They are as much feelings as thoughts; indeed, they lead their own independent life. (*CW* 7, pars. 103–4)

Elsewhere, Jung explained:

> This deeper layer I call the *collective unconscious*. I have chosen the term "collective" because this part of the unconscious is not individual but universal; in contrast to the personal psyche, it has contents and modes of behavior that are more or less the same everywhere and in all individuals. It is, in other words, identical in all men and thus constitutes a common psychic substrate of a suprapersonal nature that is present in every one of us. (*CW* 9.1, par. 3)

Like Freud, then, Jung ultimately arrived at a tristratal model of the psyche. But whereas Freud's divisions contained essentially *personal* elements—the ego, id, and superego—Jung's contained the personal *consciousness*, the personal *subconscious*, and the *transpersonal or suprapersonal unconscious* (*CW* 8, par. 321). Freud helped to lift the veil on the specific workings of the *individual* inner psyche as a biographical entity. But it was Jung who pressed on past that point until he came to that mysterious junction where the individual psyche left off—and the *collective, timeless,* and *metapersonal* psyche began. Here was that psychic bedrock for which Jung and various researchers before him had searched so long.

THE ARCHETYPES AND THE COLLECTIVE UNCONSCIOUS

Reaching the threshold of the collective unconscious and, what is more, *formulating a system* to account for it, was an important event in the history of Western psychology. In many ways, it marked the beginning of a systematically "spiritual psychology" in the modern Western tradition, leading us into those psychospiritual realms from which the religious impulse arises in all cultures and at all times despite the cultural and historical variations in the specific persons and the local imagery that are marshaled to express that impulse.

This *transpersonal* approach to psychology grants access to those in-born, primordial structures and predispositions at the deepest level of our psyches that cause us—despite personal and historical variations in language and imagery—to interpret and engage the world in much the same way from epoch to epoch and from culture to culture. For it is certainly the case that men and women have always been born with essentially the same tendencies to hope, fear, see, imagine, hate, and love the same things. The idea of the collective unconscious bears powerful witness to the essential brotherhood and sisterhood of all people at all times. But what are these universal "contents of the collective unconscious"? Jung called them *archetypes*.

Jung's detractors often attack him bitterly for being unclear about what he meant by the term "archetype." Freud said that he found the idea incomprehensible and Jung unreadable. Admittedly, from the first time he used the term in 1919, until the end of his career almost forty-five years later, the term naturally underwent some modification, which created not a little confusion—a fact readily admitted by even Jung's staunchest disciples and most perspicuous interpreters (Frey-Rohn 1974). Perhaps more than anything else, it is this fact that can make Jung so daunting to read for the first time. However, as one works his way through the twenty volumes of Jung's body of work and (what is more important) lives with and deeply experiences the reality and functioning of the archetypes, what Jung meant by "archetype" becomes not only clear but clarifying, casting light on a host of issues and problems that other depth psychologies do not address nearly as well.

There are several reasons why Jung's notion of the archetype has proven difficult for some people to grasp. First, Jung was a psychiatrist, not an academic. His job was not to provide neat theories, tightly bundled and prettily wrapped in such a way that undoing the package and looking inside would be a painless process for the casual passerby. He was a doctor. He reported what he saw, experienced, and had done in the painful, messy, and very unclear contexts of psychotherapy. Adding to this confusion was the fact that, unlike Freud, whose practice revolved around the relatively more straightforward neuroses, Jung was interested in the more volatile and vexing psychoses.

Second, Jung was a true pioneer whose life was devoted to a preliminary, empirical mapping out of territory that others had speculated about but none had explored with such persistence and thoroughness. Such a project does not permit complete, crystal-clear descriptions of the entirety of the wild land being traversed. Just to report and begin to understand what one has seen is usually enough for one lifetime's work.

And finally, it was difficult for Jung to be as precise as some would have liked regarding the nature of archetypes because archetypes are inherently difficult to define. "I admit at once that [the idea of archetypes] is a controversial idea and more than a little perplexing," Jung confessed. "But I have always wondered what sort of ideas my critics would have used to characterize the empirical material in question" (*CW* 7, par. 118 , n.15). The psychospiritual wellsprings from which our thoughts, feelings, dreams, and religions emerge are as mysterious as human life itself and in that sense defy description.

Thus, when we come into contact with an archetype, we have an experience of the divine within us, the *numinous,* as Jung called it, drawing on the Greek word for spirit, *numen*. Of the spiritual nature of this experience we are certain even if (and maybe precisely because) we cannot scientifically define it. It is because the archetype exists at the deepest levels of our moral and spiritual existence that Jungian psychology has been welcomed much more enthusiastically in the arts and humanities than the social sciences. Nevertheless, it *is* possible to talk profitably about archetypes, and Jung generally did so in language that was as accurate and authentic as possible. The ideas may be complex but his prose was not, for he abhorred what he called "the power language" of unnecessarily complex language.

At the outset of a discussion about the nature of the archetype, it is useful to say what an archetype is *not*. It is not—as some of Jung's less perceptive readers have tried to claim he was saying—an inherited image or belief system genetically passed down across many generations. True, some of Jung's *earliest* statements about archetypes did suggest that they could be inherited images, but he soon quite abandoned this Larmarckian notion (one, by the way, to which Freud clung until the end of his life). In other words, just because one's parents worship Osiris, Dionysius, or Christ, for instance, does not mean that one's children, grandchildren, or great-grandchildren will be born with a literal image of that particular god genetically embedded in their minds.

What we *are* all born with, said Jung, is the *innate predisposition* to worship a dying and resurrected god. That disposition constitutes an *archetype*—in this case, *the archetype of the savior*. Because an archetype is a human universal, one would expect to find it manifested broadly throughout history. And in this, one would not be disappointed, as Sir James Frazer (1922/1963) demonstrated in his classic mythological study *The Golden Bough*. In ancient Egypt, the archetype of the savior was embodied in the form of the god Osiris, in Greece by Dionysus, and in Roman-occupied Palestine around 30 C.E. by an iterant preacher named Jesus. But in all of these cases, the archetypal energy is more or less the same. What is variable, said Jung, are the *archetypal images* that will be used to flesh out the archetype, for this will depend on historical, cultural, and personal factors.

Another example of an archetype is the *wise old man* or *wise old woman* who, possessing secret knowledge and magical potions, comes to the aid of a young hero or heroine at particularly difficult passages in the youth's life. In ancient Greece, the *archetypal image* and personage who concretely represented this *archetype* was (among others) the blind prophet Tiresias, whose knowledge of the answer to the Sphinx's riddle and whose moral wisdom direct Oedipus to his fate at various junctures in his journey. Indeed, the notion of a heroic journey, or a road of trials, leading to some sort of growth in the hero, is itself an archetype (Campbell 1949), which manifests itself in innumerable stories, from the most ancient myths to the most recent television programs.

In Shakespeare's *Romeo and Juliet*, the wise-old-woman archetype is embodied in Juliet's nurse, to whom Juliet constantly turns for advice. Friar Laurence, who comes to the aid (alas, with a tragic lack of success) of Romeo and Juliet with a potion and plan for their escape, is a wise old man. In popular American culture, these archetypal roles are played by such characters as Obiwan and his magical Jedi sword in the movie *Star Wars* or Guinan, the millennia-old bartender with her synthetic alcoholic potions—which she freely dispenses along with her wisdom—in the television program *Star Trek: The Next Generation*. The characters and stories vary, but the archetypal basis of human experience—our propensity to see and expect people and things to fulfill certain meaningful roles and follow certain meaningful patterns—does not.

The infrastructure of psyche, then, can be pictured as shifting patterns of primary urges, predispositions, and needs—that is, as a shifting mosaic of archetypes. In their primal manifestation, these innate and universal psychic forces can be pictured as *nodes of energy*. Present in all people at all times, they permeate and shape not only the individual psyche but also those culturally foundational stories that we call religion and myth. Perhaps it was of archetypes that Goethe was thinking when, at the end of *Faust*, he wrote of "eternal mind's eternal re-creation."

We all have our psychic being in and because of our archetypes, which, because they are shared and "objective," reside in and emanate from what Jung considered to be an ontologically real *collective unconscious*. The archetypes of the collective unconscious manifest themselves today as well as anciently, individually as well as collectively, in perennial images, motifs, and stories. They may as easily appear tonight in an insurance agent's dreams as he lies in the darkness of his suburban bedroom in Denver at 3 o'clock in the morning as in the pages of an Assyrian war epic 3,000 years ago—although the specific archetypal images in which the archetypal energy embodies itself will vary according to personal, cultural, and historical circumstances. Archetypal dream analysis looks for such parallels and cultivates them, using a variety of analytic techniques to promote a heightened sense of significance and insight in the analysand (Mattoon 1984).

There are probably innumerable archetypes, manifesting themselves in such forms as the trickster, the lover, the divine child, the shadow, the magical animal, the nurturing mother, the witch, the law-giving father, the prince of darkness, the shadow, ritual sacrifice, initiation, holy matrimony, mandalas, trinities and quaternities, judgment, heaven, hell, atonement, and a great many others. The point to note at this early stage is just this: simply by virtue of the fact that we are human, we are born "hard-wired" with a wide range of dispositions to understand and act upon our world in certain typical ways. Those dispositions are the archetypes. The way they are specifically expressed is as archetypal images and motifs, which is the only way in which we can experience archetypes since archetypes in their pure form are so deeply embedded in the unconscious that we can never know them directly. Paradoxically, archetypes are both preverbal and supraverbal.

In a strikingly powerful simile, Colman (2000) has expressed the difference between archetypes and archetypal images.

> We do not know the archetypes—we only know the multiple representations of them in consciousness. To remain true to the hypothesis of archetypes, we must be true to their ultimately irrepresentable nature; that is, we must keep in mind that what we see are images. *Perhaps it is like looking at a movie screen: if we try to see where the images come from, we are blinded by the light of the projector and see nothing.* (5; emphasis added)

Of course, we do not *choose* to come into the world with an archetypal foundation already in place at the deepest layers of our being any more than we choose to have an instinct for sex or self-preservation. We are simply *born* with archetypes because we are human. Jung thus called the archetypes "autonomous" (*CW* 5, par. 467), and, in the sense that they are a primordial "given," they are the psychospiritual counterparts to our biological instincts (*CW* 8, par. 281). The theory of inborn archetypes is as far from the Lockeian and behaviorist notion of the mind as a tabula rasa at birth, an empty slate, as one could possibly get!

In sum, as Jung wrote, an archetype "is not a question of a specifically racial heredity, but of a universally human characteristic. Nor is it a question of *inherited ideas*, but of a functional disposition to produce the same, or very similar, ideas. This disposition I [call] the *archetype*"

(*CW* 5, par. 154). Archetypes underlie the "inborn disposition to produce parallel thought-formations, or rather of identical psychic structures common to all men" (*CW* 5, par. 224). They are "the stock of inherited *possibilities of representation* that are born anew in every individual" (*CW* 5, par. 264). Employing one of Jung's favorite metaphors to clarify the difference between an archetype and an archetypal image, Emma Jung (Jung's wife and collaborator) and Marie-Louise von Franz (one of Jung's most gifted disciples) likened archetypes to

> the invisible potential existence of the crystalline structure in a saturated solution. [Archetypes] first take on a specific form when they emerge into consciousness in the shape of images; it is therefore necessary to differentiate between the unapprehendable archetype—the unconscious, pre-existent disposition—and the archetypal images. [Archetypal images] are human nature in the universal sense. Myths and fairy tales are also characterized by this universal validity which differentiates them from ordinary dreams. (1960/1986, 36–37)

Archetypes, then, are "preconscious categories which [channel] thought and action into [the] definite shapes [of archetypal images]" (Frey-Rohn 1974, 93).

THE PERSONAL DIMENSION—AGAIN

With all of this talk of the collective, universal, and timeless realms of the psyche—its *transpersonal* dimension—it is perhaps a good idea to point out again that Jung never lost sight of the *personal* nature of the psyche—its strictly biographical dimension. He affirmed throughout his life that the Freudian and Adlerian models of psyche were powerful ways of explaining and treating psychic dilemmas at a purely personal level. It is simply that, theoretically and therapeutically, Jung often found it useful to analyze personal psychic functions or dilemmas in a transpersonal context. Jung's contributions to ego-psychology are substantial, however, and often overlooked because of his groundbreaking working in *trans-egoic* psychology. For instance, the reader who has ever heard the terms *persona* or *shadow* used in psychological discourse has already encountered Jungian concepts. Some neo-Freudian ego-psychologists even use a variety of Jungian terms without being fully aware that they originated with Jung.

The *persona* is—to borrow the words of the poet T. S. Eliot—the face you "prepare to meet the faces that you meet" (1971, 4). Like the mask in ancient Greek drama (to which the term literally refers), the persona is the ego-invented and ego-protecting façade that we don for others to see—to assure them, and ourselves, that we are "one of the group," that we "know the rules" and are willing and able to play by them, and, in general, that we are "doing well."

Having personas is not in itself a bad thing, according to Jung. It is, in fact, a very necessary thing since we must all negotiate the quotidian world and cooperate with others in many different ways in the course of a day—sometimes even in the course of an hour! Since we all fill so many roles in our lives, it is simply a fact of social life that an individual has not just one persona but many of them. This is what the sociolinguist Ervin Goffmann (2000) calls "face-work." The persona is thus one of the ego's most indispensable tools for being with others; it "mediates between the ego and the outer world" (Samuels 1997, 215).

Problems regarding the persona arise, however, when it no longer functions as the ego's servant but becomes its master. For the ego, being "a complex of ideas which constitutes the center of my field of consciousness and appears to possess a high degree of continuity and identity" is greater than the persona (CW 6, par. 706). As William James put it, the persona is the "me"—what others perceive when they look at me. But my understanding of the full-range of myself as a conscious being is my "I"—who I believe I *really* am. I am the one who knows that he has a persona. Optimally, the persona is only a functional part of that "complex of ideas" that comprise the total "I."

When, however, an individual becomes so preoccupied with how he appears to others that this concern comes to dominate his conscious awareness, he is *persona possessed*. We all know the type—the person who is so completely identified with his titles, possessions, and social position that there seems to be little else to him. The persona possessed person is usually considered boring or "phony" by others; he has so mistaken his masks for the face that is beneath them that, in a certain sense, he no longer has a face, or has largely forgotten what it is—like the characters in Sartre's play *No Exit*. Such a person has forfeited his individuality, becoming just a social category—and caricature.

Such a person may well find himself in the therapist's office sooner or later because of the insupportable tension between who he really is *within himself* (which can never be completely extinguished and is at some level always clamoring for recognition) and who he has become *for others*.[4] People who present in the therapist's office with a sense of emptiness or free-floating anxiety are often suffering from the effects of persona possession. Much of existentialist philosophy and therapy represents an attempt to peel off, layer by layer, the various personas that a person has put on over the years so that he can begin to see his face again in the mirror of the therapist—can begin, that is, to live authentically, or "in good faith" as Sartre put it (1956).[5]

The *shadow* is also involved with the psychology of the ego. Jung noted that his idea of the shadow was roughly equivalent to Freud's idea of the personal subconscious (*CW* 5, par. 267, n. 14), but it contains some elements that Freud's model does not. "By *shadow* I mean the negative side of the personality—the sum of all those unpleasant qualities we like to hide, together with the insufficiently developed functions, *and the contents of the personal unconscious*" (*CW* 7, par. 103, n. 5; emphasis added).

Understandably but mistakenly, many people interpret Jung's idea of the shadow to mean that it is simply the dark and boarded-up warehouse of all that is evil in us. Their picture of the shadow is well summed up in the introduction to the popular radio thriller of the 1930s that began with the words, "Who knows what evil lurks in the hearts of men? The Shadow knows!" To be sure, the Jungian shadow does contain much that is evil, for we do not like to see evil in ourselves (however ready we always seem to be to see it in others). But evil is not banished to the shadow so much because it is evil as because it—like many things, some of which are *not* necessarily evil—is something *we prefer not to acknowledge as belonging to us*. Hence, repressed memories are in the shadow. So are "qualities we like to hide."

These qualities may actually be talents, virtues, or potentials that we have hidden not only from others but also from ourselves because openly acknowledging them could place us in emotional or social peril. The young man who longs to be a ballet dancer and has talent but who denies and represses it because it would offend and even incur the wrath of his macho father, who wants *his* boy to be a running-back for the high-school football team, has been forced to cast his artistic talent into his shadow for the sake of his father's love and approval.

Also residing in the shadow are those "insufficiently developed functions" that are the very opposite of our talents. On even my best days, for example, I have very little talent with mechanical objects. Filling a tank of gas at the station, changing a tire, and putting in a new light-bulb or battery pretty much exhaust my range of mechanical skills. Hence, I shy away from such things, do not develop what abilities I might actually possess along these lines if I would only patiently try to cultivate them and not see it as a catastrophe whenever I *do* try to do something mechanical and fail. I have exiled this undeveloped part of myself to the shadow. Because I have banished this important part of daily physical existence to the psychic hinterlands, my shadow, wreaking revenge, both figuratively and literally "trips me up" quite often in the course of a day!

In the Jungian view, it is highly important that we face and integrate our shadow, or at least various aspects of it, into our conscious awareness and personality. So key is this notion of the shadow and its acceptance that it was "the *leitmotiv* of Jung's later works" (Frey-Rohn 1974, 3). But why should scraping up all of this psychic sludge from the floor of our unconscious matter so much? Wouldn't it be better to let it lie in the garbage heap of the psyche and focus our attention on more pleasant tasks that come more naturally to us instead? Life is short. Why invite such grief?

One reason to confront the shadow is that some of the dispositions and potentials that one has repressed can, if consciously acknowledged and carefully nurtured, emerge from the shadow and help one become a more complete and powerful person, more *whole*. To grow into one's full stature as a social, intellectual, and moral being by realizing as much of one's potential as possible—and not only for one's own sake but for the sake of one's family and fellows—is the great moral imperative that life lays upon us all. A truly productive life depends on overcoming the fear of irrational family censure or small-minded social disapproval in order to become the best person that one can be. This will sometimes mean inviting those elements out of the shadow that one once banished—and perhaps *had to banish* in order to survive in a family or a culture—and (re)integrating them into oneself in a way that permits a more effective, genuine, compassionate, and satisfying existence.

This is what Jung means by becoming whole. In the imperfect realm of existence in which we as fallible mortals live, the merciless drive for perfection is unrealistic and, if not put in a proper perspective, neurotic—a point that Freud often stressed, too. In the tireless push to be perfect— perfectly strong, perfectly beautiful, perfectly virtuous, perfectly orthodox, having the perfect house, perfect job, and perfect children—we make inhuman demands upon ourselves and those around us. Losing our sense of humor as well as our sense of humanity, we inevitably fall into sundry subtle traps and wind up doing ourselves and those around us great harm.

Consulting rooms are filled with people who come to therapy because their own, or their parents', or their mate's perfectionism has either frozen them into psychic immobility or forced them to act out in destructive rebellion—the latter often being the case with "black sheep" in perfectionist families where the rebellious child becomes the scapegoat who acts out the entire family's unacknowledged shadow. Such a child, the *identified patient* in therapeutic language, is essentially a symbol and scapegoat of those elements of itself that the family as a whole refuses to face (Satir 1967). I once taught at a university where the president was the sweetest man one could possibly imagine, but his secretary was an absolute witch. I always half expected to see a broomstick in her parking spot every morning. As his "shadow," she did his dirty work, institutionally and emotionally, while he basked all unaware in the false light of his artificial goodness. Shakespeare went right to the heart of the matter with his observation that "the ripeness is all"—an ageless testimony to the psychological and moral necessity of wholeness, not perfection, in attaining the full measure of our humanity.

There is yet another reason that we must confront our own shadows, and it is easily stated using another term from Jungian psychology that has become widely known—*projection.* The idea of projection is quite simple: We condemn most passionately in others what we refuse to see in ourselves. This is not exactly the latest-breaking news, of course. Two thousand years ago, Jesus said, "Why beholdest thou the mote that is in thy brother's eye, but perceivest not the beam that is in thine own eye

. . . ? Thou hypocrite, cast out first the beam out of thine own eye, and then shalt thou see clearly to pull out the mote that is in thy brother's eye" (Matthew 7:3). Not to follow Jesus' advice in this matter is to play a vicious game of psychological hide-and-seek with oneself by refusing to cast the light of honest introspection on one's own discarded, repressed, and sometimes shabby parts.

Not facing our own shadow inevitably leads to not only a psychological dysfunction but to the moral error of ascribing one's shadow-nature to another. This is not to say that whenever we see something that we consider to be disagreeable in another person or situation we are simply projecting our own shadows onto him or it. But it is to say that until we own up to our shadow, we will never know if this is the case or not. What is more, even if we do correctly perceive weakness or even immorality in another, our response to it will be tempered by an awareness of our own fallibility if we have confronted our own shadows. This will in turn engender a greater ability to forgive and help the other person, not sanctimoniously condemn him. "He who is without sin among you, let him cast a stone" (John 8:7).

Confronting one's shadow is thus vital to psychological and moral health. As such, the encounter with the shadow is more than just an abstract admission that one has a dark side. "The growing awareness of the inferior part of the personality," Jung wrote, "should not be twisted into an intellectual activity, for it has far more the meaning of a suffering and a passion that implicate the whole man" (CW 8, par. 409). It requires the moral courage to seek "ruthless self-knowledge" (CW 9.2, par. 255). Indeed, "the shadow is a moral problem" because it "challenges the whole ego-personality"—especially those personalities that are either overly sweet because they refuse to look at their own darkness or overly critical because they insist on casting that darkness upon another (CW 9.2, par. 14). Some people are both things at once, and their lilting voices and sunny smiles too often accompany deprecatory jabs and coy cuts.

Thus, there is no alternative to facing the shadow if one wants to grow. It is "the essential condition for any kind of self-knowledge, and it therefore, as a rule, meets with considerable resistance" in therapy, requiring "much painstaking work extending over a long period" (CW 9.2, par. 14). The work is worth the pain, however, for this "increasing psychological insight hinders the projection of the shadow," resulting in enhanced psychological and moral realism (*CW* 14, par. 203). In therapy, the shadow is often one of the earliest figures to emerge in the analysand's dreams, for the repressed parts of the psyche gradually begin to "sense" that they have a safe therapeutic setting in which to come forth. The consulting room provides a psychological and moral space for the "safeguarded restructuring" and "recanalization [or, rechanneling] of libido" (Stein 1984, 41).

In dreams, the shadow is usually the same gender as the dreamer and often has something dark associated with it. The dream character might have a dark complexion and/or dark hair (a fact that generally seems to be as true for analysands of color as for white analysands); the figure may be wearing dark clothes; sometimes he or she is literally standing in or peeking out of a shadow. The fact that the shadow has been "despised" by consciousness can also be symbolized in the dream by the shadow being an alien, a citizen of an opposing country, a member of a minority group, a criminal, or a beggar; or by being somehow unethical, sick, or menacing (Adams 1996). Whatever specific form it takes, when such an "outcast" figure does make an appearance in a dream, it is important to consider the possibility that it is representing the shadow and thus comes bearing important information about what needs to be acknowledged and, in some instances, *used* by the ego.

Just as the persona is the first psychic formation that greets the individual as he begins to take a long, hard look at himself in an outward direction, so the shadow is the first thing that he sees as he looks inwardly. In this sense, the shadow and the persona are the opposite poles that define the boundaries within which the ego "oscillates" in its daily transformations. That is why ego-psychologies in general often go no farther outward that the persona and no farther inward than the shadow in their theories or practices.

With all this in mind, it is now time to look at some of the specific ways in which projection works. To do so requires that we examine Freud's important notion of what he called *the transference* and Jung's subsequent expansion of that idea. Because the theory of the transference is so essential to Jungian theory and figures so prominently in the second half of this study, we will look at it in depth in the next chapter.

NOTES

1. We must, however, be careful to avoid the almost universal misconception that Freud was a solitary genius who had somehow "discovered" the unconscious and "proven" that its dynamics were primarily sexual. As Ellenberger (1970) has amply demonstrated in his massive study, *The Discovery of the Unconscious: The History and Evolution of Dynamic Psychiatry*, almost all of the elements of Freudian psychiatry had already been postulated and explored by researchers for many decades—and in some instances even a century—before Freud's first sexological works in the late 1890s and early 1900s. Not only Mesmer, Janet, and Charcot but also many other psychiatrists, psychologists, philosophers, poets, and even sociologists had argued for the existence of a subconscious whose issues and energies were primarily, even exclusively, sexual. As Ellenberger incontrovertibly demonstrates, Freud's genius lay not in proposing a radically new and widely unpopular theory but rather in putting together a wide variety of very well-known and largely accepted ideas in the form of a single psychoanalytic system—one that, far from having been rejected, generally met with approval or at least polite interest in a Vienna of the early 1900s that, far from being prudishly "Victorian," was every bit as sexually active and open as Paris at that time.

2. In fairness to Freud, it should be noted that one of his major motives in wanting to establish the sexual hypothesis as a dogma was to put psychiatry on a firm "scientific" basis and distance it from certain of its origins in spiritism, hypnosis, and parapsychology (Ellenberger 1970).

3. Furthermore, just as was the case with Freud, Jung could also draw on a rich tradition of prior psychological research—in this case, at least a century of previous studies and speculations about the possibility of certain images and structures—physiologically embedded in the brain and epistemologically determining—that were part of each individual's primordial heritage (Ellenberger 1970).

4. Existentialist philosophy draws a similar distinction between being-for-oneself and being-for-others.

5. Odajnyk (1976) claims that Jung foreshadowed a good deal of existentialist thought and that in many ways Jung was an existentialist even before Sartre and Camus appeared on the scene.

2

TRANSFERENCE AND TYPOLOGY

PERSONAL TRANSFERENCE: "THE MAIN THING"

Decades after his first meeting with Freud in March 1907, Jung recalled the event:

> After a conversation lasting many hours there came a pause. Suddenly he asked me out of the blue, "And what do you think about the transference?" I replied with the deepest conviction that it was the alpha and omega of the analytical method, whereupon he said, "Then you have grasped the main thing." (Jung 1963, 8)

What is this "main thing" that a century later continues to inform so many depth psychologies? Different theorists and practitioners have varying views of the transference, but the essential idea is summarized by Greenson, who notes that the transference, in the classical Freudian view, is

> the experiencing of feelings, drives, attitudes, fantasies, and defenses toward a person in the present which are inappropriate to that person and are a repetition, a displacement of reactions originating in regard to significant persons of early childhood. . . . For a reaction to be considered

transference it must have two characteristics: it must be a repetition of the past and it must be inappropriate to the present. (1990, 151)

In other words, the transference is, as Freud put it in a now famous phrase, "a new edition" of an old problem (1915–1917/1970, 462). It is a *repetition compulsion* in which the patient projects issues from his early childhood onto the psychotherapist, usually involving parents or other immediate caregivers. The goal of therapy—and the tricky task of the therapist—is to work with the patient's transferences in a way that will finally resolve the issue that underlies the transference, thereby eliminating the need for adult repetition of the original problem. The therapist must be able to "contain" the *transference neurosis* of the patient, therefore, in such a way that the patient can play the old issues out again but this time resolve them satisfactorily in the consulting room.

A process not suited for the faint of heart, such analytical work requires courage and commitment in both the patient and therapist. "The outcome in this struggle is not decided by [the patient's] intellectual insight—it is neither strong enough nor free enough to accomplish such a thing—but solely by his relationship with the physician" (Freud 1915–1917/1970, 453). Had Freud formulated *only* the idea of the transference and how to work with it, that alone would have been enough to secure his fame in the history of Western psychology.[1]

In classical psychoanalysis, the "significant persons of early childhood" are typically the mother and father, and the "person in the present," the analyst. Hence, a male analysand's relationship to the male or female analyst will reflect the nature of the analysand's relationship to his own mother and father in the specific Oedipal dynamics that psychically (mis)shaped him. The same dynamics are at play for the female analysand, of course, except that they revolve around the female's presumed "Electra" desire for psychophysical union with her father instead of the male's Oedipal desire for psychophysical merger with the mother. Although the theories of the Oedipus and (especially) Electra complexes have been challenged by some, most views of the transference still revolve around the classical Freudian postulation of the analysand's symbolic displacement of primary problems regarding some significant figure in his early life onto someone in the present.

Regarding Freud's insistence that the transference of psychic energy by the analysand onto the analyst is always inappropriate, various contemporary analysts have pointed out that the transferred emotions of the analysand onto the analyst may sometimes actually be very appropriate indeed as responses to the overt behaviors and/or subconscious strategies of the analyst. In any event, most theorists and practitioners concur that the transference causes crucial material to surface, which the analyst and analysand can use to understand the analysand's issues with a clarity that few, if any, other techniques can match. Henderson (1967) has called the transference *piece de resistance* of psychoanalysis.

Freud spoke of the transference as being either *positive* or *negative*, for the analysand will project either affectionate or hostile emotions onto the analyst, depending upon the analysand's original feelings toward the figure in her past whom the analyst symbolizes. "When we examine individual transference resistances occurring during treatment," Freud wrote,

> we find in the end that we cannot understand the employment of transference as resistance so long as we think simply of "transference." We must make up our minds to distinguish a "positive" transference from a "negative" one, the transference of affectionate feelings from that of hostile ones, and to treat the two sorts of transference to the doctor separately. (1990a, 32)

In the early stages of his development of psychoanalysis, Freud insisted that positive transferences, not only to the analyst but to all significant people in the analysand's life, "invariably go back to erotic sources" (1990a, 31). Although later Freudian thinkers like Marcuse (1962)—and, as we have already seen, even Freud himself—expanded the concept of *libido* to mean not only sexual energy but all psychic energy that tends toward the preservation and affirmation of life, it was Jung and his followers who first saw that the transference might involve the transmission of nonsexual, and even suprasexual, libido onto a person in the present.

For although the sexual component of the transference was "undeniable," according to Jung, "it is not always the only one and not always the essential one" (1963, 9). The transference involves other "moral, social and ethical components [of the analysand's psychic functioning] which become the analyst's allies once they have been 'purged' of their 'regressive components, their infantile sexualism'" (Fordham 1996, 115). In other words, the analysand may project "psychic contents" onto the analyst that are not necessarily (or at least not *primarily*) sexual. Indeed (and this is the crucial point) the psychic contents that the analysand projects onto the analyst may not be personal at all (or only personal in part) but *transpersonal and archetypal*.

TRANSPERSONAL TRANSFERENCE

It is not surprising that the transference should be so psychospiritually complex and, therefore, resistant to sexual reduction. For the transference is first and foremost a relationship, and "the living mystery of life is always hidden between Two, and it is the true mystery which cannot be betrayed by words and depleted by arguments" (Jung, cited in Marshak 1998, 58). This is why it is in relationship (especially in such intimate settings as love, friendship, war, therapy, and the classroom, to name only a few) that our most profound and lasting emotional and moral changes take place. This fact is also at the heart of *object-relations* theory—a neo-Freudian approach that has gained great currency in the last half-century. A basic tenet of object-relations psychology is that "relationship with an external other [i.e., an *object*] is a necessary ingredient for transformation because the unconscious needs an object onto which to project its contents" (Steinberg 1990, 49).[2]

Now, just as it is probably inevitable that an analysand will project *personal* subconscious contents onto the analyst, she will probably project *transpersonal* unconscious contents onto the therapist, too. Some Jungians even maintain that "archetypal transference" is at the heart of any therapeutic situation (Knox 1998). If this is true, then at the center of every personal "complex" (a term, by the way, which Jung, not Freud, coined) is a transpersonal, archetypal core, whose power radiates from the depths of the collective unconscious and permeates the individual's unique identity and issues.[3] It is an instance *par excellence* of the interaction of the universal and particular—the *collective unconscious*, on one hand, with the individual's *personal subconscious* and *ego consciousness*, on the other hand. Jung seemed to be suggesting exactly this kind of interaction in critiquing Freud, who, he said, observes the transference problem from the standpoint of a personalistic psychology and thus overlooks the very essence of the transference—the collective contents of an archetypal nature. . . . My handling of the transference problem, in contrast to Freud's, includes the archetypal aspect and thus gives rise to a totally different picture. (cited in Kirsch 1995, 186)

For example, it is not uncommon for a male analysand to inappropriately desire and even petulantly demand moral, psychological, and sometimes even physical nurturance from a female therapist. In this instance, the analysand is very likely projecting onto the therapist his personal Oedpial need to fuse with an all-satisfying mother. This is the sort of thing that the Freudian model can explain and handle. What it cannot deal with is the fact that the analysand may, at the transpersonal level, also be seeing the therapist in light of the seductive universal attraction exerted by the archetypal Great Mother back into the cosmic womb (Neumann 1954). Only a transpersonal analysis can bring this information to the level of ego awareness and provide ways of using it to clarify and liberate, rather than confuse and cripple, consciousness. "When archetypal images are constellated [i.e., are activated in the psyche], the analytic material reflects permeable boundaries with resultant fluidity between conscious and unconscious material, and between personal and transpersonal, archetypal material" (Machtiger 1995, 123). This interplay of ego and archetype is what, more than anything else, sets Jungian psychology apart from Freudian psychology (Edinger 1973).

PERSONAL AND TRANSPERSONAL COUNTERTRANSFERENCE

The transference is not a one-way street. Just as the analysand projects psychic issues onto the analyst, so the analyst may (and, again, perhaps inevitably does) project his psychic issues back onto the analysand. This is known as *the countertransference*, and it can be especially powerful if the analysand is projecting psychic energy onto the analyst that touches one of the analyst's own psychic wounds or complexes. In this case, "if the analyst is not aware of his or her own shadow response, real harm can be done" as the analyst projects *his or her* shadow back onto the un-suspecting and vulnerable analysand (Woodman 1995, 54). The analyst's countertransference is not always simply a response to the analysand's projections. It may also arise more or less independently of the analysand. An example of this is the male analyst who unconsciously sees all of his female analysands as "lost little girls" in need of saving. He may domineer and patronize them as an unconscious way of getting even with his emasculating mother, who continues to treat *him* like a child.

Just as the transference is a standard feature of relationships in general, so is countertransference. There simply seems to be no way around the fact that relationship always involves some sort of mutual projecting. This is especially true when one person holds more power in the relationship than the other does—when, that is, the relationship is *asymmetrical*—as it is between a doctor and patient, lawyer and client, minister and parishioner—and, of course, teacher and student (Wiedemann 1995).

The early psychoanalytic movement located transference dynamics exclusively in the analysand. It thought of the analyst as a detached scientific observer and interpreter—a sort of Olympian god whose exalted medical status prevented her from doing her own projecting in the course of therapy. Although Freud never really stopped viewing the countertransference as an impediment with little redeeming value, even he ultimately had to admit its power. With this recognition, Freud began to insist on a training analysis for all prospective analysts in which they would themselves be psychoanalyzed.

It was not until the late 1940s, however, close to the time of Freud's death, that the psychoanalytic movement began to show a widespread interest in the countertransference and its therapeutic possibilities. Not many Freudians shared then, however, and not all share even now, this positive view of the possibilities of the countertransference. For example, Winnicott, a very important object-relation theorist, has tersely restated the classical Freudian position that "the meaning of the word *counter-transference* can only be the [analyst's] neurotic features *that spoil the professional attitude* and disturb the course of the analytic process as determined by the patient" (1988, 266). Thankfully, this is rapidly becoming the minority view in the neo-Freudian literature on the countertransference.[4]

Yet well before Freudians began to show any real interest in the countertransference, Jung and his original circle of disciples had demonstrated considerable interest in its personal and transpersonal possibilities—and perils. Jung was fascinated by the countertransference largely for the practical reason that, properly interpreted and handled, it could yield enormous amounts of information to both the analyst and analysand. This theme continues to dominate a good deal of the current Jungian literature, as Samuels indicates when he writes that "realization that the analyst's feelings about the patient are communications and sources of information is the greatest advance in analytical thinking in recent years" (1997, 185).

ONE PLUS ONE EQUALS SIX

Although it may seem strange at first, it is nevertheless the case that the therapeutic relationship between an analyst and analysand involves more than two people. The complex synergy between analyst and analysand implicates not only the interaction between the analyst's conscious mind and the analysand's conscious mind but also the relationship between the analysand's unconscious and the figure of the analyst—as well as between the analyst's unconscious and the figure of the analysand. But that is not all, for, if the analyst and analysand are to understand the transferential dynamics going on within themselves personally, then each must have another relationship with her *own* unconscious mind. This adds up to the six relational interpersonal/intrapersonal vectors that are present in the analyst/analysand relationship—and arguably in *any* relationship where there is an asymmetrical distribution of power.

Jung said that such situations are so potent that they generate a special, psychically supercharged relational space that he called the *temenos*, or *sacred precinct* (Jung 1963). Wherever there is the possibility of transformative transference/countertransference dynamics (such as the consulting room or the classroom), there is also a potential *sacred space*. Some neo-Jungians even make the intriguing claim that the emergence of a *temenos* in such places as the consulting room, the meditation hall, the field of battle, the classroom, and so on, is more than merely symbolic but may involve the actual generation and interaction of psychophysical energies that form a transpersonal, quantum field in which very subtle energies of the analyst and analysand come into contact (Schwartz-Salant 1995; Spiegelman 1996). This quantum field may also foster certain paranormal and synchronistic phenomena.[5]

At any rate, most of the depth-psychology literature on countertransference agrees that Freud was wrong in saying that the countertransference is always destructive—or *dystonic*, in therapeutic parlance. Nevertheless, Freud was right in suggesting that it does have great potential for being misused in such a way that the more powerful member of a relationship can psychosexually prey upon the less powerful one. Such people as therapists, ministers, doctors, policemen, teachers, and all others who hold some authority in asymmetrical power relationships do well to heed Freud's warning about countertransference.

Despite these dangers, countertransference has many positive, or *syntonic*, uses insofar as the analyst can examine her countertransferences to see what the analysand may be doing or thinking, consciously or unconsciously, to have elicited this particular countertransference from the analyst. Hence, for the analyst (and as I will argue later, the teacher), the countertransference can be either a blessing or a curse, syntonic or dystonic, depending on how well the person in the position of authority understands and uses it. "These two thematic constructs, counter-transference as a hindrance, and the doctor's use of his own unconscious to understand the patient, have intertwined, like a double helix, throughout the historical development of psychoanalytic conceptions of counter-transference. And, we might add, the theory of treatment, itself" (Epstein and Feiner 1988, 282).

There is more to be said about the transference and countertransference, but it will have to wait until we examine it in the context of teacher-student relationships in part II. At this point, let us turn from this complicated aspect of Jungian theory to what is probably its best known, most straightforward, and most widely implemented component—namely, Jung's model of *personality types*.

JUNGIAN TYPOLOGY

First published in 1921 (*CW* 6), Jung's theory of personality types drew upon a rich cosmological and medical tradition that stretched back at least as far as ancient Greece.

Hippocrates had taught that personalities could be divided into four categories, or *humours*, reasoning that the four constituent elements that made up the cosmos—earth, air, water, and fire—must also make up, and therefore, govern the human body and personality. This hypothesis rested on the ancient belief that the human being was but a microcosm of the macrocosmic universe.

According to Hippocrates, the four humours were blood, phlegm, light bile, and dark bile. Depending upon which element a person's body tended to favor, her disposition would be *sanguine, phlegmatic, melancholic,* or *bilious.* About five centuries later, in the second century C.E., Galen said that the action of the humours was related to the digestive process, for in every food, one of the four cosmic elements predominated, and that element, when ingested and processed by "internal heat," would be released into the body.

Of course, as a twentieth-century physician, Jung could hardly credit this theory *as such.* However, he noted that its fourfold pattern exemplified a pattern that he had very often observed in his medical and literary studies, both ancient and modern. What he discerned was that many cosmological, physiological, and philosophical models divided *wholes*—both macrocosmic and microcosmic, and often depicted as a circle—into two paired opposites, represented as the two axes of a cross within the circle. This, Jung called a *quaternity*, or the unification of a double dyad (*CW* 13, par.469).

The "north-south" axis would represent one pair of opposites—say, hot and cold—while the "east-west" axis represented another pair—in this case, wet and dry. In ancient medicine, it was thought that the interaction of the force fields generated by these dialectical poles created the four elements: fire (hot and dry) and its opposite, water (cold and wet), as well as air (hot and wet) and its opposite, earth (cold and dry). In medieval and Renaissance Christian alchemy, the God-man Jesus on the cross thus represented the sacrificial redemption of *all* the cosmos, not only spiritually but also "chemically." When Jesus proclaimed, "Behold, I make all things new," he was referring not only to the human spirit but also the physical universe, which would be restored to its paradisiacal physical purity because of his atoning work on the cross (Revelation 21:5).

What particularly fascinated Jung in this connection was that some of his patients' dreams also displayed quaternities—both imagistically in

the form of mandalas and thematically in the form of characters who often "squared off" as paired opposites. Jung felt that this pattern must be
reflecting a profound secret about how archetypal energies interact and
distribute at the most primordial level. Clearly, these quaternities were
all *archetypal* images, evidencing a deeper *archetypal dynamic*.

This discovery accorded well with Jung's clinical observation that
there seemed to be four basic personality types—thinking, feeling, sensate, and intuitive , which would become the major categories of his *per-
sonological typology*. And after all, if, as Jung speculated, the quaternity
was a primary archetype of psychic functioning, was it all that surprising
that this fact should manifest itself in the form of four basic personality
types? With this hypothesis, the Jungian theory of typology was born,
and upon it rest many, if not most, of the current approaches to typology (von Franz and Hillman 1971).

In Jungian typology, the two pairs of opposing types are thinking/feel-
ing and sensate/intuitive. Before describing what Jung meant by these
terms, however, it is necessary to stress Jung's insistence that these terms
only described *tendencies* in each individual. Jung never claimed that,
say, a thinking type was that and *only that*—and that she could be ex-
haustively understood and successfully treated by simply knowing that
she was a thinking type. Far from it. Jung always made it clear that everyone had elements of all of the typological functions within herself, and
that different ones might predominate at different times, but that, *as a
general rule*, a particular person would *tend to use one particular type* in
her ways of dealing with the world. Jung called this the person's *superior
function*. Such knowledge was useful to have about the person, but it
should never be employed to pigeonhole her in what could only result as
a caricature of her existential richness and complexity. As Jung noted,
even Galen had said that everyone was a mixture of all the humours.

A further important caveat that Jung made was that no personality
type was intrinsically better than the other three. Each was simply a different way of seeing, being, and acting in the world, and each had its
own peculiar advantages and disadvantages, strengths and weaknesses.
Let us now look at Jung's definition of each of the types.

"Thinking is the psychological function which, following its own laws,
brings the contents of ideation into conceptual connection with each
other" (CW 6, par. 830). The thinking type is analytical. She employs

paradigms, models, theories, and systems to comprehend and change her world. A thinking type would usually make a good engineer, for example. Feeling, which is at the opposite pole from thinking, "is entirely a *subjective* process between the *ego* and a given content, a process, moreover, that imparts to the content a definite *value* in the sense of acceptance or rejection ("like" or "dislike"). The process can also appear isolated, as it were, in the form of a *mood*" (*CW* 6, par. 724). Feeling types see the world in terms of emotional preferences that are tied in to deeply held values. The political leader who is able to thrill an audience by the strength of her passionately held convictions might well be a feeling type.

The other paired opposites are the sensate and intuitive types. The sensate processes her world in terms of how it presents itself to her in immediate, concrete *perceptions and sensations*. The sensate type relies upon "the psychological function that mediates the perception of a physical stimulus. It is, therefore, identical with perception. . . . Sensation is related not only to external stimuli but to inner ones, i.e., to changes in the internal organic processes" (*CW* 6, par. 792). Finely attuned to the physical functioning of both her internal and external world, the sensate type typically shines in roles that range from everything from an athlete to an interior designer.

Intuition "is the function that mediates perceptions in an *unconscious way*. . . . In intuition a content presents itself whole and complete, without our being able to explain or discover how this content came into existence" (*CW* 6, par. 770). The intuitive person always seems to have an uncanny sense of how or why a situation came into being and what direction it will probably take. Her hunches, neither off-handed guesswork nor detailed analysis, generally seem to be right on the mark, although neither she nor anyone else can tell you exactly how this happens. Intuitive types often make excellent therapists. Indeed, Jung was himself an intuitive type, as many psychotherapists seem to be (Mattoon 1985).

As previously mentioned, Jung called a person's basic type her *superior function*, and concluded (perhaps as much for reasons of logical symmetry as because of actual clinical observation) that the opposite pole would represent the person's *inferior function*—that is to say, the person's weak spot. By this view, thinking types would tend to have the most problems with having, sorting out, and managing their feelings, whereas feeling types would struggle most with thinking deeply about their experiences. Sensate types, whose inferior function was intuition, would struggle with grasping the deeper causes and broader possibilities of a given concrete fact or situation, whereas intuitive types would often inhabit a world of imagination and thus not be adequately tuned in to their immediate physical realities. Additionally, each person also has an *auxiliary function*—or the thing at which she is "second best." Thus, a sensate type might also be inclined to have strong emotions about immediate situations, which would make feeling her auxiliary function.

Since thinking and feeling are mostly conscious processes that involve comparing and contrasting things in order to reach logico-ethical conclusions, Jung called them "rational functions." On the other hand, since sensing and intuiting rely on noncognitive processes, Jung called them "irrational functions." This latter term was unfortunate, however, for by it Jung did not mean that these functions were in any sense less adequate or valid than the rational functions. He merely meant to show that they resided more in the organic apprehension of something than in its cognitive assessment.

To complete his schema of personality type, Jung added one more dimension, inventing terms that—like shadow and persona—have become quite popular. They are *introversion* and *extraversion*. These were the two personality *attitudes*. Any of the four major functions could have either an introverted or extraverted attitude. Consequently, there are eight potential personality types. Jung himself was an introverted intuitive. *Introversion* he defined as

> an inward turning of *libido*, in the sense of a negative relation to the object. Interest does not move toward the object but withdraws from it into the subject. Everyone whose attitude is introverted thinks, feels, and acts in a way that clearly demonstrates that the subject is the prime motivating factor and that the object is of secondary importance. Introversion may be intellectual or emotional, just as it can be characterized by *sensation* or *intuition*. (CW 6, par. 769)

Conversely, *extraversion* is:

> an outward turning of *libido*. I use this concept to denote a manifest relation of subject to object, a positive movement of subjective interest

toward the object [an "object" in this case being not only a thing but also a situation, event, or person]. Everyone in the extraverted state thinks, feels, and acts in relation to the object, and moreover in a direct and clearly observable fashion, so that no doubt can remain about his positive dependence on the object. In a sense, therefore, extraversion is a transfer of interest from subject to object. If it is an extraversion of thinking, the subject thinks his way into the object; if an extraversion of feeling, he feels himself into it. In extraversion there is a strong, if not exclusive, determination by the object. (*CW* 6, par. 710)

Just as each of the four major types must be thought of as a tendency only, not as an autocratic force governing an entire personality in all circumstances, so must introversion and extraversion be seen as ways of relating to the external world that are "habitual," to be sure, but not exclusive (*CW* 6, par. 769). For instance, although I am basically an introvert, I am sometimes extraverted, especially when I am in front of a class. In short, these categories give us important information about a person—especially in a therapeutic setting—but they do not tell the whole story by a long shot (*CW* 16). Following Goethe,[6] Jung saw introversion and extraversion as cosmic opposites that caused all things at certain times to expand and other times to contract—the diastole and systole of the universe, as it were, and what ancient Chinese philosophy (in which Jung was also steeped) called *yang*, or the centrifugal, penetrating male principle, and *yin*, or the centripetal, receptive female principle. Here, as we have already seen elsewhere, Jung's psychology rests upon a dialectical view of the universe and psyche as powered by the tension and resolution of opposites.

This brief characterization of Jung's typology is highly simplified. His definitions contain many nuances, which it is beyond our purposes to examine in this study.[7] The interested reader can find the entire system of Jungian typology laid out in his *Psychological Types* (*CW* 6). The popular *Myers-Briggs Type Indicator* was devised on Jungian principles. Gardner's (1983) theory of multiple intelligences contains elements of Jungian typology. And even political theory has drawn upon Jung's model with the notion that conservative political theories, which stress the right of the individual over the collective, tend to be introverted, while the more liberal theories, putting prime importance on the equality of all members in a group, even if some individuals must relinquish certain goods or privileges to attain that goal, are more extraverted (Samuels 2001). Jungian typology has taken deep root in various social sciences and will undoubtedly continue to bear much fruit in the future.

NOTES

1. As with so much else in Freudian psychology, however, it is well to remember that his ideas invariably stem from historical roots and did not simply appear out of nowhere. The early Mesmerists, Magnetists, and other proto-psychiatrists, for instance, had noted the potentially dangerous phenomenon of the patient's growing attraction (often of a sexual nature) to the clinician as well as the patient's identification of the clinician with someone from the patient's past (Ellenberger 1970).

2. Rizutto (1979) has emphasized the perhaps obvious but nevertheless frequently overlooked point in some object-relation theory and practice that the object is not the external person as such but rather refers to the way that the subject has, for a variety of complex reasons, internalized that person. In other words, the object is not an external person but an internal image, based upon that person to be sure but not identical to it.

3. Although "having a complex" about something has come to mean something entirely negative in popular parlance, this was not how Jung saw complexes. As he wrote, having a complex "only means that something discordant, unassimilated, and antagonistic exists, perhaps as an obstacle, but also as an incentive to greater effort, and so, perhaps, to new possibilities of achievement. In this sense, then, complexes are nodal points of psychological life which we would not wish to do without; indeed, they should not be missing, for otherwise psychic life should come to a standstill" (CW 6, par. 925). See Ellenberger (1970) for the historical precedents of the idea of a "complex" in earlier psychiatry.

4. Winnicott's disinclination to consider countertransference a valid part of the therapeutic process may be due to the fact that his work was primarily with children, who, because they are particularly vulnerable, certainly have a special need to be protected against harmful countertransferences from the analyst.

5. As unusual as this claim appears, there is an impressive body of evidence and literature to suggest that it may actually be so, as I firmly believe to be the case from many of my own experiences as a teacher and counselor, a few of which I discuss in following chapters. Jung's phrase *sacred precinct* may be more literally descriptive than even he completely understood.

6. Jung greatly admired Goethe and was sometimes reputed (probably erroneously) to be one of his descendants, a rumor that Jung perhaps subtly encouraged while explicitly denying it.

7. Jungian typology has been quite influential in education in terms of studying and improving teachers' and students' styles of relating to each other and the curriculum. In fact, it is the only aspect of Jungian psychology that *has* been widely and systematically applied to educational issues, and it is precisely for that reason that I do not focus on it in this study.

3

FROM SUNRISE TO NOON: THE ASCENDING EGO

JUNG'S DEVELOPMENTAL PSYCHOLOGY

One of Jung's greatest contributions to twentieth-century psychology was his model of psychological development. Certainly, he was not the first modern psychologist to offer a stage theory of human growth. For example, Freud's famous paradigm of psychosexual maturation, relating to different areas of the growing infant's body, postulated an *oral stage* from birth to about one year old, an *anal stage* from one to three, a *phallic stage* from three to six, a *latency period* from seven to eleven, and the culminating *genital stage* beginning in adolescence and continuing throughout one's life. Piaget (Piaget and Inhelder 1969) believed that *cognitive* development unfolded in fairly universal and invariant steps: a *sensori-motor stage* from birth to two, a *preoperational stage* from two to six, a *concrete operational stage* from seven to eleven, and the culminating *formal operation stage*, starting around twelve years old and continuing throughout the adult's life as he continued to refine his ability to reason. Kohlberg (1987) hypothesized that one's ability to reach moral conclusions about problematic situations also unfolded in three stages: *preconventional*, *conventional*, and *postconventional*.

As useful as Jung generally found such models, he noted that they all tended to operate on the strange assumption that sometime during adolescence, the individual's growth came *substantially* to an end and that the rest of his life was more or less just an elaboration of what he had already become at that early age. To Jung, this seemed unnecessarily limiting, consigning the later years of one's life to the outer darkness of developmental oblivion—as if those years were simply a falling away from the heyday of youth, and not a legitimate and important—indeed, crowning—element of one's experiences.

If genius resides, as some have said, in the ability to see and the courage to proclaim the obvious, then Jung's theory of development is certainly the product of genius, for what could be more obvious than the grossly overlooked fact that not only the first eleven or twelve years of life but also the remaining six or seven decades evolved towards ever higher syntheses and visions? "Our life," Jung said in simple terms that would nevertheless change scientific theories of development, "is like the course of the sun."

> In the morning it gains continually in strength until it reaches the zenith-heat of high noon. Then comes the enantiodromia [or, reversal of the flow of energy—an important concept in Jung]: the steady forward movement no longer denotes an increase, but a decrease, in strength. Thus our task in handling a young person is different from the task of handling an older person. In the former case, it is enough to clear away all the obstacles that hinder expansion and ascent; in the latter, we must nurture everything that assists the descent. . . . [I]t is a great mistake to think that the meaning of life is exhausted with the period of youth and expansion, that, for example, a woman who has passed the menopause is "finished." The afternoon of life is just as full of meaning as the morning; only, its meaning and purpose are different. Man has two aims; the first is the natural aim, the begetting of children and the business of protecting the brood; to this belongs the acquisition of money and social position. When this aim has been reached a new phase begins: the cultural aim. (*CW* 7, par. 114)

By the "cultural aim," Jung meant more than just an involvement in the arts and humanities, although that might be part of it. Rather, he wanted to signify that the aging individual, moving ever closer to death and what might lie beyond it, could make and share deep psychological, moral, and spiritual discoveries. These could then become part of the collective wisdom of the family, group, nation, and even specie. A society that disprized old people, therefore, valuing only sexual, social, and financial goals (as he believed was true of American culture) was doomed to cultural catastrophe. For it ignored the elders whose wisdom was alone capable of both maintaining and enhancing the valuable traditions of the people. A modern Jungian, Michael Gellert, has used this developmental idea to critique current American society and its undervaluing—indeed, its desperate denial—of the rich process of aging. "A nation that is tyrannically gripped by the spirit of youth," Gellert writes, "will worship it and be addicted to it in a broad variety of forms. It will not be able to satisfy its appetites, live within its means, or set limits upon itself, either material or moral" (2001, 22).

Jung said that the first half of life, until about thirty-five to forty, generally was, and should be, more extraverted—dedicated to the tasks of personal and social identity formation and functioning. The second half of life, on the other hand, should lean increasingly toward the pole of introversion—as the individual plumbed the depths of his experience to mine spiritual treasures. Obviously, this does not mean that younger people should never be introspective or that older people should never play a public role. It is simply to say, as Jung sagely observed, that "what youth found, and must find outside, the man of life's afternoon must find within himself."

There can be no doubt that Freud was the pioneering modern psychologist of the early years of life, but Jung was the pioneering psychologist of life's later years (Staude 1981). Let us now look in more detail at Jung's lifespan developmental model and its wide range of educational implications.

INFANCY AND CHILDHOOD

The first stage that Jung identified was *infancy and childhood*; the second, *adolescence and young adulthood*; the third, *midlife*; and the fourth, *old age and death* (Mattoon 1985).[1]

In large measure, Jung followed Freud in his understanding of the major tasks and increments that characterized growth during this period. He felt that Freud's mapping of the child's psychosexual growth from the earliest oral phases to the concluding genital ones was more or less accurate. He strongly disagreed with Freud about the Oedipus complex, however.

Jung agreed that this complex—or something resembling it—existed but felt that it signified much more than Freud suspected. It was true, Jung allowed, that the male child wished to merge with its mother during its early years, but it was equally true, he believed, that the female child also wished to do so. What is more, this impulse toward maternal merger—although it might sometimes present itself sexually—was only secondarily sexual if at all. Rather, it represented the child's natural but regressive longing to return to the blissful comfort of the womb (and not only the physical womb of its biological mother but the cosmic womb of the archetypal great-mother) instead of having to undergo the trials of developing a differentiated ego that would one day have to stand on its own in the world.

As we saw above, Freud had at different times called this regressive tendency the death instinct, *Thanatos*, and, later, the *Nirvana Principle*. It took Jung to detect the archetypal side of this primal impulse to return to sheer absorption in the cosmos. It was this archetype of reabsorption into the great mother, not the child's desire to possess the birth mother sexually, that gave rise to Oedipal issues in the life of the child— and even the life of the adult.

Many neo-Jungian developmentalists are beginning to incorporate the thought of some of Freud's earliest disciples such as Melanie Klein (1932/1975) and object-relation theorists such as Winnicott (1992), Fairbairn (1952/1992), and Kohut (1984) into archetypal models of early childhood development. These newer models rest upon two pillars: first is the essentially Freudian notion that the way a child learns to relate to the world is greatly determined by the nature of its earliest relationship with the primary object of its passionate focus—the mother; and second is the Jungian insistence that the child's archetypal and instinctual expectations of and attitudes toward the universal mother-figure underlie and inform the child's relationship with its biological mother in many ways.[2]

Both (neo-)Freudians and (neo-)Jungians agree that the child's ego consciousness begins to "gel" around three years of age. How this happens is a subject of considerable complexity and contention. Many theorists take Melanie Klein's (1932/1975) view, however, that the primal, undifferentiated, non-egoic consciousness that is the child's at birth gradually "de-integrates" into pockets of more focused awareness in which it is forced to "de-fuse" from the mother and see her—and more and more to see the entire background world—as separate from itself. Primarily, this recognition relates to Winnicott's important notion of the mother perceived by baby as a "good breast"—that is, the mother as the ever-present supplier of the child's every feeding need upon demand—or as a "bad breast"—that is, when the mother is beginning to wean the child, thereby forcing it to "understand" that, since there is obviously a difference between its wants and the world, there must therefore be *an even more fundamental difference between itself and the world in the first place.*[3]

Learning that the world is not simply coextensive with itself, the infant begins to grasp the reality of "the other"—and, therefore, of oneself—as a discrete existential entity. The world is no longer an extension of the baby but something with which the baby must deal—sometimes unsuccessfully. As these pockets of focused, situational awareness begin to congeal—or re-integrate, as Klein says—into a functional complex, the ego is born. Not surprisingly, then, it is at about this time that the child begins to refer to it-self as "I" and not in the third-person singular. Jung early on formulated the notion that the ego is not a unitary thing with which a child is born or which it develops all at once and suddenly "has" but is rather an intricate set of shifting yet cohesive accommodations to one's biophysical and psychosocial world. In other words, the ego is not a fixed entity but a dynamic "complex."

"The ego," observed Jung, "ostensibly the thing we know most about, is in fact a highly complex affair full of unfathomable obscurities" (*CW* 14, par. 129). For an ego to be healthy requires that these multifarious elements be contained within a more or less stable and predictable "force field"—identifiable both by oneself and others as an egoic personality. This is what creates the sense of continuity between the "me" that I experience one day and the "me" that I experience the next, even though these "me's" are not exactly the same and may even be quite different. The absence of such a sense of personal continuity is what characterizes many psychoses. The Jungian theorist Erich Neumann put the matter in slightly different archetypal terms by talking of the child's evolution from the *uroboric stage* (intrauterine and neonatal fusion with the mother), to the *matriarchal stage* (increasing perception of the mother as "other"), to the *patriarchal stage* (the first stages in the development of the ego).

According to Jung, neurosis is an instability of the ego but not such a drastic one as to threaten the ego's essential core, contours, and functions. Psychosis, however, represents such a shattering inrush of personal and collective unconscious contents and forces that the ego, unable to maintain its unity, explodes into a psychic kaleidoscope of disconnected fragments (*CW* 17, par. 207). With the destruction of the ego, the psyche is thrown naked and defenseless again onto the primal ground of being. In archetypal terms, this means being consumed by "the terrible mother" of primal being, often represented in myth, dreams, fantasy, and fairy tales as the mother who eats her children, the "Mother of Death," the *mater sarcophagi*.

The proper nurturance of the child's growing ego is thus crucial to its later psychosocial competency; for, without a firm ego foundation laid in these first three years, the child will subsequently be prone to the whole gamut of neurotic and psychotic breaks. In the classic study *The Inner World of Childhood*, Jungian analyst Frances Wickes (1927/1966) examined how, from a Jungian point of view with Freudian colorations, parents and teachers could best provide such nurturance. Today, the most prominent Jungian to take a similar tack is Fordham in his work *Children as Individuals* (1994).

ADOLESCENCE AND YOUNG ADULTHOOD

Jung called adolescence the time of "psychic birth" because it is then that the young person earnestly begins to establish himself as an autonomous individual. This is accomplished through separation from the parents and the emergence of sexuality—those two crucial steps on the road to establishing one's own family and role(s) in society. Because this is the time when the young adult begins (or at least *should begin*) to put together its various psychosocial elements into the form of a relatively freestanding individual identity, Edinger (1985) calls it the *integrative stage*, considering it a fourth stage in addition to Neumann's *uroboric-matriarchal-patriarchal* stages.

Since the steps and challenges that characterize this stage are relatively constant across cultures, Stevens (1999) notes that there is an "archetypal program responsible for this elaborate transformation of the child into the adult" and that it contains four major aspects: "(1) the attenuation of the parental bond, (2) the war of the generations, (3) the activation of the sexual affectional system, and (4) initiation into the adult role" (117). Freud neatly summarized the adolescent transition as preparation for a life of "love and work."

In indigenous, preliterate cultures, the challenges of passing from youth into adulthood are effectively handled by initiation rites. These rites take many forms, of course, depending on the culture and whether or not the initiate is a male or female. Initiation rites generally seem to be more elaborate, dramatic, and dangerous for males than for females in many preliterate societies. This is probably at least partially due to the fact that a male, in order to establish his psychosexual identity, needs to end the period of fusion with his mother, whereas the female, if her relationship with her mother is good, discovers important aspects of her psychosexual identity through deepening identification with the mother (Chodorow 1978). There is doubtless significant cultural variation in this pattern (Rogoff 1984), but as a general rule it seems to hold good (Conger and Galambos 1997). Jung wrote:

All primitive groups and tribes that are in any way organized have their rites of initiation, often very highly developed, which play an extraordinarily important part in their social and religious life. Through these ceremonies boys are made men and girls women. The Kavirondos stigmatize those who do not submit to circumcision and excision as "animals." This shows that the initiation ceremonies are a magical means of leading man from the animal state. They are clearly transformation mysteries of the greatest significance. Very often the initiands are subjected to excruciating treatment, and at the same time the tribal mysteries are imparted to them, the laws and hierarchy of the tribe on the one hand, and on the other the cosmogonic and mythical doctrines. Initiations have survived among all cultures. In Greece the ancient Eleusinian mysteries were preserved, it seems, right into the seventh century of our era. Rome was flooded with mystery religions. Of these, Christianity was one, and even in its present form still preserves the old initiation ceremonies, somewhat faded and degraded, in the rites of baptism, confirmation, and communion. Hence, nobody is in a position to deny the enormous historical importance of initiations. (*CW* 7, par. 384)

The problem in (post)industrial societies is that they no longer have these initiation rites. We feel that we are too "enlightened" to engage in such "primitive nonsense." Besides, public education forces children into a lock-step march from grade to grade, and then on to some form of postsecondary vocational preparation, basically unconcerned with the subtler developmental needs of children but quite anxiously attuned to the demand of corporate capitalism for obedient and efficient "worker-citizens" (Spring 1976). Nevertheless, the *need* for initiation (and not only from adolescence into young adulthood but arguably into *any* major life stage) persists in the human psyche, for it is an archetype. Wickes (1927/1966, 253) has illustrated this point through a dream of a teenager whom she was treating:

> He was having difficulty in making his adult adaptation. He dreamed that he was on the athletic field and knocked out two front teeth. He saw them lying on the ground in front of him and stooped down to pick them up and put them in again. His instructor said, "Don't do that, if you do you will never grow up." The dreamed impressed itself so by its vividness that he repeated it, though it seemed mere nonsense. In reality it was a portrayal of his own situation. In many primitive tribes one of the ceremonies of initiation when the youth ceases to become a child and takes his place among the men of the tribe is to knock out the two front teeth. In his dream he tried to pick up the teeth and put them back. In reality he was trying not to accept the initiation into adult life but to remain a child. His instructor, who in the dream took the part which would have been taken by the medicine man, says to him when he would put back the teeth, the childish attitude, "Do not do that or you will never grow up."

Helping adolescents move into adulthood in ways that are psychospiritually authentic, exciting, and fulfilling may not serve the bottom lines of capitalism; it may even be something that the child himself occasionally resists, but it remains an unavoidable psychological and moral imperative. It is simply a fact, Jung insisted, that

> the whole symbolism of initiation rises up, clear and unmistakable, in the unconscious contents [of the modern mind no less than the "primitive"

one]. The objection that this is antiquated superstition and altogether un-
scientific is about as intelligent as remarking, in the presence of a cholera
epidemic, that it is merely an infectious disease and exceedingly unhy-
gienic. (*CW* 7, par. 385)

Jung's point is that if we do not offer our youth psychospiritually compelling and socially constructive forms of initiation (that go beyond the
paltry signposts of getting good marks on an SAT exam or landing a job
as a waiter), then they will continue to respond to the archetypal call of
initiation rites in other ways. Drugs, "extreme sports," premarital sex,
and criminal activity will rush in to to fill the archetypal vacuum when
parents and society do not. Both as parents and educators, it is important to bear in mind Mattoon's (1985) sage observation that "the 'un-
bearable age'—adolescence—might be more bearable . . . if the culture
provided an adequate initiation, comparable to the rituals of many preliterate societies" (171).

NOTES

1. Stevens (1999) offers a slightly different rendering of the Jungian model
that includes transitional substages.
2. As Samuels (1997) has perspicuously noted, this new turn in some developmental theories shows how closely Freudian and Jungian theory are related,
how fruitfully they can interact, and how possible such interaction is when each
school of thought is willing to see the truth that the other side has. It makes one
wonder just how much richer and more effective modern depth psychology
would be today if such ideological and practical alliances had been forged earlier in the twentieth century rather than later.
3. The Jungian child psychiatrist Michael Fordham has written about the archetypal patterns and de-integrations inherent in the good-breast/bad-breast
dichotomy (1994).

4

FROM NOON TO SUNSET: THE EMERGING SELF

JUNG AND THE "DISCOVERY" OF MIDLIFE

Most people know the term "midlife crisis." The idea of a difficult transition from the first to the second half of life is part of the popular repertoire of psychological concepts. What is less well known is that Carl Jung was the first twentieth-century psychologist to focus on this phenomenon. Jung is thus the first great psychologist of the time from midlife to death—from late noon to sunset. He laid the groundwork for succeeding researchers of later life, such as Erikson (1997), Levinson (1978), and Wrightsman (1994).

In naming the midlife crisis, Jung was merely rendering in modern therapeutic terms what already had been recognized by many poets and philosophers in the past. Dante's *Divine Comedy*, for instance, begins with the poet lamenting that:

> Midway in our life's journey, I went astray
> From the straight road and woke to find myself
> Alone in a dark wood. How shall I say
>
> What wood that was! I never saw so drear,
> So rank, so arduous a wilderness!
> Its very memory gives a shape to fear. (1954, 28)

In wryer tones, the mythologist Joseph Campbell has likened the midlife crisis to climbing up a very high ladder, finally getting to the top after great effort, looking around—and realizing that you climbed up the wrong wall!

We have seen that during the first half of life, there are major, compelling tasks that most people feel obliged, even eager to perform: establishing a personal identity, learning to work, finding a suitable mate, starting a family, and generally learning how to negotiate those thousand-and-one other psychosocial rules and roles that comprise the life of most young adults. These are psychosocial aims that are naturally suited to the physical resilience, emotional exuberance, and healthy ambition of youth. It is of the first importance to the survival of any culture that its youth be ready, willing, and able to take these jobs on and carry them through.

However, as a person reaches midlife (around thirty-five to forty years of age), her physical energy begins to wane and her body to lose its suppleness and responsiveness. Face lifts, tummy tucks, expensive skin creams, strenuous exercise regimens, and other costly and time-consuming things (available to only a favored few on the planet) can only delay this process a bit—for no one has ever found the fountain of youth. Decay and death are the irrevocable decrees of nature.

By midlife, too, one has already made a string of major choices that more or less define—and restrict—further options. In what might be called "the arrival syndrome," a person realizes that although some changes can be made in her life from this point on, and perhaps even a few major ones, many, if not most, of her major decisions have already been made. She must live by the consequences. The family that one has created, the networks of friends established, the experiences accrued, and the profession pursued define boundaries beyond which it is hard—and sometimes simply impossible—to go.

Given these pretty firm contours, borders, and horizons, the individual now looks at the existential landscape on which she suddenly finds herself and asks, "Is what I have created of real value? Have I been true to myself in creating it? Can it sustain me emotionally and morally through the rest of my life? If not, what changes need to be made—and what sacrifices will such changes require? Where are the new challenges that make life exciting—and, indeed, *are* there any new challenges that will make life even half as exciting as the first half of life? How can I deal with the fact that this body is beginning to sink and wrinkle and that, no matter what I do, I will never have the youthful frame or physiology that were once mine and that, physically and emotionally, carried me through so many hard times? How can I deal with the unmet expectations, frustrations, and even tragedies that life has dealt me and which can never be altered, for they are inscribed in the Book of the Past? And above all, how can I cope with the fact that my death—once such a distant, even unreal possibility—is now within sight at the end of the tunnel, approaching with what seems to be increasing velocity with the passing of each year?" No wonder the beginning of midlife is a time of increased rates of suicide and divorce (Wrightsman 1994).

Not everyone faces this passage bravely or productively. Some simply dull themselves to its reality by "keeping on keeping on" with a boring and sterile regularity from which they dare not deviate and which they refuse to examine—what Thoreau called "a life of quiet desperation." Others lose themselves in practices and substances that, briefly and pathetically, allow them to maintain the illusion of regained youth: affairs with younger lovers, exorbitant expenditures on fast cars and clothing, excessive drinking and drugs, and so on. But these are makeshifts, doomed to only a short season of dubious efficacy; by their very nature, they could never promote psychospiritual deepening and moral maturation, which Jung saw as the appropriate goal of the second half of life. He called this goal *individuation*.

INDIVIDUATION: LIFE'S HOLY GRAIL

As is so often the case with Jungian concepts, it is difficult to find a single definition of individuation that covers every sense in which Jung used the term. In large measure, this is because the process of individuation is itself a mystery not to be completely penetrated by words and theories—although they can help us understand and approach it better. Given the mysterious nature of this process, and also given that Jung's understanding of it deepened as his scholarly studies, medical practice, and personal experiences developed, it is not surprising that many Jungians construe the word in different ways—although most of these ways bear a "genetic" similarity to each other.

Late in his life, Jung (1965, xxi) claimed that individuation is not—as some have said—just a psychic process; it is a universal one, being "a biological fact—simple or complicated according to circumstances—by means of which every living thing becomes that which it was destined to become from the very beginning. This process naturally expresses itself in man just as much psychically as somatically." This characterization of individuation—reminiscent of Maslow's "self actualization" (1968)—is interesting because it combines what sometimes seem to be two competing strains of thought in Jung—namely, that (1) psychic processes are biologically grounded (not a surprising conclusion coming from a physician and a former student of Sigmund Freud, who maintained until the end of his life that psyche was ultimately a biochemical phenomenon and nothing more); and also that (2) psychic processes are morally and spiritually goal directed according to a higher power and purpose. In short, Jung was willing to allow that psyche has its roots in physiology—as all creatures must—yet he insisted that psyche is not limited to the merely physical domain but has within it the seeds of divinity. Man is a creature in nature to be sure, but he is also potentially transcendent.

Whereas the Freudian definition of psyche as ultimately just biochemical is "reductive," the Jungian idea that psyche ultimately follows a higher spiritual trajectory is "constructive." Jung made this distinction in discussing the fact that when dealing with any sort of psychological event there are two basic methods of interpretation that can be used depending on the nature of the case. The reductive approach can be useful in locating and treating the physical source of a pathology, Jung admitted. The problem with this approach is that not all psychological phenomena are pathological.

> A constructive point of view must be considered for all cases where the conscious attitude is more or less normal, but capable of greater development and refinement, or where unconscious tendencies, also capable of development, are being misunderstood and kept under by the conscious mind. The reductive standpoint . . . always leads back to the primitive and elementary. The constructive standpoint, on the other hand, tries to synthesize, to build up, to direct one's gaze forwards. (CW 17, par. 195)

This synthesizing, building up, and forward-gazing define individuation as the process of "'becoming oneself,' that is, who one really is. This suggests a balanced or optimum development" (Samuels 1997, 103).

But the human individual is not fully human, development is not "balanced or optimum," if she has no higher purpose that governs her life. The individuation process is the quest for this moral goal—it is "man's search for meaning" (Frankl 1967).

In other words, Jung's psychological theories are *teleological*. This means that they are focused more on the *purpose* of phenomena than on their physical causes, more concerned with the *ultimate moral goal* of things than with their proximate determinants, more *ethical* than merely descriptive. This focus sharply distinguishes Jung's thought from the materialist psychologies that dominated his day and ours, and has caused various critics to dismiss Jungian theory as mere "mysticism" and "pseudoreligion." Such is the joyless temper of our times that the attempt to understand psychic functioning in the light of a higher spiritual vision generally incurs academic and clinical disapproval. It has been forgotten that the world "psyche" comes from the Greek word for "spirit." Happily, this grim dogma has been yielding over the last several decades to more humane points of view in psychological theory and practice—due in no small measure to the influence of Jung himself.

THE PERSONA AND THE SHADOW
IN THE INDIVIDUATION PROCESS

Since individuation entails an ongoing journey into one's deepest truths, it follows that one must "divest the self of the false wrappings of the persona" in order to take part in it (*CW* 7, par. 269). One cannot live by the light of what the theologian Paul Tillich (1956/1987) called one's "ultimate concerns" if the clouds of inauthenticity darken the horizon. Of course, as we saw earlier, the persona is not necessarily inauthentic. Correctly used, it is a serviceable psychosocial instrument: its healthy formation and legitimate employment are central to attaining the goals of the first half of life. But in the second half of life—the individual having already established herself in various psychosocial ways—there is a decreasing need for the persona, and increasing time, opportunity, and psychic and moral capacity to lay that persona aside, to deemphasize (although never ignore) one's *social* roles and responsibilities, and to ask the very big questions. These are what Eliot (1971, 6) called "the overwhelming questions," about oneself as an *individual* in the womb of eternity and the hands of the Divine. It is time, in short, to *individuate*, to be "born again"—as Jesus said to Nicodemus (John 3:6).

In looking at the persona earlier in this study, we saw that it is the obverse of the shadow. The persona is what we want others to see and think about us. The shadow is exactly what we do not want them to see and think about us—and what we ourselves do not want to see and think about ourselves. There can be no room for the deception of self or other in the individuation process. Just as it demands that she push past the persona, individuation also demands that she push *deeper into* the shadow so as to bring it to an even higher degree of awareness, integrating those elements that have the potential to be healthily empowering while maturely working on and working through those elements that are not. But hasn't this always been the first requirement of any morally significant growth—dealing with our own darkness, with that part of us that "harbors hungry, instinctual desirousness and is contaminated with the unconscious" (Edinger 1985, 21–22), dealing what Buddhism calls "the hungry ghosts" of the ego?

The *integration of the shadow* is the psychological equivalent of baptism, according to Edinger.

> Baptism is basically a purification ritual that washes one clean of dirt, both literal and spiritual. Washings were frequently preliminary procedures in religious ceremonies, in the Eleusinian Mysteries for instance. Psychologically, the dirt or sin that is washed away by baptism can be understood as unconsciousness, shadow qualities of which one is unaware. Psychological cleanliness means not literal purity, but awareness of one's own dirt. If one is psychologically clean, one will not contaminate one's environment with shadow projections. (Edinger 1985, 72–73)

This task requires focused commitment—and cannot be achieved merely by abstract understanding or casual assent. It is a wrenching *experience* that involves the whole person. This is why Jung warned against full immersion in this process until one was mature enough. "This way of development has scarcely any meaning before the middle of life . . . , and, if entered upon too soon can be decidedly injurious" (Jung 1978, 16). "Nobody can really understand these things unless he has experienced them himself," such experiences usually being the fruits of a lifetime of effort (*CW* 7, par. 340). It is true that intimations of individuation can oc-cur throughout one's life—as Fordham (1994), who sees rudimentary forms of individuation occurring in infants, reminds us. However, it is only deep experience of the world and oneself, and the waxing longing for the divine in the face of one's waning time, that provide all the nec-essary tools and dispositions for individuation to fully unfold.

It is indicative of Jung's basic optimism that he saw individuation as an experience that is available to anyone with the psychological courage and moral maturity to cultivate it, and that he viewed this endeavor as ultimately *good*, bringing peace, fulfillment, and the fortitude to face one's aging and death with courage and hope.

> So far as we can make out, *individuation* is a natural phenomenon, and in a way an inescapable goal, which we have reason to call *good for us*, be-cause it liberates us from the otherwise insoluble conflict of opposites (at least to a noticeable degree). It is not invented by man, but Nature her-self produces its archetypal image. Thus the credo "in the end all shall be well" is not without its psychic foundation. (*CW* 18, par. 1641)

On the other hand, Jung was no Pollyanna. His was a tempered opti-mism that understood quite well the tragicomic limitations and inade-quacies of each human being. He hastened to add to the quote above that "it is more than questionable whether this phenomenon is of any importance to the world in general, or only to the individual who has reached a more complete state of consciousness" (*CW* 18, par. 1641). Jung thus discerned an "aristocratic" side to individuation because not many people will ultimately take that path. This idea has provided am-munition for Jung's critics, who want to portray him as intellectually or politically elitist. But this is not true, as we see in his insistence that

> the possibility of psychic development . . . is not reserved for specially gifted individuals. In other words, in order to undergo a far-reaching psy-chological development, neither outstanding intelligence nor any other talent is necessary, since in this development moral qualities can make up for intellectual shortcomings. It must not on any account be imagined that the treatment consists in grafting upon people's minds general formulas and complicated doctrines. There is no question of that. Each can take what he needs, in his own way and in his own language. (*CW* 7, par. 198)

THE TRANSPERSONAL NATURE OF INDIVIDUATION

So far we have been looking at individuation in terms of its *personal* dynamics, for the operations of the persona and shadow move well within the parameters of Freudian ego-psychology. If Jung had taken the process no farther than this, he would only have been adding a few interesting insights and terms to something that Freud had already substantially discovered and preliminarily mapped.

However, Jung *did* take the exploration much farther—into the regions of the *transpersonal*. As Maslow (whose researches also ultimately went beyond the realm of personal "self-actualization" into the transpersonal) also found later in his career, people can never find completion if they do not find something greater than themselves to love and serve—and something that inspires them to love and serve others, too. What Maslow found was that, above and beyond self-actualization needs, there is an inborn human need to *go beyond oneself*; to make psychological contact with "the naturalistically transcendent, spiritual, and axiological" (1968, vi). He called this religion with a little "r," since it does not require commitment to a specific religious doctrine.

With its roots in Jung's work, what would finally come to be called "transpersonal psychology" thus sprang forth and began to flower (Cortright 1997; Ferrer 2002; Wilber 2000). Said Maslow (1968) in the now famous preface to his groundbreaking work, *Toward a Psychology of Being*:

> I consider Humanistic, Third Force Psychology [i.e., the personalistic psychology of existential self-actualization, with the First and Second Forces being Behaviorism and Freudianism] to be transitional, a preparation for a still "higher" Fourth Psychology, transpersonal, transhuman, centered in the cosmos rather than in human needs and interest, going beyond humanness, identity, self-actualization, and the like. . . . Without the transpersonal, we get sick, violent, and nihilistic, or else hopeless and apathetic. (iii–iv)

In Jungian psychology, the "naturalistically transcendent" is found in the archetypal realm. Archetypes—those inborn dispositions and expectations, hopes and fears, potentials and limitations that express themselves in images and narrations that vary across persons and cultures—rest on similar *structural* foundations across all peoples and times.

Having a certain air of eternal durability about them, these structural foundations accord well with the idea of the "naturalistically transcendent." "Ingrained in man's make-up," says Aniela Jaffe, one of Jung's closest collaborators, archetypes are "unconscious operators that constantly arrange the contents of consciousness everywhere in accordance with their own structural form, thus accounting for the similarity of [archetypal] imagery" (1975, 15). They are the clusters of a priori psychic energies that interface with the most ancient and basic rhythms and realities of the universe that shape the human mind and heart.

As the capacity to perceive, pursue, embrace, and act upon that which is eternal, the archetypal capacity of the psyche makes meaning possible for the human being in what would otherwise seem to be a random, incomprehensible universe. They are what makes humans *human*.[1] Fall and redemption, death and resurrection, the devil and the savior, the great mother and the mother of death, the wise father and the despot, love and war, the magical child and the wicked spirit, the heroic call to adventure and the dark forest of trials, marriages and temples, oaths and covenants—these are but a few of the archetypes that crop up in some form in most of those religious stories that underlie and legitimate every society.

As Berger has so searchingly put it, "every human society is, in the last resort, men banded together in the face of death. The power of religion depends, in the last resort, upon the credibility of the banners it puts in the hands of men as they stand before death, or more accurately, as they walk, inevitably, toward it" (1967, 52). It is the proximity of those religions to the vivifying presence of the archetypal realm that invests them with "credibility." The archetypal realm thus allows us to structure our society and perceive our world in rich moral terms. These archetypes—not the sexual drive or the will to power—are what truly form the foundation of the psyche. Here, our psyches meet and meld with the mysteries of universal nature. Here, inner and outer reality inexplicably yet inextricably join. And so it is to this realm that we must turn, particularly in the second half of life, in order to gain the crown of individuation.

Going well beyond the limited scope of conceptual language, these eternal realities must present themselves to us in a different language from that used in merely logical analyses and propositional assertions.

They must speak to us in the transcendent language of symbols, those "time-bound expressions of timeless realities" (Henderson 1984, 249). Archetypal symbols—especially in dreams, religion, and art—are not of a lower order of reality—as our empirical, market-driven society would have us believe—but of a higher order because they point *beyond* us, and at the same time *within* us, to transcendent truths. The process of individuation thus not only invites but also requires us to embrace what Jung called "the symbolic life" (*CW* 18).

THE SYMBOL IN INDIVIDUATION

What is a symbol? At a bare minimum, a symbol is "the best possible expression for something that cannot be expressed otherwise than by a more or less close analogy" (*CW* 8, par. 148). Pointing to a reality that goes beyond the narrow boundaries of mere ego consciousness, a symbol is "the best possible expression for a complex fact not yet clearly apprehended by consciousness" (*CW* 8, par. 148). A symbol embodies a *personally subconscious* or *collectively unconscious* reality.[2] Jung suggests something of the tremendous "span" of the symbol into the realms of both our deepest depths and highest heights in observing that "the symbol is the primitive exponent of the unconscious, but at the same time an idea that corresponds to the highest intuition of the conscious mind" (*CW* 18, par. 44). It is not enough merely to *analyze* our symbols (as in Freudian psychology). We must engage in a living *interaction and dialogue with them* in dreams, art, myth, and religion. There are many techniques in Jungian psychology for doing this. One of the most important is *active imagination*.

In active imagination, the analysand, in the waking state, allows herself to continue with an image or theme of a particular dream to see where it might lead. Jung wrote:

> Continuous conscious realization of unconscious fantasies, together with active participation in the fantastic events, has, as I have witnessed in a very large number of cases, the effect firstly of extending the conscious horizon by the inclusion of numerous unconscious contents; secondly of gradually diminishing the dominant influence of the unconscious; and thirdly of bringing about a change of personality. (*CW* 7, par. 358)

Of course, Jung is not advising us to *act out* on the images from our dream life—although active imagination may lead to action that needs to be taken in one's life but that one has been unwisely avoiding for one reason or another. Rather, it is a matter of promoting a healthy alliance between one's conscious and unconscious lives—between the realm of ego and the realm of symbol—so that both might enrich and complete each other.

I often find both in myself and my clients in counseling that carrying a dream image through provides a wonderful sense of closure as well as possibility, thereby infusing the psyche with new energy for constructive action. For "the achievement of a synthesis of conscious and unconscious contents, and the conscious realization of the archetype's effects upon the conscious contents, represents the climax of a concentrated spiritual and psychic effort, in so far as this is undertaken consciously and of set purpose" (*CW* 8, par. 413). As Jung warns, however, this is a technique that, because of its psychic potency, "is perfected only after long practice" and should usually be developed only with the aid of a therapist (*CW* 7, par. 366).

Active imagination, like most Jungian techniques for accessing deeper realms, is thus a thoroughly symbolic process, for:

> an archetype expresses itself, first and foremost, in metaphors. If such a content should speak of the sun and identify it with the lion, the king, the hoard of gold guarded by the dragon, or the power that makes for the life and health of man, it is neither the one thing nor the other, but the unknown third thing that finds more or less adequate expression in all these similes, yet—to the perpetual vexation of the intellect—remains unknown and not to be fitted into a formula. (*CW* 9.1, par. 267)

Because symbols are living things, they are always transforming into something new, something potentially revelatory. Like the archetypes that they embody, archetypal symbols can never be fixed categories but must always remain pulsing mysteries. "Clear-cut distinctions and strict formulations are quite impossible" in dealing with archetypes and archetypal images, for "a kind of fluid interpenetration" characterizes them both, so that "they can only be roughly circumscribed at best. . . . Every attempt to focus them more sharply is immediately punished by the intangible core of meaning losing its luminosity." As what Jung called essentially "autonomous psychic contents," archetypes and their images "are the imperishable elements of the unconscious, but they change their shape continually" (*CW* 9.1, par. 301). Like the word of God as portrayed in the New Testament, the symbol is "quick and powerful, and sharper than any two-edged sword, piercing even to the dividing asunder of soul and spirit, and of the joints and marrow . . . , a discerner of the thoughts and intents of the heart" (Hebrews 4:12).

For Freud, a symbol was a dark token—relatively fixed and formulaically interpreted—pointing *back* to a *sexual problem*. Jung saw symbols in a broader and more positive light—pointing *forward* to a *spiritual solution*. So radically different was their understanding of the source and purpose of symbols, in fact, that some scholars see it as the primary cause of the final split between the two men (Papadopoulos 1991). Symbols *could be* problematic in Jung's view, but not, as for Freud, when we are flooded with them but when we did not have enough of them in their restorative abundance.

A person or culture becomes ill when alienated from life-giving symbols. It is this *asymbolism* that underlies the emotional and spiritual crisis of our time. "Now, we have no symbolic life," lamented Jung, in a conversation with a group of British psychiatrists,

> and we are all badly in need of the symbolic life. Only the symbolic life can express the soul—the daily need of the soul, mind you! And because people have no such thing, they can never step out of this mill—this awful, grinding, banal life in which they are "nothing but.". . . [T]here is no symbolic existence in which I am something else, in which I am fulfilling my role, my role as one of the actors in the divine drama of life. . . . That gives the only meaning to human life. That gives peace, when people feel that they are living the symbolic life, that they are actors in the divine drama. . . . [E]verything else is banal and you can dismiss it. (*CW* 18, pars. 627, 628, 630)

The Jungian view of symbols explains why the arts, humanities, and theology have turned to Jung as the twentieth-century psychologist whose finger most delicately palpated the pulse of the human soul.

"ANIMA AND ANIMUS": THE FIRST
SYMBOLS OF THE COLLECTIVE UNCONSCIOUS

We saw earlier that as ego consciousness begins to approach the threshold of the personal subconscious, the figure of the shadow begins to
make its appearance. Similarly, as ego consciousness moves beyond the
personal subconscious into the collective unconscious, it is also met by
two more "guardian figures." Jung called them the anima and animus,
the female and male forms of the Latin word for "soul." When these figures begin to make their appearance—whether in dreams, guided fantasy, artistic creation, or in some other way—we know that we are entering what Jung called "the sacred precincts" of the collective unconscious.

The anima, a female, is the figure who, for the male, symbolizes this
entrance into the archetypal realm; the animus, a male, is the figure who
symbolizes this for the female. As Jung wrote, "We know well enough
that the unconscious [of the male] appears personified: mostly it is the
anima who in singular or plural form represents the collective unconscious" (*CW* 14, par. 128). Conversely, the female's dreams, fantasies, or
artistic productions of animus figures are signs of contact with the collective unconscious.

For instance, when a man dreams of a woman about whom he feels
passionately in the dream, or, conversely, when a woman dreams of a
man about whom she has similar dream feelings, it is quite possible that
these figures come bearing messages from the collective unconscious.
Not all dreams that men have of women or that women have of men are
archetypal. Some have a strictly personal and/or erotic significance;
other dreams may have *both* personal and archetypal import, for dream
images can simultaneously operate on many different levels, perhaps as
many as ten or eleven, in the same dream (Vedfelt 2001). Yet whenever
a contrasexual figure stirs a profound emotional response in a person
(whether in a dream or waking life), there is probably some degree of
archetypal activity brewing within that person in addition to whatever
else may be going on.[3] In romances, myths, and fairy tales, the hero's
passionate pursuit of the maiden as well as the maiden's longing for the
hero both symbolize the psychospiritual desire of individual ego consciousness for connection with its own spiritual depths in the enigmatic
kingdom of the collective unconscious (Von Franz 1970/1987).

Since the collective unconscious is the ultimate psychospiritual mystery according to Jung, it is not surprising that it assumes the form of the contrasexual "other." Woman will always be the primary, mysterious "other" for man, just as man will play the same role for woman. The oldest story in the world is the mutual attraction of the sexes—and their mutual puzzlement at each other. Because the draw of the collective unconscious is so mystifying, it makes sense that female figures would embody it for men and male figures would do the same for women.

What is more, the very fact that it is a contrasexual figure who stands guard over each individual's *own depths* is already a powerful indicator that we each have a contrasexual element in our psyches. Again, it was Jung who was the first modern psychologist to explore this notion. Throughout history, various philosophers and artists have suggested that the soul has contrasexual components—just as the science of biology would later discover that everyone has both male and female chromosomes. Plato's story of the original person being a male/female in a primally perfect, circular form; the recurring idea of the hermaphrodite that figures so prominently throughout so many myths; the melding of the king and queen in alchemical lore into one triumphant bisexual figure that represents the philosopher's stone; and the fact that God commands Adam and Eve "to become one flesh" (as indeed was already implicitly the case before Eve's removal out of Adam)—these all indicate the fact that Jung merely translated into psychological parlance something that has intrigued people for time immemorial.

Learning how to integrate one's contrasexual elements without forfeiting one's primary gender identity is a major requirement of individuation in Jung's view. Paracelsus, the Renaissance physician and alchemist, wrote of the spiritual event that in Christian alchemy symbolized the internal union of the male and female principles: "When the heavenly marriage is accomplished, who will deny its superexcellent virtue?" (in CW 13, par. 199) Jung called this psychic synthesis of the male and female principles a *syzygy*, borrowing a term from St. Abelard. Jung saw the syzygy symbolized in religious texts, doctrines, and practices everywhere throughout history—the incestuous marriage of the brother-prince and sister-princess in ancient Egypt; the synthesis of the masculine principle of *yang* and the female principle of *yin* in Taoism; the spiritual seeker's quest for the Divine Beloved in yoga and Sufism; and the mystical marriage of Christ and his bride, Holy Mother Church, *sponsus et sponsa*, in Catholic dogma (*CW* 12, pars. 332–41).

Assimilation of one's contrasexual nature is a "work" that is not easily performed. Like all the aspects of the individuation process, it requires a psychic and moral commitment above what many people can imagine, much less maintain. Again, the need for this process to occur primarily *after* the midlife mark is clear. One is usually too busy in the first half of life establishing one's gender identity and performing one's gender-based roles to become overly immersed in inner contrasexual exploration. This is not to say that such exploration does not or should not happen before midlife. It is simply that it generally occurs most efficaciously and completely in the second half of life.

According to Jung, the man in the second half of life who refuses to look at his feminine side and the woman who will not do the same with her masculine side will become controlled by it. This is *anima possession* and *animus possession*, respectively, for it is an axiom of all depth psychologies that we are ultimately dominated by *any* unconscious elements that we do not integrate into consciousness. And once we are dominated by such elements, we project them onto others. The irony and tragedy of such projections is that we are hurtfully misusing unconscious energies that, if properly handled, could aid in our psychospiritual growth. The choice, as always, is ours.

The positive choice is for the man to "court" and "wed" his anima (that is, to explore and embrace his own archetypal depths) just as the woman must "court" and "wed" her animus. This will require the male to cultivate and express more delicate sensibilities and emotions than he has perhaps been used to doing—just as it will typically require the mature female to exercise more analytical precision and exert more main force than has perhaps been her wont. These are admittedly gender stereotypes, but they nevertheless suggest general terms and tasks that still seem to resonate with many people (Chodorow 1978; Belenky et al. 1986).

The negative choice is to ignore this call to moral and spiritual adventure by refusing to go as deeply within oneself as one can. When that happens, men, *anima possessed*, begin to look like a caricature of the feminine principle—snappy, sloppily sentimental, given to erratic moods. Conversely, *animus possessed* women begin to look like caricatures of the masculine principle—opinionated, stubborn, and caught in twisted webs of pseudologic.

The anima and animus stand sentry at the gates of the male and female soul. We gain entrée to the mysteries of the collective unconscious—and thus to the foundations of our very being—to the extent that we can each honor and incorporate the ancient archetypal wisdom of the other sex.

INDIVIDUATION AS A "MYSTERIUM CONIUNCTIONIS"

It is not only these gendered opposites that must meld for individuation to occur. *The unification of all sorts of opposites is an overarching task in individuation.* After all, individuation is maturity, and maturity requires looking at both sides of things, taking the best from both, and reconciling the dialectical tension in the form of a higher synthesis. This synthesis is not to be understood merely as some sort of compromise between the two extremes although compromise may be a part of what is going on. Rather, the synthesis is fundamentally a new creation, a "third," as Jung often called it, that not only combines the best of two opposing things but goes beyond them in the form of a unifying symbol—like a child who so far outshines her parents' best gifts and fondest expectations that they can only look at her in stunned admiration.

Jung called this ability to generate a higher third out of paired opposites *"the transcendent function* (*CW* 7, par. 121). He also called it a *coincidentia oppositorum*—that is, opposites coming together—(*CW* 5, par. 576), or a *unio mystica*—a mystical union (*CW* 5, par. 438). All of these terms suggest that this process is always something of a mystery, just as the cosmic operation of the *Tao* in the intercourse of yin and yang is a mystery. *Tertium non datur*—"the third is not given"—as one of Jung's favorite Latin saying goes, implying the enigma of growth itself. The force fields generated by the tug-and-pull of paired opposites are the very womb out of which all new life—physical and psychic—proceeds, but we ultimately are quite in the dark about how this actually happens. A scripture from my faith-tradition discusses this enigma:

> It must needs be that there is an opposition in all things. If not so . . . , righteousness could not be brought to pass, neither wickedness, neither

holiness nor misery, neither good nor bad. Wherefore, all things must be a compound in one; wherefore, if it should be one body it must needs remain as dead, having no life neither death, nor corruption nor incorruption, happiness nor misery, neither sense nor insensibility. Wherefore, it must needs have been created for a thing of naught; wherefore there would have been no purpose in the end of its creation. (*Book of Mormon*, 2 Nephi, 2:11–12)

Not only does dialectical tension and the creation of the symbolic "third" underlie archetypal processes in dreams, fantasies, art, and therapy, this fertile tension is *itself* an archetype, for the reality of growth through the interplay of opposites is a cosmic and psychic universal. The "third" is thus "an eternal image, an archetype, from which man can turn away his mind for a time but never permanently" (*CW* 14, par. 201). Jung saw the recurrence of trinities in religions from ancient Egypt to modern Christianity as a reflection of the archetype of "the third" (*CW* 11, pars. 169–296). The inevitability of dialectical tension and the "mystery of conjunction"—the *Mysterium Coniunctionis*, as Jung called it in the title of what many consider to be the crowning volume of his writings—are what make consciousness possible in the first place. We can only think because we can think in opposites. We only *know* something by *contrasting* it with what it is not.

Jung is not the only psychological theorist to have grasped this point. It also underlies Riegel's (1979) dialectical psychology and Kelly's (1955/1963) personal construct theory, both of which rest on the postulate that no ideation can occur in the absence of contrarieties. "Cold" would be an empty word if we had no conception of heat, light presupposes darkness, and love not only stands in stark contrast to hate but too often turns into it. Discussing the Judeo-Christian story of the creation of Adam and Eve, Jung wrote, "The splitting of the Original Man into husband and wife expresses an act of nascent consciousness; it gives birth to a pair of opposites, thereby making consciousness possible" (*CW* 9.2, par. 320). "Without opposition there is no progression," wrote William Blake—to which we might also add in Jungian tones, "Without opposition there is no cognition."

The genius of Eastern philosophy and religion—and an important part of the Buddha's message—is the recognition that everything contains the possibility of turning into its opposite. Therefore, the project of finding balance, peace, and creativity in a transcendent "third" is of the greatest importance psychically and morally:

> Unfortunately, our Western mind . . . has never yet devised a concept, nor even a name for the *union of opposites through the middle path*, that most fundamental item of inward experience, which could respectably be set against the Chinese concept of Tao. It is at once the most individual fact and the most universal, the most legitimate fulfillment of the meaning of the individual's life. (*CW* 7, par. 327)

Not only Jung's psychology but also Hegel's notion that history is a series of political theses, antitheses, and syntheses rests upon the idea of dialectical evolution. Indeed, Jung may have been influenced by Hegelian historiography (Odajnyk 1976). Yet we need not reach for such philosophical heights to understand the homespun truth that Jung was trying to convey. For it is a commonsense fact that the firmest alliances may turn into the bitterest contentions; the healthiest regimen, taken too far, inevitably breeds some sort of pathology by and by; and even the most passionate idealism (indeed, *especially* the most passionate idealism) may turn into resigned realism at best and cynicism at worst. The principle that things turn into their opposites given enough time is called *enantiodromia*. It has important therapeutic implications.

> The tendency to separate the opposites as much as possible and to strive for singleness of meaning is absolutely necessary for clarity of consciousness, since discrimination is of its essence. But when separation is carried so far that the complementary opposite is lost sight of, and the blackness of the whiteness, the evil of the good, the depth of the heights, and so on, is no longer seen, the result is one-sidedness, which is then compensated from the unconscious without our help. The counterbalancing is even done against our will, which in consequence must become more and more fanatical until it brings about a catastrophic enantiodromia. Wisdom never forgets that all things have two sides. (*CW* 14, par. 470)

Recalling Jung's theory of personality types, it is clear that individuation also entails acknowledging, examining, embracing, and trying to improve one's inferior function. Thus, the thinking physicist type would do well to cultivate her emotional side. If she does not, there will be an *enantiodromia* and her feelings will sooner or later get the better of her and—with everything from cheap sentimentalism to excessive fervency—undermine the attempt to individuate. The sensate type must learn to see beyond the immediate physical data and the sensations they stimulate in order to explore future possibilities, not merely present impressions. If she does not, there will be an *enantiodromia* and she will find herself tripped up by some situation that she might have anticipated but simply neglected to foresee.

The feeling type must learn not only to *have* deep values that inform her every decision but must *examine* them, too; otherwise, there will be an *enantiodromia* and her values may lead her into awkward, even unethical, commitments that a bit of hard-headed analysis could have avoided. And the intuitive type would do well not only to anticipate the future but also to focus more fully on present constraints and conditions, lest the reality of the present stealthily undermine the dreams of the future by means of *enantiodromia*.

If reality is dialectical, then it follows that the archetypes should also be dialectical. Thus, the archetype of the great nurturing mother has its dark flip side—the archetype of the great devouring mother. The archetype of the wise old man has as his dialectical opposite the ossified old tyrant. In myth and fairy tale, the fair visage of the lovely virgin is sometimes just a mask worn by the destructive seductress, and even a prince can be a frog. As Alice discovered in Wonderland, just step through the mirror and everything becomes its reverse. To come into living contact with the realm of archetypes, therefore, is to recognize that one is both light and dark and that one contains every good and evil human potential.

The surest antidote to a "holier-than-thou" attitude is the shocking recognition that one is, potentially, not only a saint but a sinner. "Nothing so promotes the growth of consciousness," wrote Aniela Jaffe (1975, 97), "as this inner confrontation of opposites." To realize that one has all the world within herself, its best and worst, and that the principle of *enantiodromia* makes one prone to both poles, is to know both one's mortal limitations and immortal potential. When this realization motivates acts of service performed in genuine humility and compassion, with a dollop of gentle humor thrown in, then the process of individuation is in full swing.

THE SELF AND ITS SYMBOLS

Jungians often speak of the journey of individuation as one that goes from the ego to the Self, capitalizing the latter word to indicate that the scope of the individuated "I" is greater than the limited range and self-ish interests of the mere ego. It should come as no surprise to the reader at this point to learn that there are various interpretations of what Jung meant by the term "Self." As always, the best place to start is with Jung himself.

Jung is nowhere clearer about the nature of the Self, and its difference from the ego, than in his magisterial work *The Archetypes and the Collective Unconscious* (*CW* 9.1):

> I usually describe the supraordinate personality as the "self," thus making a sharp distinction between the ego, which, as is well known, extends only as far as the conscious mind, and the *whole* of the personality, which includes the unconscious as well as the conscious components. The ego is thus related to the self as part to whole. To that extent the self is supraordinate. Moreover, the self is felt empirically not as subject but as object, and this by reason of its unconscious component, which can only come to consciousness indirectly, by way of projection.[4] (*CW* 9.1, par. 315)

In other words, the Self, that repository of ancient wisdom in the deepest realms of the psyche, can, by definition, never be fully *conscious*. However, it *can* be grasped, worked with, and assimilated through a deepening communication with the symbols that it produces. It is these "projected" archetypal images that constitute the lines of communication between ego and Self. Archetypal images are the vital means of establishing an "ego-Self" axis, around which the individuation process rotates (Edinger 1985, 1973). But what are some of the archetypal images that embody the Self?

> Because of its unconscious component the self is so far removed from the conscious mind that it can only be partially expressed by human figures: the other part of it has to be expressed by objective, abstract symbols. The human figures are father and son, mother and daughter, king and queen, god and goddess. Theriomorphic symbols [symbols of the self in animal form] are the dragon, snake, elephant, lion, bear and other

powerful animals, or again the spider, crab, butterfly, beetle, worm, etc. Plant symbols are generally flowers (lotus and rose). These lead on to geometrical figures like the circle, the sphere, the square, the quaternity, the clock, the firmament, and so on. The indefinite extent of the unconscious component makes a comprehensive description of the human personality impossible. (CW 9.1, par. 315)

The fact that we can list a few of the images that often represent the Self, Jung warns, should not lead us to believe that the list is by any means exhaustive, or that the listed symbols have fixed meanings. As we saw earlier, symbols are much more mercurial than that. Much depends on the context, timing, and emotional coloration with which the symbol makes its appearance and is reported by a person. Jung thus goes on in the same passage to stress that

the indefinite extent of the unconscious component makes a comprehensive description of the human personality impossible. Accordingly, the unconscious supplements the picture with living figures ranging from the animal to the divine, as the two extremes outside man, and rounds out the animal extreme, through the addition of vegetable and inorganic abstractions, into a microcosm. These addenda have a high frequency in anthropomorphic divinities, where they appear as "attributes." (CW 9.1, par. 315)

Intimate or powerful pairs of persons, imposing animals, insects that know the primal secrets of the underground, vegetation that in its symmetry suggests natural perfection, and certain geometrical shapes (especially squares and circles) can all symbolize the emergence of the Self—and they may appear in our nightly dreams no less than in our most ancient images of divinity. The appearance of a symbol of the Self is thus similar to a religious phenomenon. However, whether or not Jung was "religious" has been the topic of much heated and complex academic and professional debate over the last fifty years or so of scholarship about Jung.

THE SELF AS A RELIGIOUS PHENOMENON

Edinger (1973, 104) wrote, "For the modern man, an encounter with the autonomous archetypal psyche is equivalent to the discovery of God.

After such an experience he is no longer alone in his psyche and his whole worldview is altered." This is similar to Ulanov's (1999, 75) idea that the Self as the ultimate archetype—the archetype of archetypes— is constellated whenever we sense the stirrings of God within us. The Self is the archetypal echo of God's voice calling out to us *individually*, which is why Jung called the process *individuation*, for we find our- selves *as* individuals who exist *in* God *through* this process. "If we un- derstand with Jung that the Self is our greater personality, the 'diamond body' at the center of the whole psyche, which acts like a God within us," Ulanov muses,

> what connection can we draw to the God of our religion? . . . If we un- derstand the Self not to be God but rather that within us that knows about God, we can ask, with some hope of an answer, What in fact does it know? What happens to us when we experience the Self? Where does it lead? It tells us about our desire for what it leads to, which is the being that holds us in being, God's being. It tells us that our desire can be transformed into a steady, trustworthy, true loving. This is what Saint Bernard knows when he says we move, if we move this steady loving, from loving God for our own sakes to loving god for God's sake.

The question "Was Jung religious?" has been the subject of enough books to make up a small library. Some argue (as I do) that Jung *was* es- sentially religious, that the archetype of the Self is an *imago Dei* (as Jung himself often called it)—that is, the "image of God" in the human psy- che owing to its completeness, robustness, profundity, and moral grandeur. By this view, the Self is that part of man that God made "in his own image." The Self is where the mind of God and the mind of man meet. It bespeaks both the divine origin and transcendent destiny of the individual. Not a few Jungian scholars hold this position, which they be- lieve also fairly summarizes Jung's final position.[5] These scholars, more- over, believe that Jung has basically done both religion and psychology considerable good by defining a place where both fields can fruitfully in- teract.

There are many other scholars, however, who, while agreeing that Jung was trying to define a "religious psychology," maintain that he ac- tually did both religion and psychology harm by trying to make psychol- ogy too "mystical" and religion too "psychological," thus compromising the fundamental identity and virtue of each.[6] A few others argue (based, it seems to me, on an incorrect reading of Jung) that Jung never meant to make any spiritual statements at all but was speaking in strictly psychological terms (Paden 1985). And yet others see the whole question of Jung's possible religiosity as either irrelevant or unanswerable since Jung straddled religion and psychology in so many different and idiosyncratic ways throughout his career, defining a very unique space that fuses religion and psychology, that what he ultimately came up with is not "reducible" to either.[7]

This latter position is probably the dominant one in the Jungian literature—and the one that tends to be held by most of the first-generation Jungians who personally studied under Jung. Each of these positions undoubtedly contains some truth, since the way in which Jung speaks and writes about the relationship of the Self to God understandably varies. Much depends on the audience he is addressing and the context in which he is addressing them (Is he writing a letter to a clergyman, addressing a scholarly audience in an academic piece, or speaking to a group of psychiatrists at a medical conference?), the particular question that he is trying to answer (Does it have to do with a personal, clinical, historical, or philosophical issue?), and the phase of his career from which the characterization is taken (his earlier phase being more strictly medical, his middle phase more "existential," and his last phase more "religious") (Chapman 1988).

To my way of thinking, Jung finally made it quite clear that his position was an essentially religious one when, late in his life, he wrote a response to the Jewish theologian Martin Buber, who sternly accused him of psychologizing God and thus engaging in intellectual paganism. Said Jung, "Here, just for once, and as an exception, I shall indulge in transcendental speculation and even in 'poetry': God has indeed made an inconceivably sublime and mysteriously contradictory image of himself [in the archetype of the Self], without the help of man, and has implanted it in man's unconscious" (CW 18, par. 1508). Elsewhere, he suggested that the individuation process might even "unfold itself at the instigation of God's will" so that we might discover him, individually and for ourselves, in the depths of our own hearts and minds. Thus, when asked near the very end of his life in a BBC interview if he believed in God, he responded quite simply, and with a twinkle in his eye, "I do not need to believe. *I know!*"

SYNCHRONICITY: MESSAGES FROM ANOTHER REALM

Undoubtedly, one reason that Jung *knew*, and did not just believe, in the operation of the divine was because of the phenomenon of *synchronicity*, which regularly makes its enigmatic appearance when the individuation process is underway.

Synchronicity—another term coined by Jung that is now fairly well known—refers to something that most of us have experienced at one time or another. It is "the not uncommonly observed 'coincidence' of subjective and objective happenings, which just cannot be explained causally, at least in the present state of our knowledge" (*CW* 8, par. 405, n. 118). Wehr (2002) notes, "in the synchronistic occurrence, the same meaning is revealed in the psyche as well as in the arrangement of a simultaneous outer event" (253). In medieval philosophy, this phenomenon was known as "correspondence"—the mirroring of a spiritual fact in an external event or situation—and was seen as a sign from God.

As one approaches the regions of individuation and the Self—that psychospiritual space that Jung called a *temenos*, or "sacred precinct"— synchronistic events not only occur but abound. Some researchers have even found that in moments of a particularly intense encounter in therapeutic situations, there is a quantum shift in the energy field in which the participants are operating that is particularly conducive to synchronistic and other paranormal phenomena (Spiegelman and Mansfeld 1996). I have certainly found this to be true in my own practice, both in the consulting room and classroom.

Recently, for instance, a client and I were reaching archetypal realms as evidenced by a dream that she had. The dream begins with her walking into her kitchen. On the kitchen stove is a copper pot in which liquid gold is being cooked. The heat causes the gold to move circularly. For a Jungian, such an image is a "gold mine" of archetypal imagery. The dream represented a signal moment in our therapeutic work together. The next day, my wife, who is a therapist, was doing sand-play therapy with a child. This form of therapy has a child choose from many different figurines on shelves and then place them in a tray of sand in order to tell a story. In our sand-play room, we have over 3,000 figurines from which to choose. After her session, the girl chose a bucketful of figurines during her session with my wife. Afterward, as is customary in our practice, the little girl then put all the figurines she had used back on the shelf. However, she inexplicably left just one of her many figurines unreturned to the shelf, sitting on the middle of the table in the middle of the room.

Walking into the room the next day after my session with the client who dreamed of a copper pot, there, in full view to greet me, was a tiny figurine of a copper pot-belly stove—the only figurine that the girl had not reshelved. This "meaningful coincidence" clearly does not conform to any Newtonian model of cause and effect; however, I do not doubt for a moment that there is a meaningful relationship between my client's dream and the lone figurine on the table. Jung characterized synchronicity as "acausal connectedness." In the present case, this acausal connectedness—or "meaningful coincidence" as Jung also called such things—told me that my client and I were on the correct track in our pursuit of the Self. What is more, the specific nature of the synchronicity— that is, the fact that it was a little girl with a certain set of issues who left the figurine on the table—was also a clue to me that my client's image might relate to a problem from her own girlhood, which, as it later turned out, was in fact the case. Synchronistic events thus not only indicate that we are on the track of the Self but can also tell us something about what needs to be done to enhance that pursuit. Of all the early twentieth-century psychologists, Jung stood alone in having the insight to recognize and courage to study synchronicity in an intellectual milieu that dismissed such things as foolish occultism. He often pointed to synchronicity as strong evidence that there is a spiritual foundation for both our psychological problems and their solutions. Synchronicity was evidence of the intersection of the physical and the sacred, the material and the psychic.

> Since psyche and matter are contained in one and the same world, and moreover are in continuous contact with one another and ultimately rest on irrepresentable, transcendent factors, it is not only possible but fairly probably, even, that psyche and matter are two different aspects of the same thing. The synchronicity phenomena point, it seems to me, in this direction, for they show that the nonpsychic can behave like the psychic, and vice versa, without there being any causal connection between them.[8] (CW 8, par. 418)

WAS JUNG "RELIGIOUS"?

Answering the important and generative question in Jungian scholarship of whether Jung was "religious" is, for all its interest and fruitfulness, perhaps ultimately an impossible task. What we can be sure of is that Jung's concept of the Self is the crowning gem in his theory of the psyche, that it comes clothed in certain archetypal symbols and motifs, that it is available to anyone with the will and maturity to pursue it, that it represents the psychospiritual precondition of wholeness and creativity, and that, as Jung never failed to point out, no therapy ever comes to a fully satisfactory conclusion unless the person has been seized by a higher vision of what her life means in eternal terms. "Among all my patients in the second half of life," said Jung, "there has not been one whose problem in the last resort was not that of finding a religious outlook on life" (*CW* 11, par. 509).

These insights alone, not to mention the other astonishing theories and tools that he devised in the study of the psyche, mark Carl Jung as one of the greatest thinkers and physicians of the twentieth century, and perhaps of all time—one who, in the midst of the dogmatic materialism of the late nineteenth and early twentieth centuries, and in the face of considerable opposition—dared to introduce, examine, and honor spirituality in the study of the human psyche. For that alone we owe him an enormous debt of gratitude.

NOTES

1. In my rather Platonic view, archetypes are ultimately preexistent memories of where we as children of God came from and how we got here, as well as intuitions of where we are ultimately going and how to get there.

2. It should be noted that the prefixes *sub-* and *un-* in "personal subconscious" and "collective unconscious" do not mean that these psychic realities are *less than* ego consciousness but rather that they lie *beyond the limits* of ego consciousness. Rudolf Steiner, the founder of anthroposophy, was probably closer to the spirit of this truth in naming these two domains the *personal subconscious* and the *transpersonal supraconscious*, respectively (Wehr 2002). Nevertheless, I will stay with Jung's terminology.

3. Jung felt that the male's projection of his anima onto a woman with whom he then falls in love and the female's projection of the animus onto a male is frequently a cause of future marital discord, as each person comes in time to realize that his or her mate is not the archetypal figure that he or she fantasized. Coming to grips with this fact and learning to appreciate the other person for who he or she *really* is, is the only way for a marriage to grow. See "Marriage as a Psychological Relationship" in *CW* 17, pars. 324–45.

4. Jung himself and his translators often (and rather confusingly) used the lower-case "s" in rendering into English the transpersonal self (*Das Selbst*); however, for the sake of clarity I will follow the practice of various Jungians in using a capital "S" in the English spelling in order to distinguish this Self from the mere egoic self.

5. The reader who is interested in pursuing this interpretation of Jung's "religiosity" should consult the following sources: Chapman (1988), Clift (1982), Dourley (1984), Edinger (1985), Kelsey (1984), Odajnyk (1993), Spiegelman (1985), Stein (1984), Ulanov (1999), Wehr (2002), White (1952/1982).

6. This view is most forcefully presented by De Gruchy (1984), Hillman (1983), Homans (1985), and Palmer (1997).

7. See Fordham (1996), Frey-Rohn (1974), Jacobi (1959/1974), Jadot (1984), Jaffe (1989), Mattoon (1985), and Samuels (1997) for the elaboration of this argument.

8. I have always been intrigued by the similarity of this statement by Jung and the notion in my faith tradition that "the spirit and the body are the soul of man. And the resurrection from the dead is the redemption of the soul" (*The Doctrine and Covenants of the Church of Jesus Christ of Latter-day Saints* 88:15). What Jung called "the psychoid realm" (*CW* 8, par. 368)—that is, the realm where matter and psyche are reconciled and unified—would thus begin to look very like the realm in LDS theology where all people will live as resurrected beings. It would also represent, as Jung showed in his later work, the goal of the medieval and Renaissance Christian alchemists—to produce spiritual matter, alchemical gold, or the philosopher's stone (*CW* 12, *CW* 13, *CW* 14).

5

JUNG AND POLITICS

THE PRIMACY OF THE INDIVIDUAL

Jung has been accused by some of his detractors of not being political enough, or of not being political in the "correct" ways.[1]

Admittedly, in the earliest years of the Nazi regime, Jung, a Swiss, fleetingly and tangentially associated with a handful of Nazi psychiatrists—an error which he quickly and publicly admitted as early as 1935, apologizing for this brief lapse of judgment (especially to his many Jewish adherents, who, by most accounts, quickly forgave him). And he more than atoned for this passing error in his far-reaching study and genuine celebration throughout his entire career of many varied religions and cultures—and not only those of the Middle East but also those of North America, South America, Africa, India, Asia, Polynesia, and Micronesia.

Indeed, it is now beginning to be acknowledged that Jung, perhaps more than any other psychologist in the first half of the twentieth century, laid the groundwork for a truly "multicultural psychology" (Adams 1996), a fact that even many Jungians still do not sufficiently acknowledge, since they do tend to be rather apolitical in their popular and scholarly writing. Even this has been changing recently, however, with Jungians moving into sociology (Gray 1996), feminist studies (Lauter and Rupprecht 1985; Gallant 1996), cultural critique (Cowan 2002; Hauke

2000), and political theory (Samuels 2001). There have even been Jungian studies of organizational behavior and institutional change (Brown and Moffett 1999).

The fact is that Jung's vision was quite political, although, to be sure, given his commitment to those classical values that have fallen out of favor in academia, his political views have never been widely popular there. His emphasis on the primacy of the individual and abhorrence of political collectivism—especially socialism and communism—have also made him persona non grata in many intellectual circles. It should be added that he was also no great fan of corporate capitalism and would have been as unenthusiastic about Ayn Rand as about Lenin. An astute observer of a world wracked by two cataclysmic wars, Jung had very little faith in claims from either the Right or the Left that political solutions could ever bring about psychological reform or true historical progress.

When Jung addressed political issues, he did so almost exclusively from the standpoint of their psychological causes and consequences, ignoring the economic or ideological components. "Every individual needs revolution," Jung wrote,

> inner division, overthrow of the existing order, and renewal, but not by forcing them upon his neighbors under the hypocritical cloak of Christian love or the sense of social responsibility or any of the other beautiful euphemisms for unconscious urges to personal power. Individual self-reflection, return of the individual to the ground of human nature, to his own deepest being with its individual and social destiny—here is the beginning of a cure for that blindness which reigns at the present hour. (CW 7, p. 5)

Jung's approach is valuable because he examines the psychological aspects of social dynamics, something that many sociologists seem virtually to have forgotten how to do in the last half-century or so.[2] Nevertheless, it is fair to charge Jung with naivete in believing that social change could be effected in virtually all cases simply by focusing on merely individual psychological change. For all that, it is useful to heed Jung's reminder that for social changes to be deep and durable there must also be a change in people's hearts and minds. Ours is a time that seems always in search of one social program or other that will magically produce "the great society." In devising our grand schemes for cultural and political transformation, we would do well to remember Jung's pointed question, "Does not all culture begin with the individual?" (*CW* 7, par. 327).

Jung was not alone in his suspicion of collectivism. Freud was equally pessimistic about the "mass psychology" of groups. In "Group Psychology and the Analysis of the Ego," Freud (1921/1957) insisted that groups sink to the intellectual level of the least common denominator and are therefore especially susceptible to irrational ideas. Like spoiled children, groups need ever greater physical and emotional stimulation. They tend toward cruel intolerance of outsiders and slavish obedience to rulers. Subject to what he called "emotional contagion," Freud felt that groups instinctively revert to infantile states and primitive instincts and will follow whatever leader offers them the most enticing rewards or threatens them with the most dire punishments. "Groups have never thirsted after truth," was Freud's laconic conclusion. "They demand illusions and cannot do without them" (174).

In similar strains, Jung decried the evils of what George Orwell in *1984* called *groupthink*. Collectivist ideologies are "the greatest temptation to unconsciousness, for the mass infallibly swallows up the individual—who has no security in himself—and reduces him to a helpless particle" (*CW* 16, par. 225). This "leveling down and eventual dissolution [of the individual psyche] in the collective psyche (e.g., Peter's denial) occasion a 'loss of soul' in the individual, because an important personal achievement has either been neglected or allowed to slip into regression" (*CW* 7, par. 239). Put people together in large groups and what do you have? asked Jung. "Just one big fathead" (*CW* 16, par. 4). Besides, "it is . . . ludicrous to say that the individual lives for society. 'Society' is nothing more than a term, a concept for the symbiosis of a group of human beings. A concept is not a carrier of life. The sole and natural carrier of life is the individual, and that is so throughout nature" (*CW* 16, par. 224).[3]

The danger of the modern state—its overwhelming power to pound the individuality out of a person in order to shape him into a "mass man" (*CW* 17, par. 159)—underlies Jung's critique of modern education (as we shall see in part II). Jung's lament was that education has been forced to become the servant of the corporate state. Generally speaking, it does not allow children to discover their own souls but hammers them into submission to the "military-industrial complex," something that Jung understood quite well decades before President Eisenhower coined the phrase. Jung seemed to take real pleasure in citing his fellow Swiss, the pedagogical theorist Johann Pestalozzi, on the scandalous fact that mass education tended to produce "mass men" (*CW* 16, par. 103; par. 224, n. 8).

With the intellectual and moral level of the ordinary person lowered to such a dismal degree, it is hardly surprising, Jung noted, that most people fall under the mediocre sway of an "ism." We pride ourselves on having outgrown the medieval notion that the devil has horns, said Jung, but what we fail to see is that the devil has not really disappeared. As the master of disguises, he has simply traded in his horns for political doctrines. This why the worst crimes are always committed in the name of some grand political purpose or other: "Who would suspect [the devil] under those high-sounding names of his, such as public welfare, lifelong security, peace among the nations, etc.? He hides under idealisms, under –isms in general, and of these the most pernicious is doctinairism" (*CW* 9.2, par. 141).

Jung never budged from his conviction that when people fail to tend to their own psychospiritual evolution, they will inevitably wind up misdirecting their need for inner contact with the divine into outer worship of false political gods. If we do not heed the voice of God within, we will wind up serving the golden calf without. Writing from the point of view of post–World War II Europe, when all sources of valid authority seemed to be lying in heaps of smoking rubble, and when Soviet communism and American capitalism were squaring off to see whose form of corporate world governance would prevail, Jung said,

> we are rapidly becoming the slaves of an anonymous state as the highest ruling authority in our lives. Communism has realized this in the most perfect way. Unfortunately, our democracy has nothing to offer in the way of different ideals; it also believes in the concrete power of the state. There is no spiritual authority comparable to that of the state anywhere. We are badly in need of a spiritual counterbalance to the ultimately Bolshevistic concretism. It is again the case of the "witness" against the Caesar. (*CW* 18, par. 1569)

This is not to say that Jung did not understand the necessity of government. A conservative Swiss who enjoyed dressing up in his officer's uniform and parading down the street of his small village during festival days, Jung was the farthest thing possible from an anarchist. It is simply that, in accordance with classical liberal principles, he believed that the government that governed least governed best, for the reach of government should never exceed its grasp. As Odajnyk (1976) put it in his revealing analysis of the political implications of Jungian psychology, Jung felt that "the State may be a necessary means for the organization of human life, but when it becomes the primary aim the individual is cheated of his destiny . . . , 'because society, a mere condition of human existence, is set up as its goal'" (185). The first political imperative for the modern person, then, is to resist merely political programs.

This is as much a moral as a political imperative, for "morality . . . rests entirely on the moral sense of the individual and the freedom necessary for this," which is why "special attention must be paid to this delicate plant 'individuality' if it is not to be completely smothered" (*CW* 7, pars. 240–41). Individuation is not only a psychospiritual project (although it is *primarily* that) but, as conscious resistance to the specter of collectivism, also a political one. Yet in saying this much, Jung was saying no more than the great religions have always taught: the political reform of humanity must begin with the moral reform of the individual. Spirituality precedes politics, not vice versa. Rendering what is Caesar's to Caesar, we must never forget that our primary obligation is to God. And since, according to Jung, we find God first and foremost within ourselves, individuation is the precondition of all other types of broader social change.

THE POLITICS OF PROJECTION AND WITHDRAWAL

The Jungian interpreter Edward Edinger once said that individuation means the *complete* recognition and assimilation of one's shadow. The psychospiritual realism upon which individuation depends requires a person to accept his own humanity—that is, relinquish any emotionally comfortable but morally absurd claims to "purity." This "realization of the shadow releases one from the role of innocent victim and the tendency to project the evil executioner on to God or neighbor" (1973, 235). Only by maturely seeing himself for who he is, is a person able to see others for who they really are in all their moral complexity.

This is so essential politically because individuals and groups that do not acknowledge their own inadequacies but cling to a notion of divine national election will inevitably wind up projecting their denied darkness onto other individuals and groups. In Jungian psychology, projection of the individual and collective shadow is the major culprit in intolerance and racism, and withdrawal of projection is the prerequisite of peaceful coexistence. We have already looked at projection on an individual level, but group projections are arguably even more dangerous since they have the power of groups behind them—even the power of states. Recent history offers enough instances of such things that we need not look back too far for examples. Jung looked to Nazi Germany.

Impoverished and humiliated Germany after World War I, Germany, saddled with excessive reparation payments and made the scapegoat of the many historically complex European maladies leading to the Great War, tried to purge itself of its sense of humiliation and impotence by projecting its weakness, degradation, and alienation onto an "inferior race." By exterminating the Jews, Germany would be able to deny its own dark side. This is merely one example of how a cultural or national shadow can be "transferred to the outside world and experienced as an outside object. It is combated, punished, and exterminated as 'the alien out there' instead of being dealt with as one's own 'inner problem'" (Neumann 1969, 50).

Thus, "no war can be waged unless the enemy can be converted into the carrier of a shadow projection." The thrill of brutally beating one's enemy into bloody submission ultimately derives "from the satisfaction of the unconscious shadow side" (Neumann 1969, 57–58). Whenever there is hatred and suspicion of aliens, minorities, the homeless, the physically disabled or the sick, or any other "outcast," we must suspect the ominous presence of a projected shadow. In his Jungian analysis of the archetypal roots of racism, Adams (1996) has argued that minority members of a culture receive such vile treatment because they symbolize to the oppressor "the other within the self—that 'inner other' from which the self is most alienated" (136). This is often especially true regarding minorities of color since their often darker skin tones are "hooks" onto which the oppressor is especially tempted to "hang" the darkness of his own self-loathing—a practice which was *literally* the case in the lynching of blacks in the American South until not so long ago.

We look in great detail these days at the historical and socioeconomic causes of racism, as well we should. But we would also be wise to consider the *psychological analysis* of racism in our graduate schools of political science, history, social work, psychology, and education. The recognition and withdrawal of one's shadow at both the individual and collective levels is the sine qua non of psychological, political, and ethical health. It is only the individuated person who, having seen his own internal devils, can be instrumental in helping a people cleanse itself of its own hidden collective devils.

There is one more type of projection, equally dangerous politically, that is the flip side of the kind we have been discussing. It is hero worship. In hero worship, we project divine attributes onto merely political leaders. That is, we project "God archetypes" onto them. *Evita*, the musical rendition of the life of Eva Perón, the wife of the Argentine dictator Juan Perón, whom many think became more powerful than Perón himself during her short life, demonstrates this process. At her death in the last scene of the play, Argentines are praying to Eva Perón, or *Santa Evita* as she became popularly known, exalting her into the *Mater Dei* (Mother of God). These sorts of projections endow the recipients of the projections with enormous power which they may, and usually do, cultivate in a thousand mischievous ways.

If absolute power corrupts absolutely, it does so through projection—initially through the collective projection of a "Savior archetype" onto a mere political functionary of flesh and blood, who, through the absorption (or *introjection*) of the archetype, begins to believe that the projection is true. Whenever someone personally identifies with it as if he somehow specially embodied it, he has *inappropriately identified with the archetype*. In Jungian terms, this represents a *psychic inflation*. Psychiatric wards are filled with people who believe they are John Lennon, Elvis, the Buddha, Mohammed, Vishnu, the Virgin Mary, Jesus Christ, and even God the Father himself.

By way of contrast, consider the following example. Late one night many years ago, when my wife's grandfather was about to pass away, I needed a break from the deathwatch and so took a walk down the deserted halls of the Catholic hospital at three o'clock in the morning. I passed the chaplain's door, which was locked, the priest having long ago gone home. On his door was posted for public viewing a neatly handwritten note that I moved closer to read. It said the following: "Dear Father Gomez, thank you for all you do. You help many people here in the hospital and your efforts are sincerely appreciated. However, please do not believe that you have to save everyone. That's my business. (Signed) Jesus."

Here was a lovely example of a priest who knew his limitations, who loved his Lord, and indeed loved him so much that he would never presume to identify with the archetype of the Savior—an archetype that is all too often projected onto people in ministerial positions and roles (Ulanov 1999). Father Gomez's humility and humor were the antidote to the poisonous secretion and absorption of inappropriate projections. He had the good sense to *use* his office to be of the greatest service to others, but he also had the wisdom not to *identify* with it to such an extent that he lost sight of his own personal frailty and became inflated with his parishioners' "God" projections.

Unfortunately, the same cannot be said of many of our leaders, who commit the fundamental error that every truly great person in a position of authority must learn how to avoid—the error of believing one's own propaganda. For "inflation always leads to deflation in the form of neurosis or psychosis," as Jung said, which is a nice restatement of the old moral axiom that pride precedes a fall. It is therefore of the first importance politically that citizens learn to "withdraw" their projections from their leaders, just as their leaders must know how not to introject those projections (Samuels 2001). In this way, those symbioses between leaders and citizens that lead to various types of individual and collective crimes against humanity can be cut off at the root—and this can be done by using the sharpened spade of *the individuated psyche*.

INDIVIDUATION AND THE POLITICAL ANIMAL

There is another reason that individuation has a political dimension. In his treatise on *Politics*, Aristotle said that humans are political animals

by their very nature. This being so, how could anyone rise to his fully individuated stature if he had not accepted and honorably performed various social roles and responsibilities? Individuation means wholeness,
and an apolitical person is by definition incomplete. This is perhaps the
error that young people who want to enter monasteries at a very early
age commit. They hope to find God before they have matured as social
beings. Hence, many would-be monks are turned away by wise old ab-
bots, yogis, and *roshis*, who advise the passionate but naïve seekers to
come back only *after* they have had wider experience of family, work,
citizenship—indeed, of the great world in general.

Despite his errors, Marx's fundamental brilliance lay in his understanding that there is no individual who can lay claim to morally valid
happiness if he lives in an unjust state and does not try to improve it.
Our psychological, civic, and moral health are interdependent. "Man's
psychic and moral development . . . goes hand in hand with his social
and political arrangements" (Odajnyk 1976, 186). Samuels (2001) sums
the whole matter up when he writes, "Connectedness between human
beings is surely both spiritual and political," which is why "psychotherapy, politics, and religion all share, at some level, in the fantasy of providing healing for the world" (123, 131). Healing for the individual and
healing for the world presuppose each other. It is only in this synergy of
the individual and the collective that the individual and the state can
help to make each other both more human and more divine.

Man is a political, world-historical being if only because each individual bears the entire collective unconscious within him and thus also car-
ries "his whole history with him. In [each person's] very structure is written the history of mankind. This historical element in man represents a
vital need to which a wise psychic economy must respond. Somehow the
past must come alive and participate in the present" (CW 6, par. 570).
Therapy is thus a political act, and for this reason it must always be on
guard against becoming the servant of the state, which it does become
when it merely aims (as is only too true of much current psychotherapy)
to "adjust" the individual to an immoral socioeconomic order (CW 16,
par. 223; Laing 1967). Jung put it best when he wrote:

> Although the conscious achievement of individuality is consistent
> with man's natural destiny, it is nevertheless not his whole aim. It

cannot possibly be the object of human education to create an an-
archic conglomeration of individual existences. That would be too
much like the unavowed ideal of extreme individualism, which is
really no more than a morbid reaction against an equally futile collectivism. In contrast to all this, the natural process of individuation
brings to birth a consciousness of human community precisely because it makes us aware of the unconscious, which unites and is
common to all mankind. Individuation is *at-one-ment* with oneself
and at the same time with humanity. Once the individual is thus se-
cured in himself, there is some guarantee that the organized accu-
mulation of individuals in the State—even in one wielding greater
authority—will result in the formation no longer of an anonymous
mass but of a conscious community. The indispensable condition
for this is conscious freedom of choice and individual decision.
Without this freedom and self-determination there is no true community, and, it must be said, without such community even the free
and self-secured individual cannot in the long run prosper. (*CW* 16,
par. 227)

FROM JUNG THE PSYCHOLOGIST
TO JUNG THE EDUCATIONIST

Having covered the most central ideas in Jung's psychological writings,
it is now time to turn to how those ideas play out in educational terms.
In *The Development of Personality* (*CW* 17), Jung systematically presented *some* of his more conventional ideas about education. However,
it was mostly in his other studies that Jung made his most educationally
rich and suggestive observations, so it is to his entire body of work that
we must turn in order to tease out the elements of an educational vision
that could be called "Jungian."

Naturally, it is impossible in just one book to explore all of the educational ramifications of Jung's psychological precepts and practices. What
I hope to accomplish in the second part of this book is to identify and
outline some of the clearest and most applicable of those ramifications.
Hopefully, educators will thus be able to get an initial sense of them and
begin to work with them in ways that will suit their own particular needs
in both their classroom practice and professional reflectivity. The sec-

ond half of this study also aims at suggesting areas of interest that educational scholars may pursue.

In the second half of this book, the following points will be key. First, Jung believed that because there is a certain sanctity in the archetypal nature of the relationship between the teacher and student, curricularists and teachers should avoid approaches to teaching and learning that overly stress technical proficiency or abstract intellectualism, Second, the Jungian view of psyche and learning suggests that subject matter in the classroom should be mined for what it can reveal about important archetypal themes, images, and structures. Third, the intuitive function must be nurtured to a much greater degree than is presently the case in most schooling.

Fourth, students must be allowed to "fail" in productive and supportive ways that draw upon the creative possibilities of dialectical tension in promoting deep and lasting moral and intellectual growth. Fifth, it is important for teachers to understand transferential psychodynamics both personally and archetypally in order for their interaction with students to be most appropriate and fruitful. Sixth, education must be holistic, addressing the *whole child* in those many historical, cultural, and political contexts within which the child develops psychospiritually.

Seventh, education must serve the traditionalist project of helping students explore and affirm the cultural narratives that have shaped their lives, but it must also empower students to build upon those narratives to create novel archetypal images and stories that can carry them forward into a new future. And finally, teachers often experience their sense of calling and refine their pedagogical practice on the basis of archetypal energy and imagery that they can explore and cultivate for personal and professional growth.

NOTES

1. Two prominent examples of this are Carier (1976) and Noll (1994).

2. However, see Gray (1996) for a brilliant use of Jungian concepts to explore a wide range of current sociological issues. See also Progoff's 1955 classic, *Jung's Psychology and Its Social Meaning* and Odajnyk's 1976 study, *Jung*

and Politics: The Political and Social Ideas of C. G. Jung, for earlier applications of classical Jungian psychology to social questions—a line of inquiry that largely lay fallow until Gray's groundbreaking study.

3. The assumption that societies exist in the minds of their members and not as entities that have some sort of independent existence is characteristic of such phenomenological approaches to sociology as ethnomethodology (Garfinkel 1967) and symbolic interactionism (Blumer 1969).

II

ELEMENTS OF AN ARCHETYPAL PEDAGOGY

6

THE TEN PILLARS OF A JUNGIAN APPROACH TO CURRICULUM AND INSTRUCTION

In this chapter, we look at some of the major implications of Jungian psychology for education—each of which can be considered a pillar of an archetypal approach to curriculum and instruction.

FIRST PILLAR

- The teacher–student relationship is archetypal.

Perhaps the first thing to note about Jung's view of education is that he felt that *educational processes are themselves archetypal*. By this he did not *only* mean that the teacher could help the student discover archetypal truths in the subject matter but also that *"the teacher" and "the student" are themselves archetypal figures*. Their relationship is an archetypal event—just as "bride," "groom," and "marriage" are an archetypal situation; or just as "doctor," "patient," and "healing," or "parent," "child," and "family" are. The interaction between teacher and student is woven so deeply into the fabric of what it means to be a human being that it is impossible to conceive of the human situation without it. Throughout our lives, we are involved in educational acts—as teachers, students, and often both. No human culture has ever been founded or perpetuated without education about everything from how the universe came into being to how to prepare a meal. Something so fundamental to creating and sustaining individuals and cultures is necessarily archetypal.

The powerful archetypal significance of education is evidenced in the centrality of the archetypes of the Wise Old Man and Wise Old Woman, which are at the very top of Jung's list of the most historically prominent archetypes (*CW* 5, par. 611). The Wise Old Man and Woman show up in many myths, religions, and dreams, often in connection with a young hero or heroine who is engaged in a dangerous journey in order to accomplish a great but difficult task. At the beginning of the journey, the hero crosses a threshold into a perilous forest, desert, or jungle. This symbolizes the hero's acceptance of the challenge to leave childish things behind and to master those difficulties that will lead to both personal and transpersonal growth (Campbell 1949).

Soon after crossing the border into the land of dangerous adventure, the hero meets the Wise Old Man or Woman. These wise ones successfully completed their own archetypal quests many years ago when they were young and now often possess powerful amulets and knowledge about potions. Guiding the young travelers, these Wise Ones are, above all else, teachers. Their amulets and potions symbolize the fact that they are able to direct the seeker because they have had their own visions that they can now communicate to the young novitiate so that he may one day have his own experience of the transcendent. They often speak in riddles to spur their young students on to intellectual and moral growth. So closely is the Wise Old Man related to teaching, in fact, that Jung felt him to be the archetype that best "personifies *meaning*" (*CW* 14, par. 313).

There are a great many pedagogical consequences, both theoretical and practical, that stem from the fact that the student–teacher relationship is archetypal. I examine them in depth in following chapters. For now, it is enough to say that the teacher who understands the student–teacher archetype, and who is most in touch with the archetypal nature of not only his profession but his very psyche, is also bound to be an influential teacher.

Whoever speaks in primordial images speaks with a thousand voices; he enthralls and overpowers, while at the same time he lifts the idea he is seeking to express out of the occasional and transitory into the realm of the ever-enduring. He transmutes our personal destiny into the destiny of mankind, and evokes in us all those beneficent forces that ever and anon have enabled humanity to find a refuge from every peril and to outlive the longest night. (*CW* 15, par. 129)

SECOND PILLAR

- Education should not be reduced to technical rationality.

Considering Jung's view of education as being an inherently archetypal and therefore potentially sacred act, it will probably not surprise the reader to learn that he objected to any approach to teaching and learning that was essentially technical in its means and goals.

A physician and a pragmatist, Jung undoubtedly understood that education has legitimate technical goals. However, these must be secondary to the primary goal of deepening the student psychologically, politically, and morally. "It cannot be the aim of education," Jung declared in terms reminiscent of Parker, Kilpatrick, Counts, Dewey, Bode, and Bagley, as well as other American progressives of the first half of the twentieth century, "to turn out rationalists, materialists, specialists, technicians and others of the kind who, unconscious of their origins, are precipitated abruptly into the present and contribute to the disorientation and fragmentation of society" (Frey-Rohn 1974, 182). An educational system that exists simply to service the needs of a consumer society and its military-industrial machinery is not only inimical to the delicate archetypal dynamics of the student–teacher relationship but, in the final analysis, is also socially *destabilizing* despite its grand social-efficiency claims. Why is this?

It is because such forms of education do not address the whole child in all of his physical, emotional, political, cultural, and ethical complexity. The result is psychic "disorientation and fragmentation" in children, which will lead with tragic inevitability to the same things in a society whose citizens and leaders those children will one day be. Such curricula, nonholistic and antidemocratic, exemplify what Miller and Seller

(1985) have called "education-as-transmission" and Kliebard (1995) the "social-efficiency" approach to schooling. It is this type of curriculum that was championed in such documents as the Reagan administration's *A Nation at Risk* report (1983), which reflected the essential nature of many federal educational "reform" agendas in the last hundred years of American educational history (Tyack 1974).

As the authors of that document declared, "the basic purposes of schooling" must relate to the overarching goal of reestablishing America's "once unchallenged preeminence in commerce, industry, science, and technological innovation." Only these educational goals are considered legitimate. All others are seen as contributing to America's military-industrial decline. The aim of education by this view is to do exactly what Jung warned against—"to turn out rationalists, materialists, specialists, technicians."

Jung proved to be quite prophetic in issuing this warning. As Laurence Cremin (1988) would argue several decades later in his magisterial study of the history of American education, public schooling over the last 120 years has become increasingly "atomistic" and "authoritarian" in that it imposes on both the teacher and student a mélange of disconnected facts that the student must memorize—usually in order to score well on a standardized test. Such curricula are insensitive to—and indeed destructive of—those rich variations in personal and cultural perspectives and talents that are vital to psychosocial health and creativity (Jones, Jones, and Hargrove 2003).

Neo-Jungian analyst and scholar Andrew Samuels (2001) is not overstating the point, then, when he declares that education which is "confined to precise techniques learned and applied at the workplace" are "psychologically demeaning" to students, teachers—and also principals, whose unhappy task it is to enforce such totalitarian mandates at their schools (139). As Jung put it, corporate education "blots out" the individual—and it does so across the span of the person's formal education: it "begins in school [and] continues at the university" (*CW* 7, par. 240). This is immoral for several reasons: it creates the "mass man" of technocratic society and thus robs the individual of his uniqueness; it accomplishes this totalitarian goal by doing violence to the deeper personal needs of teachers, students, and administrators; and it grossly impinges upon the delicacy and sanctity of the archetypal relationship between teacher and student, wreaking psychological, social, and moral havoc (*CW* 16, par. 103; *CW* 17, par. 16).

THIRD PILLAR

- Education should not be confused with mere "intellectualism."

Jung was one of the most influential scholars of the twentieth century, researching and writing topics ranging from neurology to parapsychology, the mystery religions of Greece to the medicine men of the Navajos, the practices of alchemy to the rumors of UFOs, philology to quantum theory. His influence on not only psychology and the humanities but even sociology, physics, mathematics, and biology has been significant and is continuing to grow. The complete scholar, Jung was solidly grounded in ancient languages and literature as well as in the most recent theories in aesthetics, politics, biology, and cosmology. Here is a man who understood the life of the intellect.

Nevertheless, Jung was adamant about the danger of relying overmuch upon reason and the intellect. Certainly, rationality—and the classical forms of education meant to encourage it—has an important place. However, it was for Jung an article of faith that the mystery of how and why the psyche and, indeed, the entire universe, operate as they do far exceeds mere reason and materialistic explanations.

Like Kant, whom he studied as a very young man and deeply admired throughout his life, Jung believed that although reason provides an indispensable lens through which we see and interpret ourselves and the universe, it is, in the final analysis, simply *one* lens among many. It may *portray* a thing in terms that we can understand, but we must not fall into the trap of believing that those terms necessarily describe the ultimate *reality* of the "thing-in-itself." Jung often mentioned the Kantian distinction between the *esse in intellectu* (that is, the thing as it appears to our reason) and the *esse in re* (the thing as it *really* is). Between the two, said Jung, is a yawning chasm that our poor syllogisms can never bridge.

What we *can* know, Jung believed, is the *esse in anima*, or the thing as we *holistically experience it in our total psyche*, our soul (*CW* 6, par. 66).

Indeed, everything we know is a psychological experience, for if it were not, how could we know it? In saying this, Jung was not claiming—as he is often misinterpreted as doing—that there is no ultimate reality beyond our ideas. Such nihilism was disagreeable to Jung, leading to anarchy— the very thing he most dreaded. It is simply that we must always have the humility and common sense to recognize that reality is never obliged to conform to our models of it, even our most impressively academic and dazzlingly logical ones. The cosmos is greater than any formal propositions we can make about it.

What this means for both psychology and education is that any approach to human knowing "that satisfies the intellect alone can never be practical, for the totality of the psyche can never be grasped by the intellect alone" (*CW* 7, par. 201). Mere *intellectualism*, taken to extremes, claimed Jung, leads to ontological error, spiritual pride, and psychosocial imbalance. Extreme intellectualism is "in point of fact . . . nothing more than the sum total of all [a person's] prejudices and myopic views" (*CW* 9.1, par. 22). Like those hyperbrainy, oddball academics who live on clouds in *Gulliver's Travels*, the Laputans, the intellectualist has so grotesquely overdeveloped one of his faculties that the rest of them have fallen into laughable disarray. What is needed in the classroom no less than in the consulting room, therefore, is a "holistic approach," as Jung characterized his psychology—one that allows a person to face and appropriate reality in ways that involve his entire being, not just his mind (in Frey-Rohn 1974, 71).

Given all of this, it is not hard to imagine Jung's response to curricula that single-mindedly fixate on rationality and "higher-order cognition" as the ultimate educational goals. This is the interpretive-procedural curriculum (Mayes 2003a). It has also been called the academic-rationalist curriculum, the intellectual-academic curriculum, and the cognitive-processes curriculum (Eisner and Vallance 1974; Miller and Seller 1985, Ornstein and Hunkins 1988). Whatever name it goes by, it is the curriculum of choice of conventional developmental theorists who see the ability to think syllogistically as the culmination of mental development.

Perhaps the two most famous of such theorists are Piaget with his notion of hypothetico-deductive "formal-operations" as the apex of cognitive maturation and Kohlberg with his claim that postconventional forms of moral reasoning—in which one evaluates moral dilemmas in terms of absolute philosophical principles—is the summit of ethical development. This orientation also includes such diverse instructional approaches as schema theory (Rummelhart 1980), cybernetic models of mind (Chomsky 1968), the structure-of-the-discipline model (Bruner 1960), and the call for a return to the classical European curriculum (Adler 1982).

Jung would agree that such curricula have value insofar as they familiarize students with standard ways of posing questions and finding answers, introduce them to a canon of prestigious texts, and enlarge their understanding of some current issues in broader theoretical terms. However, Jung's model of the psyche also implies that if education does *only* this, or even just *primarily* this, then it falls short of its psychospiritual potential. Not *engaging* the person on all of the levels of his being—from the most concretely biological to the most mysteriously archetypal—such education is limiting, arid, and destructive. For Jung, intellect is an important piece of the complete pedagogical jigsaw, but it is far from the only one. Thus, Jung is rightly considered one of the founders of the twentieth-century holistic education movement (Forbes 2003).

FOURTH PILLAR

- Teachers and students can explore the archetypal dimensions of many different subjects.

Perhaps the most essential feature of a truly humane education from a Jungian vantage point is that it be archetypal—or at least that it include archetypal elements. This means that there should be an ongoing endeavor to discover in any subject matter in the curriculum its archetypal roots and fruits. This project is not only educationally possible but necessary because "the greatest and best thoughts of man shape themselves upon . . . primordial images as upon a blueprint" (*CW* 7, par. 109). In order to get to the heart of any idea, theory, model, or piece of art, therefore, it is necessary to penetrate its archetypal infrastructure. This is not to say that the archetypal approach will always be the primary educational goal. However, even when the archetypal perspective is not the core of a curriculum, it may still enliven the analysis of virtually any subject.

Rudolf Steiner's Waldorf Schools admirably accomplish this aim from kindergarten through twelfth grade. Throughout a Waldorf education, the teacher organizes much of the curriculum around archetypal images that have been drawn from an array of religious, cultural, and artistic traditions and periods. To take but one example, numbers are taught archetypally and imagistically in the early grades of Waldorf schools by associating them with fairy tales and subtly evoking their mythic significance in the hearts and minds of the children. Waldorf educationists feel that the number one appeals to the young child's intuitive sense of primal unity, two excites his unconscious sense of duality, three constellates archetypes of spirit, and four those of solid grounding and earthy rootedness (Trostli 1988).[1] By both a Jungian and Waldorf view, numbers are an occasion for cultivating "the imaginative basis for an intellectual understanding" (Trostli 1988, 345). Even basic arithmetic, then, can come alive with archetypal energy and imagery. Such an approach can form either the core of early math instruction or serve as a wonderful addition to a more conventional approach.

The later grades in a Waldorf school continue to draw upon the archetypal realm. For instance, in the eleventh grade, Waldorf students study the classic medieval romance *Parzival* by Wolfram von Eschenbach. Parzival is a noble youth of aristocratic heritage who grows up ignorant of his exalted status but later discovers and becomes the lord of the Holy Grail. This story becomes a metaphor for each of the adolescent students to explore in his search for personal identity—the fundamental psychosocial task of that developmental period (Erikson 1963). In general, many teachers and scholars of literature have found the archetypal orientation uniquely effective both critically and pedagogically, whether the students are in elementary school or graduate school (Weisinger 1974; Wheelwright 1974).

Similarly, Henderson (1991) has argued for an archetypal orientation in teaching history, for "there are layers of time in everything, including ourselves," and he observes:

> "Once upon a time," that familiar phrase, can lay them bare. When the emphasis is placed on the first of these four words, what stands out is the ab-

solute uniqueness of each person and event: once, and once only, did the light fall just so in a Constantinople landscape; once, and once only, did Paul see a blinding light on the road to Damascus. About this aspect of each episode there hangs a kind of futile finality, but there is also its complement, where constancy is the keynote. However different the context of time and place and character, "once upon a time" then promotes security, reassurance and renewal. It seems to assert that behind all appearance of change there is a pattern of perpetuation, a quality of indestructibility, which witnesses to a time different from flying sequence. (245)

In his autobiography, *Memories, Dreams, Reflections*, written near the end of his life, Jung provided the charter for this view of history and its teaching when he declared:

Life has always seemed to me like a plant that lives upon its rhizome. Its true life is invisible, hidden in the rhizome. The part that appears above the ground lasts only a single summer. Then it withers away—an ephemeral apparition. When we think of the unending growth and decay of life and civilizations, we cannot escape the impression of an absolute nullity. Yet I have never lost a sense of something that lives and endures underneath the eternal flux. What we see is the blossom, which passes. The rhizome remains. (1963)

When the teacher and student view their subject in this light—looking for the archetypal rhizome beneath the ever-shifting scenery of particular events and situations—they are engaged in an archetypal study of history.

Educators from many other fields have used archetypal terms and paradigms to frame their disciplines—from the archetypal approach to physics by the Nobel-Prize-winning scientist Wolfgang Pauli, to religious studies by Union Theological Seminary's Ann Ulanov, to sociology and cultural studies by Michael Adams and Richard Gray. The classroom teacher may draw upon these studies in order to shape an innovatively archetypal curriculum or supplement a traditional one.

It is beyond the scope of this book to do more than merely mention that these approaches exist and whet the reader's appetite for teacher-friendly expositions of them, such as Hendricks and Fadiman's (1976) practical guide, *Transpersonal Education: A Curriculum for Feeling and Being*, and Diane Whitmore's *Psychosynthesis in Education* (1986).

Hopefully, however, this small taste of the transpersonal approach to curriculum has cast some preliminary light on the Jungian notion that when subject matter is discussed and explored along archetypal lines, it vivifies classroom environments with archetypal energy. The educator who can use the curriculum as a tool to constellate archetypal energy and imagery in himself and his students has found one of the great keys to truly memorable teaching.

FIFTH PILLAR

- The symbolic domain and intuitive function are crucial to the educational enterprise.

Jung once said that concepts are ultimately stiff and empty things, like coins used to buy food, but symbols are the bread of life itself. Because Jung always stood in awe of the finally inscrutable mystery of things, he insisted that symbols can bring us much closer than theoretical speculation to those timeless truths that are able to satisfy our hearts. A Jungian theory of education emphasizes helping the student engage with his world in richly symbolic terms.

A symbol stimulates our ability to intuit a reality that transcends mere ratiocination. It points beyond itself. In doing this, it accomplishes more than a sign, which is merely an arbitrary token that mechanically *stands for* something else in a one-to-one correspondence. For instance, the sign $\int$ in the calculus means one thing *and one thing only*—namely that I must perform the mathematical operation of integration. However, the declaration in T. S. Eliot's poem *The Wasteland* that there is "fear in a handful of dust" generates many strands of interweaving and mutually enriching interpretations (1971, 38).

For instance, the clenched hand holding the dust might suggest terror, grasping, and the denial of death. The fist, unclenching, then evokes feelings of resignation, loss of potency, and the release of dust to dust, ashes to ashes. The wind that bears the dust away is an emblem of the indifferent motions of an empty universe, but at the same time it conjures up images of the breath and spirit of God. Stark terror and wise acceptance, frank futility and divine love—all of this (and a great deal more) is included in the unsettling image of fear in a handful of dust. It leads us to an *experience* of the struggle of life against death—and the hope for something beyond it.

In brief, the symbol whisks us away into an uncharted mystery while a sign ploddingly takes us from point A to B. Given the premium that Jung always placed on life as a mystery, it should come as no surprise that he saw the symbol as epistemologically a great deal more powerful than the sign. Any Jungian pedagogy, then, would have to place great emphasis upon richly symbolic ways of knowing and communicating.

As we have already seen, virtually any discipline or topic can be mined for its symbolic implications and applications. Nevertheless, it does seem easier to do this with some subjects—especially those in the arts and humanities—than with others. Unlike the typical politically motivated cries for educational reform through the imposition of standardized testing, which always cast art and literature to the edges, a Jungian curriculum stresses them. "The great secret of art . . . and the creative process" Jung observed,

> consists in the unconscious activation of an archetypal image, and in elaborating and shaping this image into the finished work. By giving it shape, the artist translates it into the language of the present, and so makes it possible for us to find the way back to the wellsprings of life. Therein lies the social significance of art: it is constantly at work educating the spirit of the age, conjuring up the forms in which the age is most lacking. The unsatisfied yearning of the artist reaches back to the primordial image in the unconscious which is best fitted to compensate the inadequacy and one-sidedness of the present. The artist seizes on this image, and in raising it from the deepest unconsciousness, he brings it into relation with conscious values, thereby transforming it until it can be accepted by the minds of his contemporaries according to their power. (CW 15, par. 130)

This Jungian view of the curriculum as psychosocially healing fits quite nicely with some important contemporary curriculum theories. Maxine Greene, for instance, sees the appreciation and creation of art as the heart of a great curriculum. Greene's emphasis is phenomenological—that is, she is concerned with the complex nature of individual experience and how to cultivate it through the use of symbols so that such experience is psychologically integrative and results in constructive social action. This is very similar, of course, to the goal of Jungian psychology, *individuation*, where the premium is also placed upon self-discovery and social responsibility through deep engagement with the symbolic realm.

According to Greene, art and its symbols offer the teacher and student many "occasions for ordering the materials of [their] world, for imposing 'configurations' by means of experiences and perspectives made available for personally conducted cognitive action" (1974, 299). But before helping students reconstruct the symbols that define their world, the teacher must first help them deconstruct some of the old symbols that have heretofore structured their comfortable daily lives. Since problematizing "perspectives" upon objects and forcing the viewer to see them in new ways was also the aesthetic goal of Cubist painting, Greene advocates a "Cubist curriculum." Its purpose is to move the teacher and student beyond the easy, standard interpretations of the subject matter in order to confront it anew with the same intensity, curiosity, and creativity with which one should examine a piece of art.

Ornstein and Hunkins have termed this and similar arts-based approaches to curriculum *humanist-aesthetic* (1988). However, it would be a mistake to conclude that only art classes promote the "expressive outcomes" of "aesthetic" curricula, for:

> any activity—indeed, at their very best, activities that are engaged in to court surprise, to cultivate discovery, to find new forms of experience—is expressive in character. Nothing in the sciences, the home or mechanical arts, or in social relationships prohibits or diminishes the possibility of engaging in expressive outcomes. The education problem is to be sufficiently imaginative in the design of educational programs so that such outcomes will occur and their educational value will be high. (Eisner and Vallance 1974, 134)

It is not only in the classroom that the aesthetic approach may come into play. It may also guide curriculum theorizing itself.

> We may want to study the aesthetic qualities of a textbook series, or of a series of deliberations and discussions leading to curriculum change, of a given teacher's classroom, or of a full degree sequence that we may be planning to alter. . . . The important point is that aesthetic inquiry into a curriculum problem must above all leave us free to *respond to qualities*

that may take us by surprise; our response to these qualities will be helped and shaped by our training and experience in seeing these qualities. (Eisner and Vallance 1975, 89)

In this approach to education, "the arts are not taught for their own sake; instead, they are taught because they allow a child to experience a subject on a level far deeper and richer than the intellectual level" (Trostli 1991, 349)—namely, the archetypal level. And this can be true of any subject, even the most traditionally scientific.

As the historian of science Thomas Kuhn (1970) observed, scientific revolutions do not take place as a result of increasingly sophisticated analyses of already-existing paradigms and problems. Rather, they occur when paradigms shift—when, that is, scientists embrace a new set of foundational symbols to frame their questions and conclusions. Einstein caught his first glimpses of the theory of relativity as a boy, wondering what it would be like to ride on the head of a beam of light. A child's archetypally rich poetic musings were the matrix out of which a whole new cosmology arose! The aesthetician Bendetto Croce made a similar point about how analytical systems begin as symbolic intuitions:

> The relation between knowledge or expression and intellectual knowledge or concept, between art and science, poetry and prose, cannot be otherwise defined than by saying that it is one of *double degree.* The first degree is the expression, the second the concept: the first can stand without the second, but the second cannot stand without the first. There is poetry without prose, but not prose without poetry. Expression, indeed, is the first affirmation of human activity. Poetry is "the mother tongue of the human race"; the first men "were by nature sublime poets." (in Vivas and Krieger 1953, 86)

A Jungian curriculum would encourage the student to explore and experience the primary, archetypal symbols embedded deep in any discipline, topic, or activity, thereby allowing him to use those symbols for personal and social transformation.

The reader will recall that one of Jung's four major personality types was the intuitive. In education driven by the corporate project of creating and dominating markets, the archetypally feminine and spiritual function of intuition receives precious little attention; however, in a Jungian education intuition is crucial because it is only in the medium of intuition that symbols can live.

This is a pity, Jung felt, because great insights often come as a result of complex *intuitions*, which, in their subtlety and multivalence, are much truer to the intricacy of life itself than mere intellectual *analysis*. Jung wrote, "My psychological experience has shown time and again that certain contents issue from a psyche more complete than consciousness. They often contain a superior analysis or insight or knowledge which consciousness has not been able to produce. We have a suitable word for such occurrences—intuition" (1938/1966, 49). Jung said that his own scholarship and practice relied upon intuition—that "irruption into consciousness of an unconscious content, a sudden idea or 'hunch'"—more than any other way of knowing (*CW* 8, par. 269). Yet again, Jung emerges as one of the great progenitors of modern holistic education, for which the cultivation of intuitive modes of seeing, being, and communicating is a primary objective. This is the goal of what the transpersonal instructional theorist Reinsmith calls "apophatic" modes of teaching and learning (1992).

Vaughan (1986) has identified four types of intuition. There is *physical* intuition, such as the somatic warning signals that our body sends us when we are in danger; *emotional* intuition, such as the "sense" we have of a person after just meeting him; *mental* intuition, such as the "mere hunch" that leads a scientist to look in an unexpected corner for evidence to confirm or disconfirm a hypothesis; and finally, *spiritual* intuition, which "is independent from feelings, thoughts, and sensations. . . . At the spiritual level intuition moves beyond dualism to experience unity directly. . . . Meditation is a technique designed to quiet the mind so that spiritual intuition can arise" (Miller 1988, 76–77). Feige (1999) has characterized the transpersonal way of knowing as an "aesthetic epistemology thriving in an aesthetic, ultimately unified world" (87).

In all of this, we see the close tie between a pedagogy that values symbolic processes and products and one that aims at nurturing intuitive ability in students. Symbol and intuition are so interrelated because "the symbol is the primitive exponent of the unconscious, but at the same time an idea that corresponds to the highest intuition of the conscious mind" (Jung 1978, 30). Naturally, it is impossible to quantify intuition. It is in many respects the very antithesis of quantification.[2] Educationists and politicians who worship the standardized test will always look upon intuition with great suspicion because it can be neither controlled nor predicted—those two great aims of "scientism" and business.

For a Jungian pedagogy, on the other hand, intuition is of the first importance. Jung readily admits that honoring and extending one's intuitive capacities may seem errant nonsense to those who cannot think outside of the box of norm-referencing. But it has always been the case, Jung reminds us, that true creativity grows out of psychic processes that small-minded people will always dismiss as mere "tomfoolery" (CW 14, par. 52). At a time when ill-informed calls for a hardnosed, back-to-basics approach to education stridently riddle the air of public discourse about schooling, and as children are increasingly being drugged to keep them quiet and submissive in classrooms that are as deadly boring as they are pedagogically absurd, it is advisable to heed Jung's reminder that

> not the artist alone, but every creative individual whatsoever owes all that is greatest in his life to fantasy. The dynamic principle of fantasy is *play*, a characteristic also of the child, and as such it appears inconsistent with the principle of serious work. But without this playing with fantasy no creative work has ever come to birth. The debt we owe to the play of imagination is incalculable. It is therefore short-sighted to treat fantasy, on account of its risky or unacceptable nature, as a thing of little worth. It must not be forgotten that it is just in the imagination that a man's highest value may lie.[3] (CW 6, par. 93)

SIXTH PILLAR

- Failure can be constructive.

Although a Jungian view of education emphasizes nurturing the student, this does not mean that he should live in a risk-free environment. One gets the feeling in reading some of the literature on teaching-as-care that it has taken the idea of nurturance too far, not allowing the student to learn how to overcome those intellectual and ethical obstacles that are necessary for growth. As we saw in part I, it is an axiom of Jungian psychology that all energy "can proceed only from the tension of opposites"

(*CW* 7, par. 34). Where there is no opposition but merely a satiated stasis, there is not only no *need* to grow but also no *way* to grow. Besides, where there is no possibility of failure, success is meaningless. Jung said that *katabasis*, a Greek term for the descent to the underworld, is requisite for psychospiritual maturation (*CW* 15, par. 213).

The student who is perpetually shielded against the developmentally necessary reality of occasional failure must ultimately succumb to a kind of psychic entropy. Or, to put it in archetypal terms, the student in a classroom whose teacher has overidentified with the archetype of the Great Mother (and this may be a male teacher as well as a female one) will ultimately find himself rocked into a moral and intellectual stupor in that teacher's excessively protective embrace. Every archetype has both a bright and dark side. The shadow of the Great Mother is the Devouring Mother, the caregiver who will not let her children go but instead spins such a web of care around them that she paralyzes them. Here is the archetypal root of the "empty-nest syndrome"—the mother's panic at the prospect of a vacant house and womb.

Not every failure in a classroom is healthy, of course. The teacher must handle the student's failure in a constructive, nonpunitive manner, patiently helping the student see how he fell short and what together they can do to help him reach his full potential in a given area—however great or limited that potential may turn out to be. I have discussed elsewhere (Mayes 2003) how techniques drawn from the cognitive therapy of Aaron Beck and Weishaar (1995) and Judith Beck (1995) can help the teacher help the student constructively reframe failure as a prelude to success. This kind of wisely handled failure leading to eventual success differs greatly from the student's impersonal and humiliating experience of failure on standardized tests. As in parenting, the best teaching strategies are neither *authoritarian* (as in standardized testing) nor *permissive* (as in an overly nurturing style of teaching). They are *authoritative*, blending judgment (the archetypally paternal) and care (the archetypally maternal) (Brophy 1994).

Not only does a Jungian pedagogy *accommodate* the student's weakness; in a sense it *encourages* it. This is to say that, in addition to cultivating the student's areas of special ability, it also pays attention to his *inferior function*. Corporate educational agendas, concerned above all else with maximizing profitability, have no room for anything less than maximal productivity from the student. They deny or repress the student's inferior function. This is psychologically damaging, for as the most unconscious element of the student's personality, the inferior function is that part of the psyche which—if ignored and unsupported—will emerge in destructive, neurotic forms and thereby undermine the child's success in other areas.

For example, if the thinking function is stressed to the virtual exclusion of all else—as is obviously the case in most postelementary public schooling and increasingly the case even in early grades—the other functions will emerge in a pathological form. The neglected feeling function will manifest itself as excessive, inappropriate, and even self-destructive emotions; the intuitive function will express itself as free-floating anxiety or reckless enthusiasm; and the sensate function, starved for attention and stimulation, will find a way to get it in the form of drug-induced highs or ill-advised sex.

For this reason, the curricularist must try to address *all* of the student's functions in order to "complete him and make him a real totality" (*CW* 17, par. 248). Because of his belief in both holistic therapy and education, Jung was perhaps the first twentieth-century psychologist to raise his voice against the invidious practice of ability grouping, which he felt ill-served all children but especially "gifted" ones, for "segregated in a special class, the gifted child would be in danger of developing into a one-sided product" (*CW* 17, par. 246).

SEVENTH PILLAR

- Education is not therapy, but it does have legitimate therapeutic roles to play.

Throughout his writings, Jung referred to the therapist as an "educator of the soul" (*CW* 7, par. 25). It was the teacher Socrates, not the physician Hippocrates, who was the first physician of the psyche, according to Jung, as becomes clear when we look at the nature of the therapeutic process. "It is a genuine old wisdom that comes to light again in the treatment, and it is especially curious that this kind of psychic education should prove necessary in the heyday of our culture. In more than one respect it may be compared with the Socratic method, though it must be said that analysis penetrates to far greater depths" (*CW* 7, par. 26). But then again, an education sensitive to Jungian principles must itself "penetrate to far greater depths" than the Socratic method if it is to promote integration and individuation. If therapy is a form of education, and if education needs to press beyond the mere inculcation of rationality, then it should not surprise us to learn that education is similar to therapy in some respects.

This is far from a novel concept, nor is it one that is limited to a Jungian perspective. Since the beginning of modern developmental psychology with G. Stanley Hall's (1904) text *Adolescence*, educationists have tried to apply the findings of psychological research and practice. The very idea of a "developmentally appropriate curriculum" is already an attempt to shape pedagogy around children's evolving psychic issues.

The junior high school, for instance, was established in order to help students make the psychologically difficult transition from early childhood to adolescence and, as such, is inherently a "therapeutic" institution (Tyack 1974). The highly significant document produced by the NEA in 1918, *Cardinal Principles of Secondary Education*, defined the public high school as a tool for psychosocially molding children during adolescence. August Aichhorn (1935/1965), a prominent Freudian psychiatrist of adolescence, argued that every teacher should know at least the fundamentals of psychoanalysis so that he could apply them in the classroom. Margaret Naumburg, the founder of the Walden School movement, asked her teachers to undergo analysis just as Freud required of analysts in training so that they could recognize and appropriately respond to their students' psychosexual dilemmas (Cremin 1964). And, of course, counseling and special education programs in colleges of education prepare people to play various therapeutic roles in the schools.

Currently, the popularity of self-esteem–enhancing curricula and literature on teaching-as-care show that many teachers and teacher educators continue to see their vocation in a therapeutic light. Indeed, the "teacher-as-therapist" is an image that some teachers think of when asked to reflect on the nature of their work with children (Mayes 2001a,b).

Like a good therapist, then, the teacher must have a personalized sense of what makes each student tick if he is to be most effective at his work. Jung claimed that "for the doctor this means the individual study of every case; for the teacher, the individual study of every student" (*CW* 17, par. 173). This is especially the case when we consider that the teacher is sometimes the object of the student's transferences and that the teacher may easily countertransfer his own issues back onto the student. This topic is discussed in considerable detail in the remaining chapters. For now, it is enough to note that transference and countertransference in the classroom was an issue that interested Jung, particularly when it came to sexual attraction between teacher and student (*CW* 17, pars. 221–22).

Object-relations psychology is also helpful in understanding teaching's therapeutic aspects. We saw earlier that an "object" is a significant person in a child's earliest experiences, primarily (but by no means always) the mother. The nature of the child's relationship with a significant object or objects is highly influential in determining how that child will eventually come to see himself and interact with others later in life. An object that is loving and supportive is called a "good object," whereas one that is rejecting, anxious, or in some other way nonnurturing is called a "bad object." Object-relationists talk of the child's "internalization" of objects. If, for instance, the mother holds, nurses, and generally deals with the infant in tender, appropriate ways, then the infant will "internalize the good object"—that is to say, the child will come to see itself as worthy of love, as *loveable*. On the other hand, a child who is treated poorly will "internalize the bad object" and come to see itself as inherently bad, as *unlovable*.

The psychiatrist W. R. D. Fairbairn (1952/1992) noted that when children internalize bad objects, their personality begins to "split" into various conflicting, self-punishing components that cannot organize in a healthy way around a stable, positive center. This does not mean that a parent must always coddle a child—must always be a completely "good object" from the infant's point of view. A certain degree of difficulty is inevitable, even healthy, in the mother–infant relationship, especially when the mother is weaning the baby, who may be quite unhappy at this process. The baby does not need perfectly "good objects" to thrive, but the mothering it experiences must be "good enough" (Winnicott 1992).

With the "good-enough mother" the baby *can* thrive. Without it, the baby is primed for a wide range of psychological illnesses as it grows.

Similarly, in the classroom, what is needed is a "good-enough teacher"— one who provides a nurturing environment for the student to thrive educationally. The student can internalize this "sufficiently good pedagogical object" and develop an image of himself as a competent and worthwhile student. This teacher need not be perfect (as some teachers, who quickly burn out, seem to believe), nor need such a teacher anxiously guard against any type of failure in his students (quite the contrary, as argued above). Rather, the teacher simply needs to be "good enough" to promote the student's psychic, academic, and spiritual growth.

As we have already seen, this entails that the teacher not promote the wrong *kinds* of failure, or excessive amounts of it, for then the student will internalize these "bad pedagogical objects." In Fairbairn's terms, this may cause the student's identity to "split" so that he becomes a problem to himself, the teacher, and the class at large. The "good enough" teacher helps promote healthy self-identity in the student. Using the sociologist Anthony Giddens' (1991) list of characteristics of what constitutes healthy self-identity, we might say that the good-enough teacher fosters in the student: (1) a sense of *unity* in his personality, (2) the feeling that he can *appropriate* what happens in the classroom in a personally relevant and satisfying manner, (3) the conviction that he has some degree of *authority* about what will happen to him and how he will respond to it, and (4) the faith that the teacher sees him as a *unique person*, not just a commodified number on a computerized list of students or a score on a standardized test.

Jung therefore felt that "it is in fact highly desirable that the educator, if he wishes to really understand the mentality of his pupils, should pay attention to the findings of analytical psychology" (*CW* 17, par. 130). However, Jung added the caveat that "the deepened psychological knowledge of the teacher should not, as unfortunately sometimes happens, be unloaded directly on the child; rather it should help the teacher to adopt an understanding attitude toward the child's psychic life" (*CW* 17, par. 100). In short, although teaching has a therapeutic aspect, the teacher should always remember that he is not a therapist (*CW* 17, par. 142).

EIGHTH PILLAR

- Reflectivity is a key component of teacher development.

Because Jung placed great faith in and responsibilities on the teacher, he was a staunch advocate of the ongoing education of the teacher. Yet, unlike many of the positivist educationists of his day, Jung put very little stock in "training" prospective and practicing teachers to follow pre-packaged "methods." For "in reality, everything depends on the man and little or nothing on the method" (Jung 1978, 9). The teacher's moral character and psychological insight are what will really win or lose the day for him with his students. The therapist and the educator are similar in that "psychotherapy has taught us that in the final reckoning it is not knowledge, not technical skill, that has a curative effect, but the personality of the doctor. And it is the same with education: It presupposes self-education" (*CW* 17, par. 240).

For Jung, this "self-education" consisted in what today is called "teacher reflectivity" (Bullough 1991; Mayes 1999). The teacher examines and critiques himself and his practice in psychological and political terms to see if he is being as sensitive and fair with all of his students as he can be, or if he has unresolved issues or prejudices that are standing in the way. "The teacher should watch his own psychic condition, so that he can spot the source of trouble when anything goes wrong with the children entrusted to his care" (*CW* 17, par. 211). In the following chapters, I discuss and give in-depth practical examples of teacher reflectivity using Jungian tools and terms. For now, let us simply note that Jung was far ahead of his time not only in his concern for teacher education but also in understanding that technical approaches to teacher education are generally unfruitful, and that for a teacher to be all that he can be requires rigorous self-analysis, personally and professionally.

NINTH PILLAR

- Education has culturally conservative as well as culturally progressive roles to play in the formation of the child.

When it comes to the sociocultural aspects of education, Jung's vision is a mix of cultural conservatism and radicalism.

On the conservative side, Jung advocated a traditional humanities curriculum as part of the student's schooling in the higher grades.

> [T]he school curriculum . . . should never wander too far from the humanities into overspecialized fields. The coming generation should at least be shown the doors that lead to the many different departments of life and the mind. And it seems to me especially important for any broad-based culture to have a regard for history in the widest sense of the word. As important as it is to pay attention to what is practical and useful, and to consider the future, that backward glance at the past is just as important. Culture means continuity, not a tearing up of roots through "progress." (*CW* 17, par. 250)

True to his conservative nature, Jung warned that "anything new should always be questioned and tested with caution, for it may very easily turn out to be only a new disease" (*CW* 17, par. 251). Besides, it is only by honoring the tried-and-true standards that have developed over time that we can rein in our instincts, many of which are—as Jung the psychiatrist well knew—psychologically and morally injurious to self and other (*CW* 8, par. 161). Those who see in Jung's fascination with archetypes a call for a return to primitivism grossly misinterpret him (Noll 1994).

Jung saw education as one of humanity's best hopes to control our animal nature and promote social and spiritual evolution. He detested "the present tendency to destroy all tradition or render it unconscious," for this must "interrupt the normal process of development for several hundred years and substitute an interlude of barbarism" (*CW* 9.2, par. 282). Besides, our personal identities are so interwoven with our individual and collective histories that we cannot know *ourselves* if we do not know *them*. This is another reason why, although education may validly include practical knowledge and skills, it should never be primarily technical, for:

> man is not a machine that can remodeled . . . as occasion demands, in the hope that it will go on functioning as regularly as before but in a quite different way. Man carries his whole history with him; in his very structure is

written the history of mankind. This historical element in man represents a vital need to which a wise psychic economy must respond. Somehow the past must come alive and participate in the present. (*CW* 6, par. 570)

We can know ourselves deeply and resist attempts at political domination only by a solid appreciation of our past. This is why "loss of roots and lack of tradition neuroticize the masses and prepare them for collective hysteria" (*CW* 9.2, par. 282).

Unlike many people who advocate a culturally conservative curriculum, however, Jung did not do so out of a sense of cultural superiority or xenophobia. As we have seen, Jung was a great student of culture—from the nearest to the most distant in space and time. He traveled from the jungles of Africa to the deserts of New Mexico to gain firsthand experience of indigenous peoples, about whom he wrote with great lucidity, genuine admiration, and unfeigned love. Hence, there is a lifetime of personal and intellectual experience in Jung's pithy observation that "the white race is not a species of *homo sapiens* specially favored by God" (*CW* 16, par. 188). It is not only the white European who needs to know about his history. Everyone must know about the great events, ideas, and hopes of his own culture, for at their heart lie those symbols that can bring out the best in him individually and socially. Education must concern itself with "the body of lore concerning the things that lie beyond man's earthly existence, and of wise rules of conduct" (*CW* 15, par. 150).

Jung was very clear that the so-called civilized cultures are not superior to the so-called primitive ones in this respect and are in some respects inferior—despite their impressive technologies and expensive toys. Indeed, as Jung saw the Westerner's faith in foundational cultural narratives eroding, he warned that "the old myth needs to be clothed anew in every renewed age if it is not to lose its therapeutic effect" (*CW* 9.2, par. 281). Sometimes, incorporating elements from "less advanced" cultural traditions is just what is needed to provide that new cultural "clothing." Decades before the modern multicultural movement, Jung argued for the value of cultural diversity, insisting that education must be culturally critical as well as culturally preserving. This blend of traditionalism and radicalism is what one would expect from someone whose focus was ever on the balance of opposites.

Furthermore, Jung believed that the idea of the shadow and projection could help teachers and students examine the darker side of their own national culture. For just as individuals have unconscious dark sides which they tend to project onto others, so do societies. As we saw in part I, a culture's shadow can be discerned in who it perceives its enemies to be, for it is onto its enemies that a culture projects what it most fears in itself. A culture's collective shadow is the flip side of its conscious values (Odajnyk 1976). Jung wrote:

> If people can be educated to see the shadow side of their nature clearly, it may be hoped that they will also learn to understand and love their fellow men better. A little less hypocrisy and a little more self-knowledge can only have good results in respect for our neighbor; for we are all too prone to transfer to our fellows the injustices and violence we inflict upon our own natures. (*CW* 7, par. 28)

Not only nations but also families, communities, political parties, and races have collective shadows that are the dark underside of their conscious, normative values. Left unexamined and unintegrated, these shadows get projected onto "opposing" families, communities, political parties, and races.[4]

Education—particularly the social studies—can help students explore cultural projection by asking such questions as the following: In a bellicose policy toward another community or state, what part of the motivation for that policy might stem from cultural projection? Conversely, in considering critiques of our own society, which of them are simply projections onto "the ugly American" and which contain truths that we must heed?

Howard Zinn's (1990) *A People's History of the United States* exemplifies the attempt to deal with one's own cultural shadow. It does this by treating its subject from the point of view of the marginalized "losers" in American history—especially people of color and poor people—so that they can be seen as real human beings engaged in important struggles and not as hooks onto which students from dominant social groups can hang their shadowy projections. By encouraging students to discover their individual and collective shadows, teachers can also help them resist political propaganda. In so doing, teachers are following the theologian Paul Tillich's (1957) counsel to resist the false gods of excessive nationalism (64).

When education helps the individual cast light on the shadow in him-self and his culture, then, guarded against the seductive prejudices of groupthink, he can become an agent in making his culture more ethical. Jung wrote:

> Every advance in culture is, psychologically, an extension of conscious-ness, a coming to consciousness that can take place only through discrim-ination. Therefore an advance always begins with individuation, that is to say with the individual, conscious of his isolation, cutting a new path through hitherto untrodden territory. . . . If he succeeds in giving collec-tive validity to his widened consciousness, he creates a tension of oppo-sites that provides the stimulation which culture needs for its further progress. (*CW* 8, par. 111)

In brief, "individuation . . . has a political aspect to it" (Samuels 2001, 23). By taking the best of the conservative and liberal views of culture, teachers can help students grow into adults who, attaining the maximum degree of integration in themselves, can promote integration in their families, communities, and cultures.

TENTH PILLAR

- Education can be spiritual in pedagogically powerful and legally appropriate ways.

Jung's view of the interaction of spirituality and culture agrees with Paul Tillich's (1956/1987) famous pronouncement that "religion is the soul of culture and culture the form of religion" (103). Every culture has "a highly developed system of secret teaching, a body of lore concerning the things that lie beyond man's earthly existence, and of wise rules of conduct" (*CW* 15, par. 150). It is from the archetypally fertile ground of these *fundamental narratives*, this "body of lore," that a society's civic and legal narratives and grow over the centuries (Bruner 1996), a point made also by the social constructivists Berger and Luckman (1967) in their assertion that "throughout human history religion has played a de-cisive part in the construction and maintenance of [social] universes"

(422). Berger (1967) has highlighted how most cultures are grounded in their (sometimes unspoken) spiritual commitments, especially regarding mortality and the promise of an afterlife, for "every human society is, in the last resort, men banded together in the face of death. The power of religion depends, in the last resort, upon the credibility of the banners it puts in the hands of men as they stand before death, or more accurately, as they walk, inevitably, toward it" (52).

But what about the academic truism that (post)modern life is "profane" or "desacralized"? As with many fashionable academic truisms, this one does not seem to apply outside the protective walls of academia—and apparently does not even really apply *there* since fully two-thirds of professors claim to have a moderate to high degree of spiritual commitments (Nord 1995). Most historians and sociologists of religion note that spirituality, in both its institutional and strictly personal forms, is as important now to most people as it ever was—and perhaps even more so (Marty 1987). This inextinguishable personal and cultural need to connect with the transcendent and to live in its light is a universal urge for individuals and peoples. As long as we must personally and collectively face what T. S. Eliot (1971) called "the overwhelming questions" of our morality and mortality, spiritual commitment is bound to be a significant issue for most people (6). Any approach to education that ignores this ethical and cultural imperative to live in the light of transpersonal truth is inadequate.

This is why, for Jung, a theory of either therapy or education that does not take spirituality into account must ultimately fail, however bright its light of popularity might burn for a brief season. For not only are archetypes inherently spiritual but *spirituality is itself an archetype*, a basic human need and capacity. In both the consulting room and classroom, spirituality must be honored and explored as the pivotal emotional, social, and intellectual force that it is. Furthermore, *morality is an archetype*, not just a social invention or sexual displacement as Freud held. Students naturally want to explore moral issues in their studies—and will feel bored and short-changed if they cannot. Ethical questions and systems are

a function of the human soul, as old as humanity itself. Morality is not imposed from outside; we have it in ourselves from the start—not the law, but our moral nature without which the collective life of human society would be impossible. That is why morality is found at all levels of society. It is the instinctive regulator of action. (*CW* 7, par. 30)

Tillich (1959) said that in the last analysis everyone has ethical and spiritual commitments because everyone has "ultimate concerns," which is another way of saying that everyone has archetypal issues, images, and impulses embedded deep in his psyche. Thus when Huebner, echoing Tillich, said we must frame our educational endeavors in "ultimate terms" (1999) or MacDonald (1995) called for a "transcendental ideology of the curriculum," they were essentially advocating for an archetypally sensitive curriculum. In this sense, too, we can interpret the philosopher Alfred Whitehead's proclamation that "all true education is religious" to mean that "all true education is archetypal." Understanding Whitehead in this light allows us to envision a pedagogy that helps students explore their own and each other's archetypal depths and thus is spiritually sensitive without being theologically dogmatic or denominationally partisan.

There is a growing body of literature about how to engage in spiritually sensitive teaching that is pedagogically powerful, psychologically enriching, and legally appropriate.[5] And it is important to reemphasize that spiritual teaching occurs not only in the humanities and arts. The social and physical sciences, too, offer many opportunities to engage in spiritually creative education; for, no less than the sculptor or novelist, the scientist and the science teacher can venture onto archetypal territory in their explorations. Attending to the archetypal realm, then, it is possible to forge an approach to curriculum and instruction that that is psychospiritually integrative, socially responsible, and capable of accommodating the many perspectives in a pluralistic democracy.

CONCLUSION

We have seen in this chapter that curriculum and instruction are greatly enriched by including the archetypal dimension, and they do this best by honoring the language of archetypes—symbols. This entails a greater stress on intuition in the classroom, both in the teacher and student, than is typically allowed or encouraged.

A Jungian approach also requires that teachers let students fail—but in ways that promote future success. It is also necessary that the teacher understand himself as a teacher deeply, which is why Jung argued for reflectivity in teacher education.

Never one to be pigeonholed ideologically, Jung was both radical and conservative in his views on the cultural role of education, arguing that education must serve both preserving and transforming functions. Confronting one's personal and cultural shadow is crucial to this project.

Moreover, an archetypal approach to curriculum and instruction allows the teacher and student to explore spiritual themes in the classroom in ways that are psychosocially enriching and legally appropriate.

TOPICS FOR GROUP DISCUSSION OR INDIVIDUAL REFLECTIVITY

1. The author implies that the archetypal dimension can be discovered and explored by teachers and students in virtually any subject matter. Do you agree or disagree with this? Are there some subjects and topics that lend themselves more naturally to archetypal approaches than others? If you believe there are, then which subjects are more archetypally rich and which are less so, and why?

2. What kinds of activities and inquiries might you structure for your students to help them develop their intuitive abilities in the subject that you teach?

3. Do you agree with the author's insistence that failure can serve constructive purposes in the classroom? Why or why not?

4. The author argues strongly that education both can and should play an emotionally therapeutic role in the life of the teacher and of the student. Some scholars and practitioners disagree with this idea, however, claiming that it is inappropriate to try to address such issues in a classroom setting, in which the focus should exclusively be on learning academic knowledge, not dealing with psychodynamics. Where do you stand in this debate?

5. Do you agree with the author's notion that the archetypal approach to education offers a legally appropriate and pedagogically fruitful way to address a student's spiritual commitments and hopes, even

in a public school? And even if you agree with this, do you agree or disagree with the author's stronger claim that the curriculum, to be complete, must nurture the student's spiritual nature and draw him or her into dialogue with other students about spiritual issues?

NOTES

1. For more on the archetypal significance of numbers, especially numbers one through four, see Jung, *CW* 8 and *CW* 9.1; see also see von Franz (1984) for a discussion of the relationship between numerical archetypes and different conceptions of time.

2. However, it should also be remembered, as the great mathematician Poincaré claimed, that the most elegant and important mathematical discoveries often first appear in a flash of intuitive insight.

3. A Jungian critique of education must also include the Montessori method in its tendency to discourage children from engaging in "mere fantasy," which Montessori saw as unproductive and even dangerous for the child. See Crain (1992) and Gutek (2000) for more on this conflict between Montessori and a Jungian perspective. Nevertheless, Montessori's idea of "sensitive periods" in a child's maturation in which certain skills and topics can best be introduced is certainly quite consistent with a Jungian developmental perspective.

4. Several years ago I had a graduate student from Russia. She told me that during the Cold War, she and many of her friends would often have dreams as children about monstrously large American soldiers in Gestapo-black uniforms coming to rape, pillage, and burn in the small town where she lived, leaving nothing but deathly horror in their wake. Of course, as a good Jungian I had often thought about how I project my cultural shadow onto other cultures. But here was an instance of somebody having projected their cultural shadow onto me! This novel experience of being not the *projecient* but the *projiciand* was very valuable for me, helping me see the process of cultural projection for the first time from both sides of the table.

5. The reader who is interested in exploring how to introduce explicitly spiritual themes and activities in public school classrooms in legally and institutionally appropriate ways may consult Brown, Phillips, and Shapiro (1976), Kniker (1990), Marsden (1997), Mayes and Ferrin (2001), Nord (1994, 1995), Warshaw (1986), and Whitmore (1986).

REFLECTING ON THE ARCHETYPES OF TEACHING

THE TEACHER REFLECTIVITY MOVEMENT

There has been a significant increase recently in research about teacher reflectivity. This term refers to a variety of processes in which both practicing and prospective teachers engage in journal work, group and dyadic encounters, and even meditative exercises in order to "surface" the deeper images and assumptions that inform their sense of calling and classroom practice. With these ideas and images made explicit, the teacher can work with them—sometimes celebrating and fostering them, other times massaging and modifying them, and occasionally replacing them with more serviceable notions about what it means to be a teacher.

Teacher reflectivity currently deals mostly with existential and political issues in the life of the teacher. What is lacking is consideration of the teacher's deeper psychospiritual dynamics. Despite its undoubted significance, the existential/political approach to teacher education does not go far enough because it fails to address the *transpersonal* domain. The seeds of "teacher reflectivity" cannot fully flower unless they are fed by the richer soil of what Jung (*CW* 14) called the "sacred precincts"— those psychic territories where archetypal winds sweep over and vitalize the otherwise dull landscapes of our daily lives. It is in such sacred precincts that many people decide to become teachers.

As the educational sociologist Dan Lortie (1975) observed, most people do not take on the difficult work of teaching for financial gain or social status (both of which they know they must more or less live without) but for what he called "psychic rewards." My twenty-five years as a teacher and teacher educator have convinced me that Jungian psychology offers some of the most powerful tools for increasing these "psychic rewards"—and in the process helps to fashion more integrated, effective teachers. In this chapter, we see how "archetypal reflectivity" is a potentially powerful means of aiding and enriching teachers as they reflect on themselves and their craft (Mayes 1999).

OFF THE PRODUCTION LINE—AND TOWARD THE ARCHETYPAL

We saw in chapter 6 that the historian Laurence Cremin (1988) said American public education has increasingly come to mirror the reigning socioeconomic agenda of turning people and nature into marketable *objects*. As Marx said, this "commodity fetishism" is the very core of capitalism. Thus, whether so-called educational reformers at the highest levels of government call themselves "liberals" or "conservatives" hardly matters, for both Democratic and Republican presidents and secretaries of education promote programs that inevitably serve to cast teachers into managerial, technocratic roles.

In these roles, teachers are forced to "deliver" a curriculum devised by "experts" in pursuit of higher international test scores and greater U.S. geopolitical competitiveness in the transnational, corporate economy—or the new "global village" as it is called in that bit of Orwellian Newspeak that has gained such currency. When teachers refuse to perform the task of turning their students into obedient "worker-citizens" (Spring 1976), they are punished with the dire institutional consequences of reduced pay and sometimes public humiliation in the newspapers, followed by termination.

In Marxian terms, all of this alienates the teacher from her students, her colleagues, and—inevitably—herself. In Jungian terms, *it leads to psychological and ethical catastrophe because it distances the teacher from the "archetypes of teaching" that spiritualize her work.* De Castillejo

(1973) has made similar observations about the psychospiritual impover-ishment of physicians, who, reeling under snowballing caseloads and bu-reaucratic demands, are losing touch with the "archetypes of the healer." She has said that physicians will find psychospiritual *mana* in their work only by recovering and reviving these archetypes. The same holds true for teachers.

In this chapter, I would like to provide a few examples of archetypal reflectivity by applying Campbell's (1949) presentation of the archetypal hero's journey to my own teaching. In doing this, I do not mean to hold up either my reflective processes or style of teaching as a standard. The individual teacher must experience and work with her own existentially unique archetypal energies and images in her own particular way. I offer myself as an example merely because I know myself as a teacher better than I know anyone else. My hope is simply that this exercise will provide an example that will encourage other teachers to explore their own ar-chetypal territories—and thereby discover their own sacred precincts.

STUDENT AS HERO, TEACHER AS SAGE

The archetypal journey commences with a call to adventure that issues from a spiritual realm. If the novitiate-hero is to develop, he must re-spond to that call in the affirmative—and not, like Jonah, try to deny the supernatural voice. Stopping one's ears to the call typically results in be-ing swallowed by the Leviathan of depression. The hero initially evi-dences acceptance of the call by his willingness to cross a perilous threshold—usually one that leads to a spooky forest or monster-infested desert. This begins the hero's quest for the grail, which symbolizes indi-viduation itself (E. Jung and von Franz 1960/1986). The hero cannot embark on this perilous quest without abandoning his previous life. Along with St. Paul, the archetypal hero must die a certain death by "put[ting] away childish things" (1 Corinthians 13:11). The person who cannot meet this challenge will always remain a psychological and ethi-cal child regardless of his chronological age—a *puer*, or in the case of the female a *puella* (von Franz 1981).

Having crossed the threshold, the hero soon meets a wise old man or woman, someone who had already completed his or her *own* archetypal quests long ago when he or she was young. As we saw previously, the wise ones tantalize their young charges with riddles, conundrums, and oracles, thereby teasing the *puer* and *puella* out of the smug certainties of their previous worlds. This requires the young hero to seek a newer world by seeking a higher wisdom. In my teaching as a professor of education, these archetypal images, characters, and motifs affect my practice in many ways.

For instance, I begin each term by courteously but relentlessly shooting holes in the excessively positive views about American public education held by my politically conservative students at Brigham Young University. Most of my undergraduate students, and not a few of my graduate students, begin the term with the incorrect idea that fiscal, instructional, and physical resources are roughly the same from school to school around the United States. I immediately disabuse them of this illusion by presenting data that indicate that public school funding in the United States ranges from about $3,000 per year per student in some rural, mostly African American regions of Mississippi to nearly $30,000 per year per student in the wealthier, mostly Caucasian areas of upstate New York (Kozol 1991; Riordan 1997).

We thus delve into sociological analyses that demonstrate with merciless clarity that this unjust distribution of "educational capital" is a function of race, ethnicity, and socioeconomic status. The rich get richer and the poor get poorer in the United States, and this grim reality is embedded in the very structure of American public education. I somewhat scandalize my students by making it clear that, although I have recently found myself becoming more conservative as I age, I spent many years involved with the socialist view that American education perpetuates class differences more often than it provides a "level playing field" where a child can succeed "if only she tries hard enough!"

To further upset my students' already shaken ideological world, I relentlessly drive home the message that in the study of American education we are dealing with issues of such intractable complexity that there simply is no such thing as the "Truth" (with a capital "T") about these questions. All we can hope to attain are functional, lower-case-t "truths," each of which will allow us to understand and act affirmatively in the schools in certain respects, but which will also foreclose other points of view and breed its own set of local dilemmas. With this realization, it dawns on my students that I was actually serious during the first class when I said that the goal of our time together would be for *each student* to wrestle—individually and authentically—with these problems in order to come to her *own* conclusions about them. They learn the wisdom of Kenneth Burke's (1989) great pronouncement that "every way of seeing is also a way of *not* seeing."

I have dared the academic *puer* or *puella* to cross the threshold of ideological adventure, to enter the "perilous forest" of political and philosophical complexity, where there are few answers but increasingly compelling questions. As if all of this were not shocking enough to my conservative students, they are hearing these ideas from a co-religionist professor in our church's flagship educational institution (indeed, the largest religious university in the United States) who has also held a few responsible ecclesiastical positions. To negotiate my class successfully, the students will have to answer the archetypal call to abandon their naively celebratory notions about American education and achieve more considered points of view.

As I have reflected on my practice, I have seen with increasing clarity that I am embodying the archetype of the Wise Old Man for my students, challenging them in academic terms to embark on a mythic quest in search of a valid ideological grail. Like any good old "sage," from Lao Tzu to Yoda, I (sometimes rather brusquely) require them to forsake their *puerish* and *puellish* misconceptions. I have drawn a line in the dirt, and have then made matters worse by daring them to cross it—to cross this threshold of academic adventure—in order to find the complex elixir of their own ethical vision.

WHEN CHARLIE CHAPLIN MET DARTH VADER

Most of my students do rise to the occasion of the archetypal call by literally and symbolically "crossing the threshold" at my office door for afterclass discussions. Still, there are inevitably some students who refuse to resonate to the call, entrenching themselves even more deeply as *puers* and *puellas*—as "good boys" and "good girls" who too often confuse the simple certainties of provincial political conservatism with religious virtue. To them, my leftist views regarding the politics of American education also invest me with the archetypal energy of the Ogre as well as the Sage. That is to say, although they *want* to like me and are (in spite of themselves) excited by the fact that I am inviting them into new philosophical territory, they also see me as a "dangerous presence dwelling just beyond the protected zone of the village boundary. . . . The emotion that he instill[s] in human beings who by accident [venture] into his domain [is] 'panic' fear, a sudden groundless fright" (Campbell 1949, 81). I am personally interesting and ideologically attractive, but I am also marginal and menacing.

At this juncture early in the term, some students, psychically and ethically unable to bear this paradox, will march into my office, brandishing a "drop slip" (as if it were the sword of truth itself!) and imperiously inform me that they are transferring into another section that is taught by a much older colleague whose credentials as a conservative are impeccable. Of course, such moments as these are often very hurtful to a teacher, who will see his students' dropping the class as a personal rejection. For, just as in therapy the analysand has great power to emotionally wound the analyst, who is so deeply involved personally in her patient's processes, so the student can wound the teacher, who also invests a great deal of herself in her students.

Here is a place where archetypal reflectivity can come to the rescue— saving the teacher psychic pain by granting psychic insight. I have come to see that most of these negative reactions to me are not really *to me* at all, for I am not finally an individual person to such students so much as I am an archetypal paradox—a paradox that finally resides in *them* and that they are projecting onto me. I am a helpful Wise One but also a Dark Magician, the *sol niger* (or black sun) of the alchemists, who is endangering their simple certainties by the weird conceptual chemistry of his suspicious academic art. The black robes I wear at commencement are emblems of both my role as guide *and* tempter.[1] Because I understand that certain of my students are projecting this archetypal conflict onto me, I can respond to them with greater compassion and clarity. This knowledge enables me to help them negotiate the alluring yet spooky, dangerous yet vivifying forests of academia. Archetypal reflectivity makes me a better teacher.

Adding to the complexity of my students' archetypal projections is the fact that they are also projecting onto me the closely related archetypal energy and imagery of the Clown and Trickster. I must confess that these are roles that I *do* shamelessly cultivate. My Jewish grandmother was a vaudeville comedienne in the Yiddish theater, and my mother was constantly "on stage" around the house, so I grew up in a constant rain of one-liners, broad slapstick, and subtle irony—all of which I now bring to the classroom. Particular favorites with the students are my "Jimmy-Does-Jimi" Series, in which I imitate Jimmy Stewart singing the music of Jimi Hendrix; and my widely celebrated "ear imitations," including Mr. Spock, Lyndon Johnson, George W. Bush, Vincent Van Gogh, and Evander Hollyfield.

Such humor (often purposefully at my own expense) goes a long way in assuring my students that I truly care about them and that, even though I bear some resemblance to that archetype of the prankster, Coyote, in Native American mythology, I will not lure them into ethical catastrophe and doctrinal heresy with my shape-shifting tricks. They are *beginning* to believe me—but I can still feel their shadows all over me.

THE TEACHER IN THE STUDENT'S SHADOW

I sometimes invite prospective teachers or administrators to engage in Gestalt dialogues in front of class (Mayes 1998b). In these exercises, the person sits across from an empty chair on which we imagine such invisible, school-based characters as "My Best Teacher in High School," "My Worst Teacher in High School," "The 'Perfect' Student," "The 'Problem' Student," "The Best Principal I Ever Knew," "The Worst Principal I Ever Knew," and others. As in most Gestalt exercises of this sort, the volunteer first sits in the chair that represented her own identity, but after that she has to move into the other chair to become the imaginary person she has been addressing, who now talks to her "self." One of these dialogues stands out vividly in my mind because it exemplified so clearly how a student can cast his shadow onto a teacher.

On this particular day, I asked for volunteers to speak to and then *become* their "Worst High School Teacher." A very bright and willing young man—a drama education major who was always eager to please—quickly raised his hand, anxious, I suppose, to perform for the class. It did not take long, however, for this to become much more than just another role for him. He soon found himself overwhelmed by some of the repressed rage that he had never allowed himself to feel as a "perfect student" as well as a "good boy" in the church and community. By getting mad at his worst teacher, this student was getting in touch with a larger sense of rage at always having been molded into someone else's image of what he should be.

Yet even more poignant were his responses when he moved into the "bad teacher's" chair. We were all surprised to discover how very vulnerable this (imagined) teacher was and how genuine his distress in discovering that he was oppressing his students. After switching chairs a few times, it became clear that this teacher's pedagogical problems stemmed from a deeper psychological inability to commit to relationships. Whether or not this was true of the actual teacher was, of course, beside the point. My concern was not with that teacher, about whom I could know nothing, but rather with that introjected aspect of *my student's identity as a teacher.* I also happened to know that my student's father had just divorced his mother for a younger woman. My student had previously confided to me in my office that he felt his father was "a nice guy and I love him a lot. But he's also a jerk. *He can't keep commitments.*"

Here, in one of those rare "Aha!" moments, it flashed upon me that my student's image of the Bad Teacher and the Bad Father were virtually identical—for both were men who could not, or would not, enter into emotionally responsible relationships with people in their care. What is more, as my student explored this theme throughout the term in meditation, journal work, and group processes, he came to the even deeper and more courageous insight that this weakness was so threatening and repugnant to him precisely because *he had discovered it in himself!* He had come into contact with his own shadow—in this case, both the personal shadow of his father and the archetypal shadow of the False Teacher who shows up in so many religious narratives—those "hypocrites [who] are like unto whited sepulchers, which indeed appear beautiful outward, but are within full of dead men's bones, and of all uncleanness" (Matthew 23:27).

In subsequent work with the archetype of the Shadow Teacher—much of it involving active imagination—we explored many ways in which to acknowledge and explore that archetype and thus to consciously possess it instead of being unconsciously possessed *by* it. By the end of the term, my student reported in his class journal that he had learned a great deal about how *not* to be controlled by the shadow teacher in his own practice—as well as how to harness aspects of it that were genuinely powerful and, if rightly handled, potentially good and useful. These aspects would invest him with healthy combative energy that might occasionally prove useful to him in maintaining discipline in the class and preserving his own emotional boundaries. Being all sweetness and light is as false and off-putting in the classroom as it is in every other situation.

As a further benefit of this shadow work, I felt that my student would be able to respond more skillfully when—as a male teacher and therefore inevitably a father figure to many adolescent students—he would sometimes be perceived as a Shadow Teacher and a Dark Father (or *Darth Vader* as George Lucas put it in a self-consciously Jungian move). This projection of the Shadow Father onto older males is especially frequent with students who have had a troubled relationship with their fathers. Jung warned teachers that they could be the objects of their students' parental projections, specifically advising male teachers to be aware of the fact that they often receive the personal and archetypal Shadow Father projections of female students who have previously been abused by an older male. Similarly, female teachers should be aware of Shadow Mother projections from their male students who have had troubled relationships with their mothers.

THE STUDENT IN THE TEACHER'S SHADOW

Students not only project their shadows onto teachers; teachers project their psychic darkness onto students. This can lead to dire classroom consequences. It can even result in the teacher acting out with her students in ways that can be sexually, morally, and politically harmful. Psychospiritual reflectivity can be invaluable in helping the teacher avoid this by examining her own personal and archetypal issues.

As the only child of a troubled marriage, I became for my mother the source of the affection that she did not adequately experience with my father. Some years ago in reflecting on my practice, I became aware of the disconcerting fact that I was focusing most of my time and care on the females in my classes. The males I essentially ignored. Each term I was quite certain that I was receiving subtle signs from a great many of my new female students that they were in some sort of distress and that they were crying out to me to save them. This caused me to try to "rescue" these women—most of whom (I can now see) were quite healthy psychologically and did not need a rescuer. All they wanted was a teacher! It is only by reflecting archetypally on this "pedagogical Oedipus complex" that I came to see that I was allowing myself to be consumed by both patterns in my personal past as well as by the transpersonal Devouring Mother, who is the archetypal core of the child's personal experience of her biological mother (Neumann 1954).

Indeed, what we see and expect in our biological parents is often much more a result of our archetypal projections onto them of the Great Father and Great Mother than it is a realistic reflection of who they *actually* are in all their natural human frailty. "The parental imago [i.e., archetypal image] is constituted on the one hand by the acquired image of the personal parents, but on the other hand by the parent archetype which exists *a priori*, i.e., in the pre-conscious structure of the psyche" (*CW* 16, par. 212, n. 2). Consequently, "X's idea of his father [or mother] is a complex quantity for which the real father is only in part responsible . . . ," the same being true of the idea of the mother (*CW* 9.2, par. 37). A large part of maturing consists in seeing that one's parents are just people who could never have fully embodied the archetype of Heavenly Parents. The mature person sees that her parents may well deserve forgiveness for what she at the time perceived to be their horrible inadequacies but may really have just been their inevitable human limitations.

At any rate, when we consider Jung's observation that teachers are typically the first nonparental figures to receive the parental-projections of children—in which the male teacher is seen as a "substitute for the father" and the female "for the mother" (*CW* 17, par. 107a)—it is understandable how *personal* parental, *archetypal* parental, and *pedagogical* roles and functions can get mixed up with each other and result in a confusing classroom brew. This is what had happened with me.

I had spent my childhood registering and satisfying the emotional needs of my own mother. I knew how it felt to be in the arms of the Devouring Mother, the sweetness and the terror of being in a hold that is at once a loving embrace and a desperate clutch. I understood that one found peace—even if only conditional and fleeting—in doing whatever was necessary to address the Devouring Mother's needs. And this is just what I was doing now with my female students. Enshrouding my female students with shades of the Great Devouring Mother—imagining them to be emotionally needy, and then struggling to satisfy those "needs" with an excessive concern for them—I was conducting my classes in a way that was as instructionally fruitless as it was emotionally inappropriate. Only in working through these dilemmas in their personal and archetypal aspects was I able to respond to *all* of my students, female and male, with much more authentic sensitivity to their real needs, not my projections.

Hopefully this example of my own archetypal reflectivity has suggested how recognizing and harnessing the power of various archetypes can contribute to a teacher's psychospiritual health and professional development. "It is important," said Jung, "that the teacher should be conscious of the role he is playing" (*CW* 17, par. 107a). Each teacher must uniquely interpret and carry out her task with this knowledge always before her. But I believe that she can best do so when, like Jacob in the Old Testament, she authentically wrestles with the archetypal dimensions of herself as a teacher and thus receives a blessing. The blessing will be twofold. First, it will help her be more effective and sensitive in how she addresses her students' multifaceted needs. Second, it will infuse her practice with archetypal energy and spirituality, increasing the chances of her classroom becoming a psychologically and morally "sacred precinct" in which she and her students may be transformed intellectually and ethically.

THE ARCHETYPE OF ICARUS IN THE COMMUNITY OF LEARNERS

It has become very clear over the last several decades that the best classrooms are those in which the teacher is not an authoritarian taskmaster who presumes to know all the answers but rather is an authoritative facilitator—one who poses questions and suggests directions but who is also a *co-learner* with her students in a "community of learners" (Brown, Collins, and Duguid 1988). This requires that we as teachers must be willing to change, we must be capable of doubt, and we must sometimes reform or even reject our own passionately held paradigms. Archetypally, we must be not only the Sage but also the Novitiate.

Seeing ourselves as learners who, like our students, are engaged in a lifelong journey of learning guards against the psychic "inflation" that comes from an excessive identification with and possession by the archetype of the Wise One or the related archetypes of the Great Mother and Great Father. In Jungian psychology, such possession is called *inappropriate identification with the archetype*. Armed with this knowledge, the teacher can learn to free herself from the impossible burden of feeling that she must have all the answers to her students' questions and problems (a common enough syndrome in teachers, leading to inflation, enmeshment, and burnout) for, however much she may draw on archetypal energy to enliven her practice, she must always keep squarely before her the fact that *she is not the archetype itself*, merely one of its very imperfect, very fleeting embodiments.

In our own ongoing heroic journeys, we must not only be showing the way to the grail, we must always be searching out new paths for ourselves, seeking, in T. S. Eliot's (1971) words, "a further union, a deeper communion" with our students, our discipline, and the powerful curricular questions which should be affecting our lives (129). If we are in humility truly learning along with our students, their questions will often become our questions too—questions that we cannot avoid by hiding behind an omniscient, teacherly persona (Craig 1994). Lacking this humility, we will fall into the grip of the archetypal image of Icarus, and our wax wings will melt in the unforgiving daily sun of classroom reality. However, by honoring and participating in our students' archetypal quests, we as teachers (drinking deep from the same psychospiritual springs that our students do) will be renewed by the same archetypal elixir.

THE TEACHER AND THE ETERNAL RETURN

In this chapter, we have looked at some of the most salient components of the archetypally heroic journey: the call to adventure, the acceptance or refusal of the call, the rebirth just after crossing the

threshold, the ogre or seducer just beyond the threshold, and the prof-
fering of supernatural aid by a teacher who appears as a Wise Old Man
or Wise Old Woman. Let us conclude by looking at the final stage of
the epic journey—the hero's return to society—and its implications for
the teacher.

The Hero returns to society from the underworld *to teach* his people
about what he has learned there (Campbell 1949). This suggests that the
Hero and the Teacher are so similar in their ultimate goals as to be finally indistinguishable. Perhaps this is why, when the awestricken Mary
Magdalene first recognized the risen Lord Jesus (to me the greatest historical instance and archetypal embodiment of the Hero returning from
the dead to bring new life to the community), she called him *Rabboni*,
which the Greek translation of John's Gospel renders as "Teacher." The
saving, archetypal vocation of the Hero and Teacher is to pass on his re-
demptive vision to the people—to bring new life to the community. "I
am come," said Jesus, "that they might have life, and that they might
have it more abundantly" (John 10:10). Here, at last, we see the culmination of the Hero in the form of the Teacher, who announces the "good
news" of eternal life and proffers cues for finding it.

Just as the mythic hero must become a teacher, then, so may the
teacher learn to become a mythic hero. This sustaining psychospiritual
wine is abundantly available to teachers. Originating in the vineyards of
the collective unconscious, it flows out of the winepress of archetypal reflectivity.

AN EXERCISE IN ARCHETYPAL REFLECTIVITY

The author used Campbell's "Hero's Journey" to reflect on his teaching.
Would this paradigm help you reflect on your own teaching? Is there another mythical story, character, or pattern that might better serve that
purpose for you? Using whatever "mythic construct" works best for you,
reflect on your sense of calling and some important aspects of your
classroom practice. This reflectivity might take the form of meditation,
active imagination, dyadic or group discussion, journal work, or an essay.
As in the author's reflectivity, you might wish to include biographical,
political, cultural, and spiritual elements.

NOTE

1. Some time ago at a BYU graduation ceremony, a man who is probably the most respected scholar in the 180-year history of our church, Professor Hugh Nibley, referred to our professorial gowns as "the robes of a false priesthood." This is a statement that many found funny, some scandalous, and some simply mystifying. What almost everyone failed to appreciate, however, was the profound archetypal wisdom of his cryptic pronouncement.

PERSONAL AND ARCHETYPAL TRANSFERENCE IN THE CLASSROOM

TEACHING AND THE TRANSFERENCE

In this chapter, we explore in greater depth the classroom implications of transference and countertransference from both personal and archetypal perspectives to see how understanding transferential psychodynamics sheds light on certain issues in teaching and learning. The transference in the classroom possesses an intensity that may equal, and sometimes even surpass, that which occurs in the consulting room.

That the classroom may be a theater for archetypal dramas should not surprise us. Everyone tends to more or less project his or her needs, fears, and expectations onto others in those "attachments of daily life" that make up our everyday world (Stone 1988, 273). And we all do so especially regarding authority figures like teachers, who stimulate the most multivalent and passionate projections because we see these figures as powerful—and thus "attractive" in almost an electromagnetic sense. Freud said that "psycho-analysis shows us that people who in our real life are merely admired or respected [are often] sexual objects for our unconscious" (Freud 1990a, 33). As we have already seen, these "admired or respected" people are also archetypal "objects for our consciousness."

Speaking of how teachers are transferential objects, the great Freudian psychiatrist of adolescence August Aichhorn wrote:

> We know that with a normal child the transference takes place of itself through the kindly efforts of the responsible adult. The teacher in his attitude repeats the situations long familiar to the child, and thereby evokes a parental relationship. He does not maintain this relationship at the same level, but continually deepens it as long as he is the parental substitute. [With a neurotic child] with symptoms of delinquency . . . , the tendency to transfer his attitude toward his parents to the person in authority is immediately noticeable. (1990, 97)

This lends the classical idea of the teacher in loco parentis a whole new dimension. For better or worse, the teacher is often the displaced object of the student's desires and antipathies regarding her own parents. If that child comes from a dysfunctional setting (and more and more do), it is all too likely that those hopes and fears may play out in the classroom in ways that may be problematic for both the student and the teacher. The ten-year-old boy who has been psychologically beaten into submission by an authoritarian father may be unresponsive to the teacher if he is a male. Yet the same boy, perhaps also enmeshed in Oedipal dynamics with a needy mother and thus hypersensitive to her psychosexual dynamics, may be finely attuned to a female teacher's slightest emotional shifts and may strive to respond to them with a diligence which, although initially pleasant, is increasingly disquieting and puzzling to the teacher.

These different attitudes in the boy may have little if anything to do with the quality of the teacher but almost everything to do with the dynamics of the transference. For this reason, Aichhorn, like Jung, thought it imperative that every teacher understand at least the basics of the transference. Such instruction should occur in all teacher education programs, for it is a very rare prospective teacher in a college of education who ever hears a word about the transference, much less its potential applications to questions of interpersonal classroom processes.

In light of the transference, we could, for instance, help our prospective teachers understand that a student will occasionally challenge them—and sometimes quite forcefully—in a manner (or lack of manners!) that seems to go quite beyond the academic point being discussed in class. Prospective teachers need to know, in more than simply a vaguely intuitive way, that, especially in adolescent students, this "resistance to instruction" can be a healthy sign of the increasing need of children at this developmental stage to sever the ties with the personal Oedipal mother and the archetypal Devouring Mother. This is something that a child must do in order to establish an autonomous psychic and even spiritual identity. It might save teachers, especially novices, some considerable grief to know that the teacher is typically the parental surrogate onto whom the child transfers much of this rebelliousness. Jung called the student's transference of archetypal images, issues, and complexes onto the teacher "perfectly natural" (CW 9.2, n. 16), but by "natural" he clearly did not mean invariably pleasant and wholesome but simply an inevitable consequence of the asymmetrical power relationship between student and teacher.

THE CASE OF JEAN—OR, "WILL YOU (STILL) LOVE ME?"

In the therapeutic process, it is important for the analyst to know that the analysand's transferences will often be related to that analysand's developmental stage. A child will be more likely to cast parental archetypes onto an analyst than will a middle-aged analysand—although, to be sure, such projections can occur at any developmental stage. Adolescents are also more likely to project the archetypal figures of the wise old tribal master onto the analyst because of the fact that adolescence is the time of so many rites of passage. Moreover, the analysand may (and probably will) project both luminous savior imagery as well as tenebrous tempter imagery onto the analyst in the course of therapy—and not infrequently in the course of one hour of therapy.

The same thing happens to teachers. How many of us as teachers have had students who seemed to instantly love us at the beginning of the term and wanted to be our bosom friends—only to find that, by the end of the term, they are inexplicably casting poison glances at us from hooded eyes? Perhaps the teacher has actually done something wrong to cause this Kafkaesque metamorphosis in the student. But it is just as likely that the teacher has quite innocently said or done something that constellated the bright savior archetype and then, through an equally innocent statement or action, reversed the process and constellated the student's dark-destroyer archetypal projection onto the teacher.

Of course, it is not always necessary to go to archetypal depths to understand unusual fluctuations in the student's attitudes toward the teacher. Jung himself always insisted that one should not analyze a problem at an archetypal level if a merely biographical analysis will do the trick (CW 4). As an example, consider the well-established fact that many analysands have a love–hate relationship with their analysts. Sometimes this is due to the fact that one or both of the analysand's parents forced their own needs on the child so completely that they never allowed the child to understand and meet her own needs and form a viable self. On one hand, the child hates the parent for this. On the other hand, the child's only experience of her "self" is in relation to the parent, who thus becomes the source of all reality and identity; hence, the child also idealizes the parent. This oscillation between hating and idealizing a parent is typically projected onto authority figures such as analysts, teachers, coaches, ministers, bosses, and superior officers.

Even in the best of scenarios, the analyst should always expect that the analysand's attitude toward her is bound to shift somewhat from time to time since, as the early Freudian analyst Ferenczi noted long ago, a certain sine wave between love and hate is to be expected as the analysand faces her issues regarding the original parent. Thus, it is not surprising that some students occasionally alternate, without any obvious cause, between positive and negative feelings about their teachers, for this is the very rhythm of the transference, especially in psyches that are still in such highly formative stages as adolescence.

This makes it unrealistic to expect—as too many teachers, especially beginning teachers, do—that their students will always love them. There is, for instance, the first-year-teacher syndrome of the novice who simply cannot understand why her students do not always love her despite the fact that she loves them and does the best she can. It would save her a great deal of grief, and might prevent a great deal of teacher burnout, to know that her students' occasional fickleness may be stemming from a psychodynamic over which she has little control— especially in students who already have difficult psychological issues regarding their parents. An example from my own experience as a teacher may help illustrate this.

About ten years ago, I had an undergraduate student who psychically latched onto me very early in the term. This student, whom I will call Jean, was overweight and rather dour. After the second or third class meeting, she asked if she could stop by my office a little later even though I was not having office hours at that time. It was an inconvenient time for me, but I told her to go to my office and wait for me while I checked my mailbox. When I came in, I found her looking through the files in my filing cabinet! Throughout the term, Jean continued to demonstrate this pattern of trying to get close and then immediately doing something irritating that seemed designed to anger me. I noticed that she would then scrutinize me with almost clinical attention to gauge my response to her erratic behavior. She seemed particularly interested in whether I would get angry at her. Unfortunately for both of us, I never did.

At the time, I had trouble making sense of Jean's paradoxical behavior. I was especially puzzled when she once said to me during one of her too-frequent office visits, "People don't really care about you. They always let you down in the end." I attributed this odd statement to the fact that because Jean was slightly overweight and not particularly attractive, she had perhaps been an unpopular girl in school and was bitter. However, even then I suspected that this explanation was too simple—not to mention sexist. It certainly did not adequately account for the jarring contradiction of Jean's grim attitude about people with her deep religious beliefs, which were rooted in our very optimistic and communally oriented theology.

How could I make sense out of these different elements in the puzzling picture that was Jean—how understand her apparent need to be close to me versus her deliberate attempts to alienate me, her religious commitment versus her lack of faith in people? Even more puzzling, how could I make sense of my own responses to Jean? I cared about her, but I was also exasperated with her and just wanted her to go away. Inevitably, the relationship went sour. As I recall, she said something to me during one of the last classes (I forget what) that I found inappropriate and mean-spirited. I responded to her with a mordant cynicism that is extremely rare for me. At the end of the term, her class evaluations of me were witheringly negative, despite my positive evaluations from most of the other students. In those evaluations, she even suggested that

I had let the class down not only as a teacher but also emotionally, morally, and spiritually as a member of our church.

Over the years I thought of Jean and her sad proclamation—uttered with that vague yet needy cynicism that was her emotional signature: "People don't really care about you. They always let you down in the end." I have come to believe that the key of the transference could help me open and see beyond the slammed door that was Jean.

Given Jean's rigidly moralistic and highly dogmatic religiosity, which she revealed during our early discussions, in addition to suggestions she let slip about her family life, I am fairly certain that she was raised in a home that was correct in every "religious" particular but emotionally repressed through and through. All of her life, she had probably learned from her parents' lack of emotional nurturance and authenticity that "people always let you down." Early in our conversations, I had pieced together enough evidence to satisfy me that Jean's developmental needs as a child probably mattered much less to her parents than did their compulsion to create a programmatically controlled and "doctrinally correct" home. As Jean had once told me, if she as a child showed the slightest anger at her parents for anything at all, their response was always moral condemnation and a deepening of the emotional freeze.

This is the classic set-up for the dissociation of the child from her emotional needs—Fairbairn's (1952/1992) "splitting"—and the setup for passive–aggressive as well as approach–avoidance behavior. The child is learning that the formation and nurturing of her identity is not important—or at least not as important to the parents as their other agendas. She has internalized a whole host of "bad objects." In extreme cases, the child may develop into a "borderline personality" characterized by bizarre emotional fluctuations, antisocial behavior, and a tenuous reality function (Comer 1998). Even in less dramatic instances of this phenomenon, such as in Jean's case, the person's rage at having been emotionally abandoned does not disappear. It simply takes on other forms—such as abstractedness, depression, cynicism, and an ongoing attempt to provoke other people to show and speak the anger that the dissociated personality could never directly express.

And so it was with Jean. In a biting mixture of despair and hope, Jean was constantly testing her hypothesis that "people always let you down" by trying to evoke an anger that would both mirror her own unexpressed rage at the parental figure as well as test to see if that person cared enough about her to do what never happened in her home—namely, authentically express an appropriate emotion which, however negative, would ultimately be followed by the fundamental relational fact of love. As an academic and ecclesiastical authority figure to Jean, I was a perfect hook for this projection.

In her relationship with me, Jean ultimately did not find disconfirming evidence for her gloomy hypothesis about people. Ultimately, I, too, after several months of strained patience, forced smiles, and dwindling interest in Jean and her contradictions, wound up "not caring." However, if I had understood at the that time that I was the object of a parental projection in desperate search of disconfirmation—I might have helped both of us by honestly expressing both my anger at her games as well as my genuine care for her and faith in her potential.

It would have been useful to have understood at that time the classroom implications of three basic therapeutic facts about the analysand who consistently inspires anger in the analyst. First, this analysand will often try to inspire anger as a way of seeing if the analyst really cares enough to demonstrate the clarity followed by charity that her parents never did; second, she will sometimes try to provoke the analyst as a vicarious way of expressing her own deeply repressed anger; and third, she may use approach–avoidance contradictions to break the analyst down (Jacoby 1984). In many ways, these three points summarize the story of Jean—a story that I might have helped her rewrite (even if only in a small way) if I had known more about the drama of the transference in the classroom.

TRANSFERENCE AND THE PASSIVE STUDENT

There is another kind of student who is a problem precisely because she seems to be no problem at all. Most of us would rather deal with a student who is too compliant than too aggressive. The student who never challenges our authority, opinions, or arrangements in the classroom may cause us to think that we are smarter, wiser, and more powerful than we really are, and it is a rare teacher who is impervious to that temptation! Still, an excessively obedient and admiring student may be evidencing a psychological dysfunction and distress that is every bit as deep as Jean's.

The first problem with a student's overflowing affection is that it may not be completely real—however much the student may think that it is. Many depressives, for instance, especially those with overly demanding fathers and mothers, have learned to literally "swallow" their anger towards their parent(s). As Woodman (1995) has shown in her analysis of eating disorders, the person does this in order to remain the loving and obedient child. Because such people are the "emotional food" upon which their parents eat, they themselves either refuse to eat or overeat as a way of resistance and as a call for help.

The result of this inward-turning rage is often excessive compliance to authority figures, on one hand, accompanied by covert acts of self-destructiveness, on the other hand. This is called the "compliant patient syndrome" (Steinberg 1990, 203). The analysand may be masking unconscious hostility toward the parental authority figure of the analyst by, paradoxically, being too pliable. The same analysand may also express anger against the parental figure of the analyst by subverting any progress in therapy—remaining, of course, very polite and superficially obliging during each therapeutic hour.

A related phenomenon may sometimes be occurring with those students who, although agreeable in the classroom, never seem to live up to their potential. Such students might be showing signs of a similar transferential dynamic—let us call it "the compliant student syndrome." She may fail to perform well in class although she seems intelligent—or, in a related phenomenon, may consistently deny that she is doing well despite evidence to the contrary. Consequently, the child will either not permit herself to succeed or will deny success if it occurs. This behavior may carry through in the child's relationship with any authority figure, as Steinberg has shown in drawing an explicit connection between this kind of student in the classroom and analysand in therapy:

> Further analysis of these individuals indicated a . . . fear of outer achievement—a pattern that included work inhibitions, a failure to complete tasks, the denigration of positive attributions and accomplishments and an inability to make decisions. I found that people who fear psychological development sabotage all potential successes including

friendships, romances and explicit or implicit contests involving skill, talent, attractiveness or popularity. . . . Such people have difficulty completing tasks. In school, they do not hand papers in on time, do not prepare adequately for tests or cram furiously at the last minute. (1990, 57)

Bullough (2001) offers many heart-wrenching examples of this type of transference in the classroom. One of the most poignant is a little boy named Mark:

> "Are you a good student?" I asked Mark. "No." "You aren't? What kind of grades do you get." "I used to get F's and then I went up to B's. . . . I just go up." "So, you're getting better and better?" "Yeah, now I'm on A's and B's." "So you are a good student, then, aren't you?" Mark wouldn't grant this. Without hesitating, he said, "No." I then tried to get him to think of himself as a student differently, and asked: "Okay, tell me why you aren't a good student." "I go too fast, like my multiplying things, I go too fast and when I read, well, I don't know about reading. I don't pay attention in class. I do all kinds of things that aren't very good." "But you know, Mark, I watch you in class. I've watched you maybe ten or fifteen times." He was amazed. "You have?!" "Yes, and you seem to me to be working hard, and your hand is up, and you ask good questions. You know, you are reading Mark Twain and a lot of kids your age couldn't read Mark Twain." "I guess," he responded, "I'm not normal." "Well, what would make you a better student?" "I guess if I'd pay attention and not rush into everything, and let some answers for other people." "And do what?" "Let answers for other people." "I don't understand." "Well, see, I'm always raising my hand and the teacher gets mad at me sometimes for raising my hand every single time." "But you raise your hand because you know the answer, right?" "Well, I think. I think I know the answer." "Isn't that what good students do?" "Yeah." "Well, are you a good student?" "I guess." (61)

Knox's (1998) description of "the empty patient" also seems to describe Mark: He constantly counters any praise with the strategy of "emptying himself" of ability and worth. Like the analyst, the teacher may have good grounds for suspecting that the "flat affect" such as that in Mark may be due to damage in a parental relationship, to the internalization of many "bad objects." The teacher's experience of such a student will then parallel the analyst's experience of the analysand:

In the case of the stagnated patient the analyst experiences a void, like an unbridgeable gap between them, perhaps because the stagnated patient has unconsciously abolished the analyst/mother and therefore cannot depend on, relate to, or demand of her. There is then no transference in that, by abolishing the analyst/mother, the patient avoids relating to her with either love or hate. (Knox 1998, 80)

Armed with this knowledge, a teacher may do whatever she feels appropriate in order to begin to establish contact with such a student. But without this knowledge, the teacher may inappropriately blame herself for a lack of connection with the student and thus impose an impossible burden on herself. "If only I try harder, I know that I can save him! If only I continue to lavish praise on him, he'll see how good he really is! I will love my student into existence—whatever it costs me emotionally!" A teacher may pour tremendous psychic energy into the student in an attempt to undo a complex that, years in the making, cannot be rectified overnight and certainly not just in the classroom. Understanding the transferential issues at stake here will help the teacher be less sentimental and thus more helpful in relating to her student.

Extreme compliance also extends beyond the realm of the personal into the archetypal—namely, *the archetype of redemption through submission*. This archetype is central to many religions. Submissiveness, however much a virtue in relationship *to God*, will nevertheless preclude the kinds of risks that the student must take to make progress in his psychological and intellectual growth *in the classroom*. The analysand or student who is possessed by the archetype of submission often focuses it onto such displaced and misplaced "deities" as the savior-analyst or savior-teacher (Machtiger 1995).

As a teacher at a religious school, where the archetypes of redemption constellate and operate with a special intensity, I occasionally feel students (particularly my undergraduate students) archetypally projecting this image onto me and onto other professors. How shocked those students would be to know that they are not so much expressing respect for a professor as engaging in a classroom idolatry of the professor. Such a student is pliable, ever so quick to agree with my points of view. But, despite the unwholesome pleasure I—or any teacher—might take at being seen as superhuman, that wicked delight must give way to a realistic appraisal of the pedagogical and moral consequences of such imposture.

For there is an obvious contradiction if I am relating to my students in this psychologically and spiritually exploitative way while, at the same time, I am inviting them to stand on their own, to challenge platitudes, to forge their own vision.

And, even if the student does engage in my classroom in the critiques of American education that I am trying to encourage, how do I know that she is not doing it simply to please me? Indeed, the other side of the compliant student syndrome could be called the "dependently independent student syndrome." As in therapy, such a student will be fiercely independent—but only because that is what she thinks the teacher wants, not out of any felt need to break free. Of this sort of analysand in therapy, Steinberg has said:

> They will often behave in a manner of exaggerated independence when they are not in a depressive downswing. They always have at least one seriously depressed parent, usually the mother. They understood at an early age that their mothers could not tolerate their dependency needs and withdrew in response. These mothers taught their children to be independent but in a dependent way; that is, the children learned to act independently, even when they were feeling dependent, so that their mothers would not withdraw. Their independence became a form of submission in return for love. (1990, 139)

Hopefully, these few examples have suggested how knowing about these particular aspects of the transference can be helpful to the teacher in better understanding and responding to a student who possibly has similar issues that she may be projecting.

EROS IN THE CLASSROOM

Little boys fall in love with their first-grade teachers and we smile. We even look back wistfully on our own infatuations with our elementary school teachers. I know that I will always carry a torch for my fourth-grade teacher, Mrs. McFarland—the only perfect woman who ever graced this planet with her presence!

These classroom romances are usually harmless enough, yet in some cases they are not without their shadow side, for they may also be extensions of the boy's attachment to and desire for both the personal and archetypal mother. In some instances these romances are anything but harmless as, once the child has reached puberty, they may develop into actual sexual contact of one form or another between the student and teacher. Although somewhat rare, such occurrences are not rare enough, and even small-town newspapers such as those where I live carry a story or two each year about such goings-on in our local schools. Transference in the classroom can be a serious matter—and all the more so when the teacher, unaware of its dynamics, acts it out in anything from a furtive kiss in the darkness of the auditorium between a drama teacher and her handsome young student-assistant-director to a torrid and tawdry affair that ends in lifelong psychological damage to the young person.

More common is the opposite scenario—the seduction of a female student by a male teacher. Female analysands who have had unhealthy relationships with their fathers are often especially vulnerable to the advances of the male therapist as the displaced father-object of their Electra desires (Schwartz-Salant 1995). Indeed, it is something of a therapeutic truism that many female analysands choose male analysts in the first place for Electra-related reasons, just as Oedipal issues often guide males' decision for a female analyst. Electra-complex issues also may result in the analysand or student "dressing, acting or speaking in a provocative manner" in order to see if the male analyst or teacher, by *not* responding, will prove himself an emotionally trustworthy person who can serve as a positive father figure with whom she can psychologically rest—and grow (Steinberg 1990, 47–48).[1]

That the teacher needs to know such things is implied in Freud's warning that "it is *not* a fact that transference emerges with greater intensity and lack of restraint during psycho-analysis than outside it" (1990a, 30). Accordingly, we can expect to find "transference love" in the Electra-bound female's relationship with other male authority figures such as her male teachers. The psychosexually knotted relationship with her father may make this female student particularly susceptible to the seductive behavior of an unscrupulous male teacher, whose advances promise the psychological and physical closeness with the father that she never experienced in a healthy way.

We must wonder how many male teachers—some consciously aware of what they were doing, others perhaps responding with an instinctual cunning—have preyed on their female students' Electra needs in a process that, starting with a few seductive glances in the classroom, ends in the bedroom. And who does not know of at least one male professor who has not manipulated some of his female students—away from home for the first time—in just this way? I have seen such things at both state and religious universities, and I suspect many others have, too.

As teacher educators, we can be helpful to both practicing and prospective teachers by teaching them about how it is possible that they may have at least a student or two for whom they will become a sexually charged parental substitute. Equipped with such knowledge, the teacher has a marvelous opportunity to contribute to his students' psychosexual growth by responding in an appropriate manner. This clearly means no overt sexual behavior. But that is not all. On a subtler level, it also entails neither sending out nor responding to subliminally seductive energy involving one's students. Freud said that analysis should always be carried on "in celibacy"—meaning both physical and psychological. The same is true in education. This is a psychologically exacting but morally necessary task—one which the teacher can do best with a good working knowledge of how personal and archetypal Oedipal and Electra dramas can play out in the theater of the classroom.

COUNTERTRANSFERENCE IN THE CLASSROOM: SYNTONIC AND DYSTONIC

We saw in part I that most of the literature on countertransference is in agreement that Freud was wrong that the countertransference is always counterproductive—or *dystonic*. Still, we concluded that such people as therapists, ministers, doctors, policemen, teachers, and all others who hold some authority in asymmetrical power relationships ignore Freud's warning about countertransference at their own professional and moral peril.

For example, I once knew a teacher who was famous for being a power-monger in the classroom. He once let drop in an unguarded moment in a conversation that his father would frequently tease him because he was small and clumsy as a boy—not at all the athletic paragon that his father had himself been in his glory days. Could it be that, now that he was the more empowered member of the teacher–student dyad, he had assumed the role of "father," countertransferring his father's castrating aggression onto his vulnerable "children–students"? If this hypothesis is true, then it would certainly classify as the kind of countertransference which Horney called "infantile repetition compulsion." In pedagogical terms, this hypothesis simply states in countertransferential language what most people know at an intuitive level: Teachers can exploit their authority to satisfy neurotic power needs.[2]

Despite these dangers, countertransference has many positive, or *syntonic*, uses (Orr 1988). The example that I gave above about Jean provides an example of a dystonic countertransference but one which, if I had handled it better, could have been syntonic. I noted that when Jean asked me after the first class if she could visit me, I agreed although I was actually quite busy since it was the beginning of the semester and these were not my office hours. I remember thinking at the time, however, that I would "stuff" my irritation at her and the insistent, needy, dark tones in her voice. Why didn't I just tell Jean that I was in a rush now but could see her later in the day at 3:00 during office hours? The answer is *countertransference*.

How much better would my relationship with Jean have been had I not fallen under the sway of my countertransference but, rather, had used its emergence as a sign that something was wrong with Jean to which I was unconsciously resonating? I would have realized that she was crying out to be saved but that responding in my usual way would simply ensnare us both in a symbiosis that she did not need any more than I did! When the analyst or teacher does not act out the countertransference but, rather, uses it as information about his and the student's psyche, then it can serve syntonic purposes. Indeed, the teacher's intuitions about a student may ultimately be countertransferential information that the teacher's unconscious mind is revealing about the student

Hence, for teacher and analyst alike, the countertransference can be either an advantage or a problem.

How can we as teachers know when we are involved in a countertransference—and, if so, whether it is syntonic or dystonic? Probably in the same way that analysts do. Many teachers will probably resonate to Tower's common evidences of dystonic countertransference in therapy, which, *mutatis mutandi*, also describe teachers' relatively common attitudes towards some students in the classroom. These signs are "anxiety in the [classroom]; disturbing feelings toward [a student]; stereotype in feelings or behavior toward [a student]; love and hate responses toward [a student]; erotic preoccupations, especially ideas of falling in love with a [student]; carry over of affects from the [class period]; dreams about [a student]; and acting-out episodes" (1988, 133).

Where these psychic phenomena *exist*, and especially when they *persist*, there is strong evidence of a teacher's dystonic countertransference onto the student. Most teachers could easily provide examples of each of the above feelings that they have had about at least one or two students in their careers. This is not to say that any countertransference that one feels toward a student is useful and valid simply because one feels it. Countertransference may sometimes arise quite independently of the specific character and issues of the other person in the relationship. This is what Jacoby has called "illusory countertransference" (1984, 42).

It is also possible that a teacher's countertransference onto a student may be a mixture of both valid perceptions about the student and the teacher's own issues for which the student is just a handy hook. This underscores the great importance of our learning to understand, manage, and master our own countertransferential energy. "Physician, know thyself" then becomes "Teacher, know thyself." Clearly, our countertransference hunches must be validated by further interaction with and observation of the student, especially since "counter-transferences are always both illusory and syntonic, at one and the same time. And yet these discriminations need to be made if we are ever to raise consciousness about the contents and dynamics of counter-transference" (Stein 1995, 70).

COUNTERTRANSFERENCE AND INFLATION: THE ARCHETYPE OF THE GREAT MOTHER

The Great Mother as Nurturer and Enabler

"Most teachers are motivated by such 'psychic rewards' as a sense of social mission, gratification at increased emotional intimacy with their students, and delight in seeing students spiritually blossom under their care" (Mayes 1998b, 17). This sense of calling seems rather common not only in teaching but in all those helping professions such as nursing and social work that (perhaps providentially) do not offer the same worldly rewards as do the "elite" professions (Sheridan, Wilmer, and Atcheson 1994).

As we have seen in previous chapters, the idea of teaching as care arises from the archetype of the Nurturing Great Mother (Neumann 1954)—the archetype that embodies the human need for and experience of all that is fecund, loving, receptive, and wholesome in the cosmos. We see—and more importantly, *feel*—this archetypal maternal energy and its calming, cradling effect when we look at the prehistoric fertility figurine of *The Venus of Willendorf* just as we do in the tender portrayals of Mary in Giotto's *The Annunciation* or DaVinci's *Madonna of the Rocks*. It is powerfully present in the character of Rose-o'-Sharon, who literally suckles a starving man in Steinbeck's *Grapes of Wrath*. We also see a teacher-incarnation of the Great Mother in the poignant figure of the terminally ill yet self-sacrificing young female teacher in the film *October Sky* or the tough but loving female-Marine-turned-teacher in *Dangerous Minds*.

This archetypal energy is probably more common among female teachers than male teachers; however, it is not unusual for male teachers also to become conduits for the energy of the Great Mother. Mr. Keating in *Dead Poets' Society*, Jaime Escalante in *Stand and Deliver*, and Mr. Holland in *Mr. Holland's Opus* embody the popular vision of the male teacher as Great Nurturers. An archetypal connection with the nurturing Great Mother can sustain both men and women teachers in their difficult jobs, infusing their practice with compassion and their psyches with a sense of higher spiritual purpose in helping, and sometimes even healing their students in their psychological, political, and spiritual struggles.

However, even the life-giving, life-sustaining archetype of the nurturing Great Mother casts a shadow, and the shadow that it casts is the archetype of the Devouring Great Mother. This mother will not let her children go because, possessed and inflated by her role as matriarch, she fears emotional and spiritual death if they leave her. Like a snake (in primitive and ancient art, she is often portrayed wearing a wreath of snakes), the Devouring Mother recoils and then strikes out in a fearing, fearful rage at the prospect of being left alone. For her, the alternative to caring for her children is not to set them free but, Medea-like, to murder and eat them. In this act, a diabolical parody and reversal of birth, she consumes them with gruesome finality so that they will always be hers. Males of whatever age who still wrestle with difficult Oedipal issues are often in the psychic throes of this mother at both personal and transpersonal levels (Jacoby 1984). Some females with eating disorders also stand in the shadow of this (appropriately named) *devouring* matriarch (Woodman 1995).

If the therapist and teacher—especially women—are aware that they are tapping into archetypal Great Mother energy and learn how to use and contain it within appropriate bounds, the results can be healing. According to Woodman, it is not uncommon for females in care-giving professions to take on the role of the nurturing Great Mother with positive results. In her treatment of women with eating disorders, the female analyst may

> become a medium for the archetype of the Great Mother, she who re-mothers without the original conflict, the mother who is accepting, somewhat directive, loving and non-judgmental. Often a very powerful dream of the Great Mother shakes the analysand's rational roots. "I don't know what is going on," she will say. "I'm not a religious person, but now I have this inner sense of peace. I know somebody up there loves me." During this phase, the analysand can be brought to deal with her eating disorders by trying to incorporate the Good Mother into herself: nourish herself with good food, love her body, cherish herself as a woman in a way her mother was unable to do. (1995, 59)

I studied fifteen prospective administrators, who had been teachers for an average of ten years, about their sense of calling as teachers and, now, as prospective public school administrators (Mayes and Blackwell-Mayes 2002). The responses of the eight female participants in the study contained many more images of the teacher/administrator as a nurturer than did those of the seven males. The females' interviews abounded with references to the students as "my little ones," "my children," and, with elementary school teachers, "my babies." Such characterizations of students were rare from the male teachers.

As did Woodman in describing herself as an analyst, many of the women in my study spoke about themselves as teachers in terms that combined gender, care, and divinity, reflecting the fact that many female therapists and female teachers may be similarly inspired by the archetypal energy of the Great Mother. For instance, one veteran teacher, a forty-five-year-old African American special education teacher who had grown up in the Philadelphia projects, confessed that the intensity of her care for her students would be insupportable without her faith as a Roman Catholic, tearfully confiding during our interview:

> I've had so many experiences with my kids, my life has been so touched by them. I once lost a student because she was murdered. I let my feelings show in class—just like now. I thought it was important for her classmates to know that people care. I've taken in a child because his mother didn't want him. And there are other things, too, that I've done in my life for my students. And I do think that if I didn't have God in my life right now that I couldn't make it—couldn't continue being a teacher.

This wonderful woman, now a principal at a large school, exemplifies the teacher and administrator as the Nurturing Great Mother, whose calling stems from her communion with a spiritual, archetypal source.

The Great Mother as Devourer and Witch

The shadow of the nurturing mother archetype is the analyst/mother who unconsciously undermines her analysand's progress in order to keep the analysand dependent on her. The devouring side of the Great Mother

> is experienced by the analyst as hostility towards the patient's development, together with an impulse to interfere with the therapeutic process. Such impulses are usually repressed as the analyst naturally tends to identify with the nourishing aspect of the Great Mother. By way of compensation, this causes the desire to devour to exert its effect unconsciously and all the more strongly. (Steinberg 1990, 58)

At first blush, it may seem difficult to imagine classroom parallels to this syndrome. Yet it is by now an educational truism that a student's academic failure may be more a result of the teacher's issues and inadequacies than the student's. I believe this may sometimes be due to the fact that the teacher, possessed by the archetype of the devouring Great Mother, may actually (if unconsciously) be encouraging the failure of a student whom the teacher psychically needs to keep in her maternal grasp. At a bare minimum, it is arguable that the teacher who infantilizes her student by being condescending, overprotective, or hypercritical may be trying to keep that person a dependent child, whose maturation would pose a psychic threat to the teacher's dystonic countertransference as a controlling Great Mother.

Another problem for the teacher or therapist who is possessed by the shadow Mother is simply that it is exhausting! Nurturing is hard—even appropriate nurturing. Dysfunctional nurturing depletes. As we have seen, all that is necessary is Winnicott's "good-enough mother"—one who nurtures functionally, which means neither deficiently nor excessively. Wolstein has called the practitioner who nurtures beyond healthy limits "the overprotective therapist" (1988, 227). He has warned that such practitioners easily burn out or break down. We cannot know precisely how many teachers leave teaching because, inflated and then consumed by the role of the Great Mother, they have emotionally overextended themselves, but it is a fair guess that this is true of more than just a few of them.

In one's personal life as well as in one's classroom life, individuation is a hard process. But on those occasions when the archetypes are clearly and cleanly alive in the sacred precinct of the classroom, then it is indeed a *temenos*, a sacred precinct, where teaching becomes "mysterious" (Reinsmith 1992, 40). When this happens, the classroom becomes a space where the transpersonal and the personal merge. In this way, teacher and students alike may experience "the intersection of the timeless with time" (Eliot 1971, 136).

Spiegelman and Mansfield describe these classroom epiphanies in more technical language in their presentation of the "physics and psychology of the transference as an interactive field."[3] In his research, Spiegelman has scientifically demonstrated how energy fields measurably change in moments of emotionally charged interaction:

> By interactive field condition we mean the two parties are embedded in an imaginally perceived whole situation. They experience the unconscious or archetypes both "around" and "between" them, as well as "within"

them—an encompassing, infusing and mutually interactive field. This occurs when the collective unconscious is . . . "constellated." (1996, 186)

As we saw in part I, whenever an archetype is constellated, it creates an environment in which synchronicities frequently occur. Spiegelman and Mansfeld have given us some of our first empirical glimpses into how this occurs. I previously offered an example of synchronicity from my counseling experience. I would like now to give one from my classroom practice, for every term I have at least one synchronistic event between a student and me—and usually more.

Several years ago, I dreamed that I was singing Beethoven's "Ode to Joy" in German with a student. This student, Mark, was, in fact, emerging as a leader in our classroom, which was just beginning to come together into a tight and intimate cohort—the kind of situation that would generate Spiegelmann and Mansfield's quantum field. What is more, I had already developed a special sense of closeness to Mark because of our similar age, experiences, and general view on life.

When I told the students about my Beethoven dream the following day so that we could all have a good laugh out of it, everyone *did* laugh—everyone except Mark. When he heard the dream, his mouth dropped open and he went a little pale. I asked him why. He told me that last night he had been trying to learn how to read music on the guitar and had been practicing by repeatedly playing the famous tune from Beethoven's "Ode to Joy." These kinds of events, so frequent in my experiences as a teacher, are strong evidence of the reality of archetypal transference and countertransference in the classroom.

Whatever the explanation of *how* such things take place, it is clear that *when* they do—when, that is, the archetypes constellate between and within the teacher and student—then both may experience that clarity and charity which, for many of us as teachers, *is* our Holy Grail.

TOPICS FOR GROUP DISCUSSION
OR INDIVIDUAL REFLECTIVITY

1. In talking about his former student, Jean, the author analyzed how he was involved in a transferential relationship with her that he

could have handled better if he had been more aware of what was going on. Do you feel that you have ever been the object of a student's projections? Has a student ever been the object of your projections? How did you deal with that situation or those situations at the time? Has this chapter helped you understand the situation(s) better now than you did then? If so, how would you have negotiated the situation(s) differently in light of what you have learned in this chapter?

2. In this chapter, it was proposed that both "the passive student" and the "dependently independent student" might both be resisting the teacher's help for reasons that have to do with that student's emotional needs and wounds, not his or her intellectual ability or interest in the subject matter? Do you agree with this? Can you think of examples of this from your own experiences in the classroom?

3. The author mentioned various films in which the hero or heroine is a teacher who embodies the Great Mother archetype. Can you think of any other films, books, or television programs where this is so? Does envisaging that character in the archetypal terms presented in this chapter lead to deeper and richer insights into him or her? If so, what are some of those new insights?

4. The negative side of the Great Mother archetype is the Devouring Mother. Can you think of any teacher (or someone who is fulfilling some sort of educative function) in either a fictional work or your own experience who has played the Devouring Mother role? How can awareness of the Great Mother archetype help a teacher be, on one hand, effectively nurturing while also, on the other hand, be able to create and maintain healthy emotional boundaries between him and his students?

5. Have you ever had a synchronistic experience with a teacher or student? What was it, and what might its deeper meaning have been?

NOTES

1. The idea that the patient "tests" the analyst in the consulting room in various ways to see if he is "safe" so that the patient can begin to truly work

through issues without fear of psychological or physical seduction is an important idea in both the theory and practice of psychotherapy at Mt. Zion Hospital in New York (Eagle 1984). If the patient does conclude that the analyst is safe, then the consulting room can become what Fairbairn has called a "holding environment," in which the patient experiences the safe feeling of being held appropriately by the mother in a way that did not happen—or did not happen often enough—in childhood (Fairbairn 1952/1992). I believe that a classroom can also become a safe "holding environment" for students, especially troubled students, if they perceive that the teacher is neither "buying into" nor generating any psychosexually seductive energy. This allows the student not only a better environment in which to learn but also one in which to heal in the light of the teacher's positive regard and untainted nurturance.

2. Another school-related example comes from Grumet (1981) who has argued that female teachers caught up in an Electra complex may be excessively deferential to a male administrator (the sexualized father-object of their transference), who then takes on and plays out this role with his female teachers (the sexualized daughter-objects of his countertransference) in order to autocratically impose his will on the teachers and their classroom practice.

3. For a survey of the most recent scientific literature regarding the empirical demonstrability of the existence of archetypes and archetypal fields in domains ranging from molecular biology to astrophysics, see Gray (1996).

9

THE TEACHER AS AN
ARCHETYPE OF SPIRIT

We have seen throughout this book that spirituality is often embodied in the archetypal image of the Wise Old Man or Woman. Other images that served the same function are the Magician, the Doctor, and the Priest or Priestess. In this concluding chapter, the focus is on the archetypal image which Jung felt in many ways most effectively embodied the archetype of "the spirit" itself—the archetypal image of the Teacher. Many of the images of teachers that have emerged in the teacher-reflectivity literature in the last two decades present four different archetypal facets of the teacher as an archetype of spirit. These are: (1) the teacher as philosopher, embodying what might be called *scholastic spirituality*, (2) the teacher as federal-prophet, or *civic spirituality*, (3) the teacher as Zen master, or *ontological spirituality*, and (4) the teacher as priest, or *incarnational spirituality*. Since all archetypes have a light and dark side, we will look at both aspects of each of these archetypal images.

THE TEACHER AS PHILOSOPHER:
SCHOLASTIC SPIRITUALITY

We have already come across this Socratic image of the teacher and therapist in previous chapters. The teacher as philosopher helps the student discover the universe of propositional truth that is revealed by classical scholastic methods. One of the most ancient archetypal forms of teaching in the Western tradition, it still underlies many recent visions of what the teacher and student should be or may become. Adler's (1982) *Paideia Proposal* and Lipman's (1988) *Philosophy Goes to School* exemplify scholastic spirituality, which aims at bringing "a greater degree of rational order than currently exists into the curriculum" (Lipman 1988, 252). In this pedagogical approach, the teacher is supposed to show students how to use "sequential procedures" to interpret texts and events. The result, says Lipman, will be the fostering of "cognitive excellence" and "higher order thinking."

From a Jungian perspective, the teacher as philosopher is the most marginal spiritual archetype, for it is balanced on the dividing line between the rational and transrational domains. In saying this, I do not mean to suggest that this model is not valid. Nor am I suggesting that such teaching always misses the mark. Quite the contrary. It is often precisely on target. For example, in presenting the major modern sociological models in my sociology of education classes, I do so in a linear and analytic fashion. A poetic and subjective exposition of, say, structuralism, a highly analytical school of sociological analysis, would do very little to help my students understand the structuralist analysis of U.S. public schooling. It is sometimes quite appropriate for teachers to fill the archetypal role of the teacher as philosopher—to be the archetypal sage who is initiating the novice student-scholar into an established community of inquiry.

However, an overidentification with this role can too easily keep the teacher and student from entering the *transrational* regions—which, of course, are not to be confused with irrationality, for it is from the transrational realm of spirit that the archetypes emerge and it is back to that realm that they point—back, that is, to a more poetic domain, where the archetypes live, move, and have their being.

The critique of the model of moral reasoning discussed in chapter 2 is applicable here, for, like Kohlberg, the teacher as philosopher makes the limiting assumption that classical rationality is the highpoint of both academic and ethical development. Taken to the extreme, the image of the teacher as philosopher negates the physical, emotional, naturalistic, artistic, and spiritual ways of knowing and acting that are such vital elements of the *whole* teacher and student.

Another way of understanding the limitations of this archetype is by turning to the Eastern seven-tiered model of consciousness in Hinduism—a model whose psychospiritual subtlety greatly interested Jung (1978) and continues to interest some Jungians (Spiegelman 1985). Using these terms, we see that the teacher who primarily "images" himself archetypally as a philosopher operates at the third level of consciousness, *manomayakosa,* or mere rationality. But in order to explore and extract the "good mana" (Wilber 1983) of *all* the psychospiritual dimensions of teaching, teachers need to move themselves and their students into the fourth level of consciousness, *vijnanamayakosa,* which is "higher mental or transrational or intuitive cognition, the beginning of actual spiritual insight" (Wilber 1983, 24).[1]

Of course, some instructional theorists, teacher educators, and teachers may feel neither the need nor the inclination to "go transrational" (Wilber 2000) in their approach to teaching. It may suit neither their philosophical commitments nor their understanding of their craft. But for teachers who want to invest their practice with higher forms of spiritual presence, it is difficult to see how they can do so without moving into deeper archetypal territories than the image of the teacher as philosopher allows.

THE TEACHER AS NATIONAL PROPHET: CIVIC SPIRITUALITY

"Prophecy in its root meaning," wrote Lawrence Cremin (1977, 77), is "the calling of a people, via criticism and affirmation, to their noblest traditions and aspirations. Prophecy, I would submit, is the essential public function of the educator in a democratic society." Cremin is not talking about prophets as such. Indeed, it would be a mistake to confuse his use of the term with its more classical sense in Isaiah, for example, who received his calling when he

> saw also the Lord sitting upon a throne, high and lifted up, and his train filled the temple. Above it stood the seraphim. . . . And one cried unto an-

other, and they said, Holy, holy, holy is the Lord of hosts: the whole earth is full of his glory. . . . Then said I, Woe is me! For I am a man of unclean lips, and I dwell in the midst of a people of unclean lips: for mine eyes have seen the King, the Lord of hosts. (Isaiah 6:1, 6:3, 6:5)

Cremin's *civic* prophet deals not in ecstasy but in political "criticism and affirmation." He is a *federal prophet.*

Still, it is clear from Cremin's morally impassioned language in describing the teacher as prophet that there is *spiritual* significance in this role—just as there is a *political* dimension to Isaiah's epiphany. Cremin offers an idealized political vision of the teacher, whose function is to call—or rather recall—a people to "their noblest traditions and aspirations," in this case, the "traditions and aspirations" of democracy. Cremin's use of the phrase and his invocation of the archetype of the teacher as prophet are spiritual because this prophet, although secular, has a message of great historical significance to deliver to a chosen people who have betrayed a collective, even divine political mission.

This distinctly American vision of the teacher fulfilling an almost ministerial instrument of divinely inspired national renewal predates Cremin. It clearly motivated Horace Mann in the early 1800s and invested his vision of public schooling with religious purpose (Messerli 1976). The same sense of national destiny caused many people to become teachers throughout the nineteenth century in the United States (Mattingly 1975). Such extraordinary and inadequately celebrated women as Catherine Beecher, Emma Willard, Zilpah Grant, and Mother Mary Seton even saw this prophetic teaching role as basically a female one. They felt that women teachers had a special talent and calling to purify the republic by educating its children to such high standards that it would be prepared for its historical mission and destiny—to serve as the base and home for Jesus Christ as he returned to establish his millennial kingdom first in this land and then throughout the world (Sklar 1973). In the examples of these women, one sees embodied the archetype of the teacher as a federal prophet, whose mission is to announce the good news of historical redemption through democracy.

In *Protestant, Catholic, and Jew,* Herberg (1954, 77) said this federal gospel was the result of the "triple melting" of those three faiths in the crucible of American society. The result, said Herberg, has been a synthesis of the sacred and secular in the form of an *"American religion*, undergirding life and overarching American society, despite indubitable differences of religion, section, culture, and class" (77, emphasis added). The advocacy of this U.S. "civil religion," as the historian of American religion Sydney Ahlstrom (1972) has called it, is what Cremin means by the teacher's prophetic function.

This prophetic advocacy can be conservative, as in former U.S. Secretary of Education William Bennett's view that schools must lead the way in helping a degenerating America rediscover its forgotten ideals; or it can be radical, as in the critical theorist Peter McLaren's insistence that schools be a place where the United States finally makes good on the ideals that it has consistently betrayed. Yet in both visions, the standard of American democracy is a divine message translated into political terms. And in both cases, it is the teacher who is ordained to the prophetic role of calling the people to repentance and reform.

Another example of this is George Counts' (1932) famous call for schools to create a socialist economy in the United States because this form of *economic* democracy was most consistent with its commitment to *political* democracy in which power was (theoretically) shared equally among all the people. Jung would probably point out that Counts' vision of the teacher remains so compelling not simply for political reasons but also because it is invested with the transpersonal power of the social aspect of the teacher as an archetype of spirit.

Prophecy has probably always been more or less a blend of the transcendental and political—at least in the major monotheistic traditions. As it is written in the Koran, "O my people! Enter the holy land which Allah hath assigned unto you, and turn not back ignominiously, for then will ye be overthrown, to your own ruin" (Surah 5, Al Ma'idah 4:21). Micah proclaimed, "What doth the Lord require of thee, but to do justly, and to love mercy, and to walk humbly with thy God? The Lord's voice crieth unto the city" (Micah 6:8–9). And Amos enjoined the Jewish nation to "hate the evil, and love the good, and establish judgment in the gate" (Amos 5:15). Carrying on this work *with* children in the public school classroom by carrying this message (in secularized form) *to* them is the task of the teacher-prophet (Bullough, Patterson, and Mayes 2002).

It is my belief that even today many teachers have this sense of moral and social mission, powered by the archetypal dynamics of the teacher as national-prophet. Certainly, this would help explain why most teachers take a very dim view of relativistic values-clarification curricula. In a study of how teachers picture themselves and their work, Joseph and Efron (1993, 203) found that teachers "overwhelmingly . . . affirmed that moral values should be defined as guidelines for behavior in which moral choices are not preferences but are definite rules for right and wrong." This should not be surprising, for the republican teacher-prophet, as the social incarnation of the archetype of teacher as spirit, does not, indeed *cannot*, traffic in relativism. His task is to recall his students to the ethical foundation of their collective being.

But there is also the shadow side of the teacher as a federal prophet. Nash has noted that some of these teachers, possessed by the dark aspect of this archetype, may too easily speak and teach from a smug sense of

> absolute moral certainty. [This archetype] gives automatic moral preference to those whom it designates as oppressed. It bestows unchallengeable moral authority on those whose political pronouncements are somewhat left-of-center, preferably leaning toward a humanistically rejuvenated type of Marxism. It shows a presumptive bias against merit, wealth, individual achievement, and liberty, because it thinks these are capitalist, racist vices. And it insists that those who dissent from the doctrine that social justice entails perfect equality be immediately cast out of the community and declared as heretics. (1999, 99)

There are equally dangerous shadow prophets on the political Right—although we hear them less frequently in academia due to its general affinity for the Left. In both cases, people who are drawing from the power of the archetype of the teacher as prophet must learn to guard against the "shadow teacher-prophet," who, always lurking in psychic nooks and crannies, can too easily turn a teacher's sense of political commitment and calling into intolerance, self-righteousness and even fanaticism.

THE TEACHER AS ZEN MASTER/THERAPIST: ONTOLOGICAL SPIRITUALITY

The next archetypal image of the teacher as spirit is one that shows up quite often in the literature on teacher reflectivity—the teacher as a Zen master.

In his analysis of teaching styles, Reinsmith (1992) portrays this form of teaching as the highest form of teaching. Just as the Zen master, *by* his sheer presence and *as* sheer presence, draws the novice out of her illusory mental formations into a realm of self-existent Being, so too may the teacher as Abiding Presence both embody and reveal sheer presence— what the poet Wallace Stevens simply called "mere being." Such a teacher is both a still point and a mirror that orients and reflects the novice to herself in such a way that she is *revealed* to herself and thus *liberated* from her egoic self into an experience of her transpersonal Self, which, in a sense, is "no-self."

> Teaching in this sense becomes mysterious; the teacher's "non-doing" par-
> adoxically brings a feeling of fulfillment unlike that in the previous forms.
> Her "influence" has markedly decreased, yet in another way it is more re-
> fined, subtle, unself-conscious. Becoming totally student-centered, the
> teacher is moving toward a certain egolessness. (Reinsmith 1992, 140)

The teacher as Zen master provides for her students a model of egoless fulfillment through being completely present in the moment.

Writing of his own deepening reflectivity and evolving practice, Tremmel has discussed how practicing presence can lead to great acts of teaching. "I am beginning to see that paying attention, not only to what is going on around us but also within us, is not only a necessary step towards mindfulness and Zen, but it is also the better part of reflective practice. For both Zen students and education students, without their paying attention, no skillful action of any kind can occur" (1993, 447).

Coming from a Roman Catholic perspective influenced by Zen practice, O'Reilley explores the parallels between the teacher as Zen master and the Benedictine rule of hospitality. She notes that the teacher must be present to each student in all his particularity—and not just see them as standardized faces in the classroom crowd—in order to be a compassionate teacher.

> Hospitality calls me to consider the singularity of each person, the diversity of needs. The discipline of presence requires me to *be there*, with my senses focused on the group at hand, listening rather than thinking about what I'm going to say—observing the students, the texts, and the sensory world of the classroom. This is harder than sitting *zazen* [which is the act of sitting in meditation in the Zen tradition]. In *zazen*, nobody talks back to you. Hospitality, by contrast, implies reception of the challenging and unfamiliar: that student with spiked hair who has written on her card, "I'm the one with tattoos all over my body." (1998, 9)

It is in the archetypal light of the teacher as a Zen master that we can best appreciate Nel Noddings' insistence on an "ethic of care" in the classroom. For, implicit in her vision of the teacher as caregiver is the idea of being delicately attuned to the psychospiritual needs of the student with whom she is *presently* engaged. Because this is also the traditional role of the counselor and mother, these frequent images of the teacher are, in a sense, variations of the image of the Zen master.

The images of teacher as counselor and caretaker exemplify a "relational approach . . . rooted in the natural relation of mothering, subjective experience, and the uniqueness of human encounters" (Valli 1990, 43). With this tender archetype of the teacher, we begin to move beyond the somewhat impersonal roles of philosopher and federal prophet into more intuitive, maternal dimensions. Valli has noted that "while this approach does involve moral deliberation, its rootedness in receptivity, relatedness, and responsiveness rather than in moral reasoning precludes it being subsumed under the category of moral deliberation. . . . [R]elationships are more important than rationality, empathetic understanding more important than abstract principles" (1990, 43).

In other words, this is a movement into a more spiritually *complex* atmosphere of spontaneous responsiveness to the psychospiritual needs of the Other as those needs present themselves *in this particular moment, in this particular classroom, with this particular student*. The teacher who embraces this archetypal image is helping his students find emotional stability, mature identity, and spiritual awareness. For teachers who pictures themselves and their sense of calling in this latter way, the link between therapy and spirituality is quite explicit in their Buddhistic attempts to help students find balance through the discovery a "transcending identity," a suprapersonal "I" that, as in the Eastern form of meditation known as *vipassana*, "is a detached observing center of awareness and identity which transcends psychosocial identity" (Whitmore 1986, 149).

Of course, this archetype has a negative as well as a positive pole. In what he calls "the failure of the alternative spiritualities narrative," Nash (1999) has noted that it can too easily degenerate into "elitism and anti-intellectualism" because it often "[goes] to bizarre lengths to reject the value of critical analysis and logical thinking . . . in [the] pursuit of *'dharmakaya'* (raw experience) or the 'thatness' of 'reality'" (132, 135).

In archetypal terms, this is an important reminder of the Jungian point that the individuated personality does not sacrifice political considerations but holistically includes them. While pointing out that social activists such as Mahatma Gandhi and the Vietnamese Zen monk Thich Nhat Hanh grounded their radical political action in Hinduism and Buddhism respectively, Nash nevertheless notes that, in its more faddish forms, alternative spirituality as practiced by Western dilettantes results in such an obsessive concern with self-transformation that one loses sight of social injustice. Jung also felt that Westerners should basically stick to Western forms of spirituality, however much they might borrow from Eastern forms. Despite his profound respect for and frequent appropriation of certain aspects of Eastern spirituality, Jung wrote:

> The usual mistake of Western man when faced with [the] problem of grasping the ideas of the East [is that he] contemptuously turns his back on science and, carried away by Eastern occultism, takes over yoga practices word for word and becomes a pitiable imitator. (Theosophy is our best example of this.) Thus he abandons the one sure foundation of the Western mind and loses himself in a mist of words and ideas that could never have originated in European brains and can never be profitably grafted upon them. (*CW* 11, par. 108)

Whatever one might make of Jung's controversial assertion that no Westerner could ever fully understand or correctly follow any form of

Eastern spirituality, Jung practiced what he preached. Although fascinated by Buddhism, Jung, an astute student of many Eastern religions, ultimately focused his research, practice, and personal spirituality on the archetypal images of the Judeo-Christian tradition.[2]

Nash's and Jung's critiques carry home the important message that becoming possessed by the archetype of spirituality as presence—and neglecting the philosophically and politically oriented archetypes—will produce *shadow* masters/mothers/counselors who are oblivious to theory or political reality.

THE TEACHER AS PRIEST:
INCARNATIONAL SPIRITUALITY

In U.S. public schooling, there are, as we have already seen, many historical precedents for teachers seeing themselves in clerical terms. There is, for example, Catherine Beecher's mid-nineteenth-century model of the common-school teacher as a sort of Protestant lay clergywoman ministering to the youth and preparing them for the return of Christ (Sklar 1973) or the postbellum image of the white Northern female teacher as a minister of "light and love" working with the recently freed slaves (Jones 1980). Beecher called on women to assume the quasi-ecclesiastical job of the teacher-evangelizer and prepare America for its millennial destiny, which seemed just around the corner. Throughout the nineteenth century, women thus moved in large numbers into teaching, which some came to look at as a female religious vocation (Bailyn 1960).

Various authors from different faith perspectives continue to explore sacerdotal imagery about teaching. For instance, Harris (1991) has teased out the pedagogical implications of sacramental Roman Catholic worship. From a Jewish perspective, Wexler (1996) has illustrated how Kabalistic mysticism may offer a model for bringing a sense of the holy to teacher education and public school education. Palmer's (1998) ecumenical Protestant commitments have shaped his vision of the sacredness of teaching as an act of prayer. And Gatto (1997) has even likened teaching to an apostolic calling.

There is this common thread running through all the literature on teaching as priestly: All the authors have shaped their highest vision of teaching and learning around their specific theistic commitments, which they then attempt to "incarnate" in approaches to teaching that someone from any faith perspective, or even no faith perspective, might use to spiritualize classroom dynamics. "Ontological spirituality" and "incarnational spirituality" are similar in their transrational focus and their desire to base their compassion on "ultimate concern." However, "incarnational spirituality" differs from "ontological spirituality" in that the former rests on *specific doctrinal commitments* involving a personal God whereas the latter is nontheistically interested in cultivating *ontological presence as such* in the classroom. This lends a different coloring and texture to the image of the teacher as priest, compared with the teacher as master/mother/counselor.

For example, in strains that echo St. John's proclamation that "God is love" (1 John 4:8) and St. Paul's promise that in a celestial future the individual will "know even as also he is known" (1 Corinthians 13:12), Palmer (1983) insists that the teacher must learn to take a view of knowledge that is very different from the prevailing passion for technical rationality in the U.S. "A knowledge that springs from love will implicate us in the web of life; it will wrap the knower and known in compassion, in a bond of awesome responsibility as well as transforming joy. . . . We must recover from our spiritual tradition the models and methods of knowing as an act of love" (9).

Similarly, Wexler (1996) combines imagery drawn from the Jewish Diaspora as well as the fiery inner workings of Jewish mysticism to suggest some of the transcendental possibilities of all classroom interaction:

> Social interaction is revitalized by a movement outward, toward the supramundane. It is reenergized by glimpses of eternity and obliged by the task of reversing the exilic dispersion of energy that exists in the world as concealed potentialities. . . . The cycle of ecstasy, union, interpretation and revelation is incomplete without the ingathering and uplifting of the holy sparks. . . . This mysticism is innerworldly not only in the way that it can be assimilated into secular social theory, but also in its obligation to transformative action and education. (129–31)

It is in these images of *incarnational* spirituality that one comes closest to the throbbing, brilliant center of the Jungian archetype of the teacher as spirit. Yet cautions about the shadow apply to the archetype of the teacher as priest no less than to any of the other archetypes. In many ways, indeed, these warnings are especially important here.

Teachers who envision themselves in ministerial terms must resist the evangelizing tendency to overtly or covertly direct the curriculum and discussion in the classroom along the lines of their own religious allegiances—a point made quite clearly in two important Supreme Court decisions, *Abington v. Schempp* in 1963 and *Lemon v. Kurtzman* in 1971. In fact, an important reason for encouraging archetypal reflectivity in prospective teachers is that it can help them identify and examine their own spiritual commitments, or lack thereof, so that they do not unconsciously project their opinions about religion onto their students in the increasingly multicultural U.S. public school classroom. Furthermore, through group exercises in spiritual reflectivity, prospective and practicing teachers may learn a great deal from each other about how various perspectives impact a teacher's practice. These teachers may even use elements of those other perspectives in order to enrich their own worldviews, leadership styles, and pedagogies.

THE TEACHER AS SPIRIT—THE TEACHER AS *EVOLVING* SPIRIT

In this chapter, we have seen that spirituality in teaching can be looked at as an archetypal continuum ranging from scholastic spirituality to incarnational spirituality. Ideally all of these aspects of the teacher as an archetype of spirit will be active and interactive within a teacher. When they do not interact at least to some degree, they run the risk of degenerating into their shadows.

When the four aspects of the teacher as an archetype of spirit integrate and operate in a teacher, his classroom is much more likely to be a sacred precinct where mutually enriching forms of communication and presence occur. In such an environment, the teacher will inevitably feel that his work is more exciting and satisfying.

Offering many rich possibilities for personal and professional refreshment and betterment, archetypal reflectivity is a powerful tool for teacher development. An archetypal approach helps the teacher become not only a guide to his students but also a fellow traveler, not only the liberator but also the liberated. The archetype of the teacher as spirit, then, is also the teacher as an archetype of an *evolving* spirit—one whose professional growth is intimately related to his and his students' overall intellectual and spiritual progression.

A TOPIC FOR A REFLECTIVE ESSAY

After discussing what he believes to be the four major aspects of the teacher as an archetype of spirit—the philosopher, federal prophet, Zen master, and priest—the author concluded with the assertion that "when the four aspects of the teacher as an archetype of spirit integrate and operate in a teacher, his classroom is much more likely to be a sacred precinct where mutually enriching forms of communication and presence occur. In such an environment, the teacher will inevitably feel that his work is more exciting and satisfying."

Write an essay that deals with each of these four archetypes in terms of their suitability to how you see yourself as a teacher and how you see the subject that you teach. Are all of these archetypes appropriate to you in your situation? Some of them? None of them? Can you imagine ways in which you might either grow into or grow out of one or some of these archetypes as you mature as a teacher or educational leader?

NOTES

1. Ajaya (1983) and Rama, Ballentine, and Ajaya (1976) also offer both Hindu and Buddhist models of mind with reference to Jung that provide extremely helpful tools for parsing different sorts of psychospiritual knowledge and experience.

2. This is reminiscent of T. S. Eliot, who was also deeply immersed at various points in his life in both the scholarly and spiritual pursuit of Eastern religion. He is reputed to have said that he ultimately had to give it up because, if he had not, he would have been "lost to the West"—and to his commitment to the Church of England.

(10)

JUNG THE EDUCATIONIST

We have covered a great deal of ground in our inquiry into the psychology of C. G. Jung and its educational implications. Naturally, there is much more to be said on this topic than can fit into just one book—especially an exploratory study such as this one. After reviewing some of the major ideas contained in the present study, therefore, let us conclude by looking at some of the directions that the theory and practice of an archetypal pedagogy might take.

JUNG THE PSYCHOLOGIST

The fundamental difference between Jung and Freud was Jung's postulation that beyond the personal subconscious lies another dimension of psyche—the collective unconscious, the realm of the archetypes. Timeless and intrinsic to every human being, the archetypal domain is the most central element of our psychic functioning, causing each of us to see, be, interpret, and create things in ways that are relatively constant across all cultures and epochs. The Resurrected God, the Evil One, the Wise One, the Trickster and Teacher, the Lovers and their inevitable travails, the Heroes and Heroines and their salvific journeys—all of these and more are the foci around which our experiences turn and toward which they tend.

Historical, cultural, political, and personal factors shape those archetypal energies into an endless array of archetypal images, motifs, and narratives. Indeed, that is the only way in which we can experience archetypal energies, which are unknowable *as such*. But underneath all of the tremendous variety of these images is the archetypal base, which, like the rhizome under a field that blooms with a spectacularly rich array of plant life, forms the dynamic foundation of our psychic reality. It is therefore *from* the collective unconscious that all our experiences essentially arise, and it is *to* the collective unconscious that they ultimately point.

Given its psychic ultimacy, the experience of the collective unconscious has a spiritual character. When a person or culture loses touch with this spiritual dimension, it becomes morally eviscerated and disoriented—and soon finds itself in a crisis. Ours is such a time, Jung felt—an epoch "without a soul." Finding our individual souls—becoming *individuated*, becoming more than an ego but a *Self*—is the great precondition of not only personal renewal but also political and cultural rebirth since, said Jung, a society is little more in the last analysis than the individuals who comprise it. This stress on the primacy of the individual clearly aligns Jung with classical liberalism. Yet on the other hand, his reverence for the great variety of cultural-spiritual traditions, and his insistence that renewal must happen in the terms and contexts that those traditions provided, places Jung with some of the most contemporary multiculturalists.

For all of his focus on the collective and universal, however, Jung, a psychiatrist in daily clinical practice, was also deeply involved with the workings of the personal subconscious. Jung even added important theoretical concepts and clinical tools to the repertoire of ego psychology. Such terms as *the persona, the shadow*, and *extraversion and introversion* have become standard not only in psychoanalytic practice but even in everyday conversation. Jung's parsing of personality types into four major functions—thinking, feeling, sensate, and intuitive—and the two different attitudes of extraversion and introversion—pioneered the twentieth-century study of personality types. And his theory of *projection* is not only very widely known but also used in fields ranging from political analysis to quantum physics.

Also of enormous value in the theory and practice of psychotherapy has been Jung's notion of countertransference, which required therapists to see that *their own* psychodynamics are relevant, even determining, in the therapeutic process—and that, as always, it is of capital importance that the physician heed the injunction: "Heal thyself." Hence, the *withdrawal of projections* is as necessary for the therapist as for the patient.

Jung posited as well that everyone has *contrasexual* elements in his or her psyche, the *anima* or *animus*, which, left untended and unintegrated into one's total psychic functioning, will exact vengeance by wreaking emotional havoc, especially in the second half of life. Indeed, the second half of life is filled with many different dilemmas, projects, and potentials, and Jung was the first twentieth-century psychologist to address that topic in depth.

Furthermore, just as no one is totally male or female, so no one is totally good. Everyone has her dark side, which one must acknowledge, even honor and appropriate, in order to harness its energy for the good—and not be possessed by in pious ignorance. To do this—indeed to bring all opposites into productive dialectical opposition—is the key that opens the door into the chambers of the individuated Self, that holy of holies wherein the individual experiences and communes with the God-within.

JUNG THE EDUCATIONIST

Perhaps the most fundamental implication of Jungian psychology for education is that there is a certain sanctity in the teacher–student relationship. Jung often raised his voice against any educational theory or practice that would tend to violate the fundamental sacredness of the art and act of teaching. His ire was particularly aroused against education that overly stressed technical proficiency or abstract intellectualism. To be psychosocially viable, Jung felt that education must address the whole student in all of her physical, emotional, political, and spiritual complexity. To do less was to do immediate damage to the student as well as long-term damage to both her and society. Thus, a sane and ethical approach to education will rest on an archetypal foundation—or at least significant archetypal elements.

An archetypal approach to education is constantly engaged in searching out personally and socially constructive answers to such questions as the following. What does the subject or topic I am studying tell me about the fundamental images and narratives that power my life as well as other people's lives? Where do those narratives and images agree with each other, and where do they diverge? How can we learn from each other's psychospiritual commitments in a way that is mutually beneficial—or that at least promotes a generous and genuine tolerance?

What are the assumptions about nature, society, and the individual's place in and responsibility to both that are implicit in what I am studying or doing? Do I agree with those assumptions? If so, what must I do to construct a self and a society that are more consistent with those assumptions? If not, then how can I, both individually and in solidarity with others, work to resist those assumptions and replace them with more humane ones?

How can I learn to reconcile internal and external oppositions so as to help me become passionately committed in my beliefs yet genuinely open to others, sensitive to the symbolic realm yet earnestly involved in the practical world, always engaged in inner exploration yet pursuing it through service to others? Furthermore, how can I synthesize what I have learned, from physics to physical education, in order to create a more integrated, productive, loving, and peaceful self? And moreover, does what I am studying tell me anything about where I originally came from, where I am ultimately going, and how to carry this journey on most sanely and productively?

To *ask* such ethically and spiritually essential questions as these, and then to *act* on the answers that one receives from deep within oneself or from communion with others requires both humility and intuition. Proud reason by itself not only cannot *answer* such questions; it will often not even dare to *ask* them. This is why Jung believed that reason must be harnessed in the service of those more fundamental psychospiritual needs and hopes that comprise our moral nature. Jung fully subscribed to the theological notion that intellect is most valuable when it is engaged in the search for faith.

These are objectives and issues that, being so far-reaching and conse-
quential, will sometimes cause students to stumble, fall short of the
mark, or just plain fail. Such temporary "failure" can be a good thing if
handled by the teacher in a way that is both enlightened and enlighten-
ing. A teacher will be all the more able to perform this delicate task if
she understands the therapeutic dimensions of her relationship with the
student. Understanding transferential psychodynamics is key in accom-
plishing this, as is deep reflectivity on her unique sense of calling and
practice as an educator.

In a word, education must be *spiritual*. But by spirituality, Jung did
not mean self-absorption or airy disengagement from the world. One
finds oneself as a *whole being* only by seeing oneself in the historical,
cultural, and political contexts that have been crucial in generating the
images, providing the stories, forging the tools, and setting up the goals
that define one's ethical life work. With due reverence to the traditions
that have shaped an individual, she must also have the courage to *reform* those traditions so that they will better answer her needs and
those of others as, individually and collectively in their particular world-
historical circumstances, they pursue psychological and cultural
growth—happily engaged in a process that we in the Mormon tradition
call "eternal progression."

NEW DIRECTIONS IN JUNGIAN PEDAGOGY

There are at least several directions that both educational theorists
and practitioners might take in pursuing and practicing an archetypal
pedagogy.

The first concerns the potential of Jungian psychology to deepen our
reflectivity as teachers, for this is one of the surest roads to helping
teachers become more genuinely satisfied and effective in their important role. Thus, there is a great need for more work—both theoretical
and practical—in "archetypal reflectivity" (Mayes 1999). In colleges of
education as well as in individual and group exercises during retreats or
in-services, teachers and teacher-educators can explore the many un-
tapped potentials that Jungian psychology in particular and the transpersonal psychologies in general offer for personal and professional growth.

The second avenue to pursue regards transferential dynamics between teachers and students. In dealing with personal transference and archetypal inflation in the classroom, I focused mostly on the dangers inherent in them. However, I only hinted at some of the positive effects that can accrue by stimulating archetypal energies in the classroom (Mitchell 2003). Thus, for instance, teachers may ask themselves such questions as the following: At the elementary school level, how can the child's primal proximity to archetypal energy be best nurtured and shaped so as to lay the groundwork for future psychospiritual health? At the same time, how can teachers help their young students transition smoothly as they begin to move out of the realm of undifferentiated, raw archetypes and into the more mundane world of social identity formation?

At the secondary level, how can the teacher help students constellate the hero/heroine archetypes within themselves so as to help them embark on healthy heroic journeys of self-discovery and political involvement? Regarding the difficult physical and psychosocial changes that begin to occur as one approaches age forty, how can societies create and sustain ways of educating midlife adults so that they can view their crises of transition as opportunities for spiritual enlargement, not existential despair? And with the aged, how can late-life education help the individual frame his existence in the terms of an archetypal narrative, one that is personally unique yet also tied into universal, timeless realities— a narrative that make sense out of his past and provides acceptance and hope for what lies ahead?

And finally, there is the challenge of actually creating archetypally sensitive curricula in different subjects and at different grade levels— tasks that I could only hint at in this book and that specialists in other fields must work out. How, for example, can Pauli's archetypal understanding of physics or von Franz's of mathematics be incorporated into elementary school, high school, and graduate school curricula? What would be the commonalities among those curricula, what would be the differences?

Additionally, it would be useful to look in more detail at the question of whether there are some fields in which archetypal approaches are more suitable than others. For instance, there have been many archetypal approaches to literary studies and few, if any, to, say, sociology. Perhaps this demonstrates that literature is more amenable to archetypal analysis than sociology. But perhaps not. Several exciting new works in cultural studies have appeared recently that show not only the relevance of an archetypal approach to old sociological questions but also its power in generating a wide range of new questions. The same is true in biology. In short, the fact that some fields seem less suitable to an archetypal pedagogy than others may say less about the fields themselves and more about the need to take a broader view of those fields.

In these and many other ways that future exploration may yet reveal, we can confidently continue to turn to the work of Carl Gustav Jung—and to the archetypal heartlands that he intrepidly charted—to restore our energy and revision our roles as teachers and educational leaders.

REFERENCES

Abington Township, Pennsylvania, et al. v. Schempp et al., 374 US 203 (1963).

Adams, M. 1996. *The multicultural imagination: "Race," color, and the unconscious.* London: Routledge.

Adler, M. 1982. *The Paideia proposal: An educational manifesto.* New York: Macmillan.

Ahlstrom, S. 1972. *A religious history of the American people.* New Haven: Yale University Press.

Aichhorn, A. 1935/1965. *Wayward youth: A psychoanalytic study of delinquent children, illustrated by actual case histories.* New York: Viking Press.

———. 1990. The transference. In *Essential papers on transference.* Ed. A. Esman, 94–109. New York: New York University Press.

Ajaya, S. 1983. *Psychotherapy East and West: A unifying paradigm.* Honesdale, Pa.: Himalayan International Institute.

Almon, J. 1999. From cognitive learning to creative thinking. In *Education, information, and transformation: Essays on learning and thinking.* Ed. J. Kane, 249–69. Columbus, Ohio: Merrill.

Bailyn, B. 1960. *Education in the forming of American society: Needs and opportunities for study.* New York: W.W. Norton.

Beck, A., and M. Weishaar. 1995. Cognitive psychotherapy. In *Current psychotherapies.* Ed. R. Corsini and D. Wedding, 229–61. Itasca, Ill.: Peacock.

Beck, J. 1995. *Cognitive therapy: Basics and beyond.* New York: Guilford Press.

Belenky, M., B. Clinchy, N. Goldberger, and J. Tarule. 1986. *Women's way of knowing*. New York: Basic Books.

Berger, P. 1967. *The sacred canopy: Elements of a sociological theory of religion*. New York: Doubleday.

Berger, P., and T. Luckmann. 1967. *The social construction of reality: A treatise in the sociology of knowledge*. New York: Anchor Books.

Blumer, H. 1969. *Symbolic interactionism: Perspective and method*. Englewood Cliffs, N.J.: Prentice Hall.

Bly, R. 1990. *Iron John: A book about men*. Reading, Mass.: Addison-Wesley.

Book of Mormon, The: Another testament of Jesus Christ. 1986. Salt Lake City, Utah: Church of Jesus Christ of Latter-day Saints.

Boorstin, D. 1985. *The discoverers: A history of man's search to know his world and himself*. New York: Vintage Books.

Bridges, W. 1992. *The character of organizations: Using Jungian type in organizational development*. Palo Alto, Calif.: Consulting Psychologists Press.

Brophy, J. 1994. *Motivating students to learn*. Boston: McGraw-Hill.

Brown, G., M. Phillips, and S. Shapiro. 1976. *Getting it all together: Confluent education* Bloomington, Ind.: Phi Delta Kappa Educational Foundation.

Brown, J. S., A. Collins, and O. Duguid. 1988. Situated cognition and the culture of learning. *Educational Researcher* 18:32–42.

Brown, J., and C. Moffett. 1999. *The hero's journey: How educators can change schools and improve learning*. Alexandria, Va.: Association for Supervision and Curriculum Development.

Bruner, J. 1960. *The process of education*. New York: Vintage.

———. 1996. *The culture of education*. Cambridge, Mass.: Harvard University Press.

Bullough, R., Jr. 1989. *First-year teacher: A case study*. New York: Teachers College Press.

———. 1991. Exploring personal teaching metaphors in preservice teacher education. *Journal of Teacher Education* 42 (1): 43–51.

———. 2001. *Uncertain lives: Children of hope, teachers of promise*. New York: Teachers College.

Bullough, R.V., Jr., C. Mayes, and R. S. Patterson. 2002. Wanted: A prophetic pedagogy: A response to our critics. *Curriculum Inquiry* 32 (3): 311–30.

Bullough, R.V., Jr., R. S. Patterson, and C. Mayes. 2002. Teaching as prophecy. *Curriculum Inquiry* 32 (3): 341–48.

Burke, K. 1989. *On symbols and society*. Ed. J. Gusfield. Chicago: University of Chicago Press.

Campbell, J. 1949. *The hero with a thousand faces*. Princeton, N.J.: Princeton University Press.

Carier, C. 1976. The ethics of a therapeutic man: C. G. Jung. *Psychoanalytic Review* 63 (1): 115–46.

Chapman, J. 1988. *Jung's three theories of religious experience.* Lewiston, N.Y.: Edwin Mellen Press.

Chinen, A. 1989. *In the ever after: Fairy tales and the second half of life.* Wilmette, Ill.: Chiron Publications.

Chodorow, N. 1978. *The reproduction of mothering: Psychoanalysis and the sociology of gender.* Berkeley: University of California Press.

Chomsky, N. 1968. *Aspects of the theory of syntax.* Cambridge, Mass.: MIT Press.

Clift, W. 1982. *Jung and Christianity: The challenge of reconciliation.* New York: Crossroad.

Cohen, M. 1988. Countertransference and anxiety. In *Essential papers on counter-transference.* Ed. B. Wolstein, 64–83. New York: New York University Press.

Colman, W. 2000. Models of the self. In *Jungian thought in the modern world.* Ed. E. Christopher and H. Solomon, 3–19. London: Free Association Books.

Comer, R. 1998. *Abnormal psychology.* 3rd ed. New York: Freeman Press.

Conger, J., and J. Galambos. 1997. *Adolescence and youth: Psychological development in a changing world.* New York: Longman.

Corsini, R., and D. Wedding, eds. 1995. *Current psychotherapies: Basics and beyond.* Itasca, Ill.: F. E. Peacock.

Cortright, B. 1997. *Psychotherapy and spirit: Theory and practice in transpersonal psychotherapy.* Albany, N.Y.: State University of New York Press.

Counts, G. 1932. *Dare the school build a new social order?* New York: John Day.

Cowan, L. 2002. *Tracking the white rabbit: A subversive view of modern culture.* London: Routledge.

Craig, R. (1994). "The face we put on: Carl Jung for teachers." *The Clearing House.* March–April, 189–91.

Crain, W. 1992. *Theories of development: Concepts and applications.* Englewood Cliffs, N.J.: Prentice-Hall.

Cremin, L. 1964. *The transformation of the school: Progressivism in American education, 1876–1957.* New York: Vintage Press.

———. 1977. *Traditions of American education.* New York: Basic Books.

———. 1988. *American education: The metropolitan experience.* New York: Harper and Row.

Dante Alighieri. 1954. *The inferno.* Trans. John Ciardi. New York: Signet Classics.

De Castillejo, I. 1973. *Knowing woman: A feminine psychology.* New York: Harper and Row.

De Gruchy, J. 1984. Jung and religion: A theological assessment. In *Jung in modern perspective: The master and his legacy*. Ed. R. Papadopoulos and G. Saayman, 193–203. Lindfield, Australia: Unity Press.

Doctrine and Covenants of the Church of Jesus Christ of Latter-day Saints, The. 1986. Salt Lake City, Utah: Church of Jesus Christ of Latter-Day Saints.

Dourley, J. 1984. *The illness that we are: A Jungian critique of Christianity*. Toronto, Ont.: Inner City Books.

Dusek, J. 1994. *Adolescent development and behavior*. New York: Macmillan.

Eagle, M. 1984. *Recent developments in psychoanalysis: A critical evaluation*. Cambridge, Mass.: Harvard University Press.

Edinger, E. 1973. *Ego and archetype: Individuation and the religious function of the psyche*. Baltimore: Penguin Press.

———. 1985. *Anatomy of the psyche: Alchemical symbolism in psychotherapy*. La Salle, Ind.: Open Court Press.

Eisner, E., and E. Vallance, eds. 1974. *Conflicting conceptions of curriculum*. Berkeley, Calif.: McCutchan.

Eliot, T. S. 1971. *T. S. Eliot: The complete poems and plays: 1909–1950*. New York: Harcourt, Brace and World.

Ellenberger, Henri F. 1970. *The discovery of the unconscious: The history and evolution of dynamic psychiatry*. New York: Basic Books.

Epstein, L., and A. Feiner. 1988. Countertransference: The therapist's contribution to treatment. In *Essential papers on counter-transference*. Ed. B. Wolstein, 282–303. New York: New York University Press.

Epstein, M. 1995. *Thoughts without a thinker: Psychotherapy from a Buddhist perspective*. New York: Basic Books.

Erikson, E. 1963. *Childhood and society*. New York: Norton.

———. 1997. *The life cycle completed*. New York: Norton.

Fairbairn, W. R. D. 1952/1992. *Psychoanalytic studies of the personality*. London: Routledge.

Feige, D. 1999. The legacy of Gregory Bateson: Envisioning aesthetic epistemologies and praxis. In *Education, information, and transformation*. Ed. J. Kane, 77–109. Columbus, Ohio: Merrill/Prentice Hall.

Ferenczi, S. 1990. Introjection and transference. In *Essential papers on transference*. Ed. A. Esman, 15–27. New York: New York University Press.

Ferrer, J. 2002. *Revisioning transpersonal theory: A participatory vision of human spirituality*. Albany: State University of New York Press.

Forbes, S. 2003. *Holistic education: An analysis of its nature and ideas*. Brandon, Vt.: Foundation for Educational Renewal Press.

Fordham, M. 1994. *Children as individuals*. London: Free Association Books.

———. 1996. In *Analyst-patient interaction: Collected papers on technique*. Ed. S. Shamdasani. London: Routledge.

Frankl, V. 1967. *Man's search for meaning*. New York: Washington Square Press.

Franz, Marie-Luise von. 1981. *Puer aeternus*. Santa Monica, Ca.: Sigo Press.

Frazer, J. 1922/1963. *The golden bough: A study in magic and religion*. New York: Macmillan.

Freud, S. 1900/1965. *The interpretation of dreams*. New York: Avon Books.

———. 1914/1957. "On narcissism: an introduction." In J. Rickman (Ed.). *A general selection from the works of Sigmund Freud* (pp. 104–23). Garden City, New York: Doubleday Anchor Books.

———. 1920/1957. "Beyond the pleasure principle." In J. Rickman (Ed.). *A general selection from the works of Sigmund Freud* (pp. 141–68). Garden City, New York: Doubleday Anchor Books.

———. 1921/1957. Group psychology and the analysis of the ego. In *A general selection from the works of Sigmund Freud*. Ed. J. Rickman, 169–209. Garden City, N.Y.: Doubleday.

———. 1923/1960. *The ego and the id*. (Tr. Joan Riviere. Ed. James Strachey). New York: W. W. Norton & Company.

———. 1923/1957. "The ego and the id." In J. Rickman (Ed.). *A general selection from the works of Sigmund Freud* (pp. 210–35). Garden City, New York: Doubleday Anchor Books.

———. 1924/1970. *A general introduction to psycho-analysis*. New York: Pocket Books.

———. 1949/1975. *Three essays on the theory of sexuality*. New York: Basic Books.

———. 1990a. The dynamics of transference. In *Essential papers on transference*. Ed. A. Esman, 28–36. New York: New York University Press.

———. 1990b. Observations on transference-love. In *Essential papers on transference*. Ed. A. Esman, 28–48. New York: New York University Press.

Frey-Rohn, L. 1974. *From Freud to Jung: A comparative study of the psychology of the unconscious*. New York: G. P. Putnam's Sons.

Frye, N. 1957/1966. *Anatomy of criticism: Four essays*. New York: Antheneum.

Gallant, C. 1996. *Tabooed Jung: Marginality as power*. New York: New York University Press.

Gardner, H. 1983. *Frames of mind*. New York: Basic Books.

Garfinkel, H. 1967. *Studies in ethnomethodology*. Englewood Cliffs, N.J.: Prentice Hall.

Gatto, J. 1997. Education and the Western spiritual tradition. *Holistic Education Review* 10 (3): 17–25.

Gellert, M. 2001. *The fate of America: An inquiry into national character.* Washington, D.C.: Brassey's.

Giddens, A. 1990. *The consequences of modernity.* Stanford, Calif.: Stanford University Press.

——. 1991. *Modernity and self-identity: Self and society in the late modern age.* Stanford: Stanford University Press.

Gilligan, C. 1982. *In a different voice: Psychological theory and women's development.* Cambridge, Mass.: Harvard University Press.

Glazer, S., ed. 1999. *The heart of learning: Spirituality in education.* New York: Jeremy P. Tarcher.

Glover, E. 1956. *Freud or Jung?* New York: Meridian Books.

Goffman, E. 2000. On face-work: An analysis of ritual in social interaction. In *The discourse reader.* Ed. A. Jaworski and N. Coupland, 306–20. London: Routledge.

Graves, R. 1959. *The white goddess: A historical grammar of poetic myth.* New York: Farrar, Straus, and Giroux.

Gray, R. 1996. *Archetypal explorations: An integrative approach to human behavior.* London: Routledge.

Greeley, A. 1974. *Unsecular man: The persistence of religion.* New York: Delta Books.

Greene, M. 1974. Cognition, consciousness, and curriculum. In *Heightened consciousness, cultural revolution, and curriculum theory.* Ed. W. Pinar, 69–83. Berkeley, Calif.: McCutchan Publishing.

——. 1995. Care and moral education. In *Critical conversations in the philosophy of education.* Ed. W. Kohli. New York: Routledge.

Greenson, R. 1990. The working alliance and the transference neurosis. In *Essential papers on transference.* Ed. A. Esman, 150–71. New York: New York University Press.

Grumet, M. 1988. *Bitter milk: Women and teaching.* Amherst: University of Massachusetts Press.

Grumet, M. 1981. Pedagogy for patriarchy. *Interchange, 12*(2–3), 165–87.

Gutek, G. 2000. *American education: 1945–2000.* Prospect Heights, Ill.: Waveland Press.

Hall, G. S. 1904. *Adolescence: Its psychology and its relations to physiology, anthropology, sociology, sex, crime, religion and education.* New York: D. Appleton.

Hall, J. 1985. Differences between Jung and Hillman. In *Essays on the study of Jung and religion.* Ed. L. Martin and J. Goss, 144–64. Lanham, Md.: University Press of America.

Harris, M. 1991. *Teaching and religious imagination: An essay in the theology of teaching.* San Francisco: HarperCollins.

Hauke, C. 2000. *Jung and the postmodern: the interpretation of realities.* London: Routledge.

Henderson, J. 1967. *Thresholds of initiation.* Middletown, Conn.: Wesleyan University Press.

———. 1984. The Jungian interpretation of history and its educational implications. In *Jung in modern perspective: The master and his legacy.* Ed. R. Papadopoulos and G. Saayman, 245–55. Lindfield, Australia: Unity Press.

———. 1991. "The Jungian interpretation of history and its educational implications." In R. Papadopoulos and G. Saayman (Eds.). *Jung in modern perspective: the master and his legacy* (pp. 245–55). Garden City Park, N.Y.: Avery Publishing Group.

Hendricks, G., and J. Fadiman, eds. 1976. *Transpersonal education: A curriculum for feeling and being.* Englewood Cliffs, N.J.: Prentice-Hall.

Herberg, W. 1954. *Protestant, Catholic, Jew: An essay in American religious sociology.* New York: Doubleday.

Hillman, J. 1976. *Re-visioning psychology.* New York: Harper and Row.

———. 1983. *Archetypal psychology: A brief account.* Dallas, Tx.: Spring Publications.

Holy Koran, The. New Revised Edition. Trans. and commentary by Abdullah Yusuf Ali. Brentwood, Md.: Amana.

Homans, P. 1985. C. G. Jung: Christian or post-Christian psychologist? In *Essays on the study of Jung and religion.* Ed. L. Martin and J. Goss, 26–44. Lanham, Md.: University Press of America.

Huberman, M., M. Gronauer, and J. Marti. 1989. *The lives of teachers.* Trans. J. Neufeld. New York: Teachers College Press.

Huebner, D. 1999. *The lure of the transcendent: Collected essays by Dwayne E. Huebner.* Ed. V. Hillis. London: Lawrence Erlbaum.

Jacobi, J. 1959/1974. *Complex/archetype/symbol in the psychology of C. G. Jung.* Princeton, N.J.: Princeton University Press.

Jacoby, M. 1984. *The analytic encounter: Transference and human relationship.* Toronto, Ont.: Inner City Books.

Jadot, L. 1984. From the symbol in psychoanalysis to the anthropology of the imaginary. In *Jung in modern perspective: The master and his legacy.* Ed. R. Papadopoulos and G. Saayman, 109–18. Lindfield, Australia: Unity Press.

Jaffe, A. (1975). *The myth of meaning: Jung and the expansion of consciousness.* (Tr. R.F.C. Hull). New York: Penguin Books.

———. 1989. *Was C. G. Jung a mystic?: And other essays.* Trans. D. Dachler and F. Cairns. Einsiedeln, Switzerland: Daimon.

Jamal, M. 1996. *Deer dancer: The shapeshifter archetype in story and in trance.* New York: Arkana.

Johnstone, R. 1997. *Religion in society: A sociology of religion.* 5th ed. Upper Saddle River, N.J.: Prentice-Hall.

Jones, J. 1980. *Soldiers of light and love: Northern teachers and Georgia Blacks: 1865–1873.* Chapel Hill: University of North Carolina Press.

Jones, M., B. Jones, and T. Hargrove. 2003. *The unintended consequences of high-stakes testing.* Lanham, Md.: Rowman and Littlefield.

Joseph, P. and S. Efron. 1993. Moral choices/moral conflicts: Teachers' self-perceptions. *Journal of Moral Education* 22 (3): 201–20.

Jung, C. G. 1967. *Freud and Psychoanalysis: Collected works.* Vol. 4. Trans. R. F. C. Hull. Bollingen Series XX. Princeton, N.J.: Princeton University Press.

———. 1967. *Symbols of transformation: Collected works.* Vol. 5. Trans. R. F. C. Hull. Bollingen Series XX. Princeton, N.J.: Princeton University Press.

———. 1921/1971. *Psychological types: Collected works.* Vol. 6. Trans. R. F. C. Hull. Bollingen Series XX. Princeton, N.J.: Princeton University Press.

———. 1938/1966. *Psychology and religion.* New Haven: Yale University Press.

———. 1953. *Two essays on analytical psychology: Collected works.* Vol. 7. Trans. R. F. C. Hull. Bollingen Series XX. Princeton, N.J.: Princeton University Press.

———. 1960. *The structure and dynamics of the psyche: Collected works.* Vol. 8. Trans. R. F. C. Hull. Bollingen Series XX. Princeton, N.J.: Princeton University Press.

———. 1959. *The archetypes of the collective unconscious: Collected works.* Vol. 9.1. Trans. R. F. C. Hull. Bollingen Series XX. Princeton, N.J.: Princeton University Press.

———. 1959. *Aion: Collected works.* Vol. 9.2. Trans. R. F. C. Hull. Bollingen Series XX. Princeton, N.J.: Princeton University Press.

———. 1964. *Civilization in transition: Collected works.* Vol. 10. Trans. R. F. C. Hull. Bollingen Series XX. Princeton, N.J.: Princeton University Press.

———. 1958. *Psychology and religion: West and East: Collected works.* Vol. 11. Trans. R. F. C. Hull. Bollingen Series XX. Princeton, N.J.: Princeton University Press.

———. 1967. *Psychology and alchemy: Collected works.* Vol. 12. Trans. R. F. C. Hull. Bollingen Series XX. Princeton, N.J.: Princeton University Press.

———. 1968. *Alchemical studies: Collected works.* Vol. 13. Trans. R. F. C. Hull. Bollingen Series XX. Princeton, N.J.: Princeton University Press.

———. 1963. *Mysterium coniunctionis: Collected works.* Vol. 14. Trans. R. F. C. Hull. Bollingen Series XX. Princeton, N.J.: Princeton University Press.

———. 1966. *The spirit in man, art, and literature: Collected works.* Vol. 15. Trans. R. F. C. Hull. Bollingen Series XX. Princeton, N.J.: Princeton University Press.

————. 1967. *The practice of psychotherapy: Collected works*. Vol. 16. Trans. R. F. C. Hull. Bollingen Series XX. Princeton, N.J.: Princeton University Press.

————. 1954. *The development of personality: Collected works*. Vol. 17. Trans. R. F. C. Hull. Bollingen Series XX. Princeton, N.J.: Princeton University Press.

————. 1954. *The symbolic life: Collected works*. Vol. 18. Trans. R. F. C. Hull. Bollingen Series XX. Princeton, N.J.: Princeton University Press.

————. 1978. *Psychology and the East*. Trans. R. F. C. Hull. Princeton, N.J.: Princeton University Press.

————. 1965. *Memories, dreams, reflections*. New York: Vintage.

Jung, E., and M. von Franz. 1960/1986. *The grail legend*. Boston: Sigo Press.

Kaestle, C. 1983. *Pillars of the republic: Common schools and American society, 1760–1860*. New York: Hill and Wang.

Kelly, G. 1955/1963. *A theory of personality: The psychology of personal constructs*. New York: Norton.

Kelsey, M. 1984. Jung as philosopher and theologian. In *Jung in modern perspective: The master and his legacy*. Ed. R. Papadopoulos and G. Saayman, 182–92. Lindfield, Australia: Unity Press.

Kirsch, J. 1995. Transference. In *Jungian analysis*. Ed. M. Stein, 170–209. Chicago, Illinois: Open Court.

Klein, M. 1932/1975. *The psychoanalysis of children*. Trans. A. Strachey. New York: Delacorte Press.

Kliebard, H. 1995. *The struggle for the American curriculum, 1893–1958*. 2nd ed. New York: Routledge.

Kniker, C. 1985. *Teaching about religion in the public schools*. Bloomington, Ind.: Phi Delta Kappa.

————. 1990. Teacher Education and Religion: The role of foundations courses in preparing students to teach about religions. *Religion and Public Education* 17 (2): 203–22.

Knox, J. 1998. Transference and countertransference. In *Contemporary Jungian analysis: Post-Jungian perspectives from the society of analytic psychology*. Ed. I. Alister and C. Hauke, 73–84. London: Routledge.

Kohlberg, L. 1987. *Child psychology and childhood education: A cognitive-developmental view*. New York: Longman.

Kohut, H. 1984. *How does analysis cure?* Chicago: University of Chicago Press.

Kozol, J. 1991. *Savage inequalities: Children in American schools*. New York: Harper.

Kuhn, T. 1970. *The structure of scientific revolutions*. Chicago: University of Chicago Press.

Laing, R. D. 1967. *The politics of experience*. New York: Pantheon Books.

Lauter, E., and C. Rupprecht. 1985. *Feminist archetypal theory: Interdiscipli-nary re-visions of Jungian thought.* Knoxville: University of Tennessee Press.

Lemon v. Kurtzman, 403 US 602 (1971).

Levinson, D. 1978. *The seasons of a man's life.* New York: Ballantine.

Lipman, M. 1988. *Philosophy goes to school.* Philadelphia: Temple University Press.

——. 1996. In *Philosophical documents in education.* Ed. R. Reed and R. Johnson, 241–72. New York: Longman.

Lortie, D. 1975. *Schoolteacher: A sociological study.* Chicago: University of Chicago Press.

Maccoby, E., and C. Jacklin. 1976. *The psychology of sex differences.* Stanford, Calif.: Stanford University Press.

Macdonald, J. 1975. A transcendental developmental ideology of education. In *Heightened consciousness, cultural revolution, and curriculum theory.* Ed. W. Pinar, 85–116. Berkeley, Calif.: McCutchan Publishing.

——. 1995. *Theory as a prayerful act: The collected essays of James P. Mac-donald.* Ed. B. Macdonald. New York: Peter Lang.

Machtiger, H. 1995. Reflections on the transference/countertransference process with borderline patients. In *Transference/countertransference.* Ed. N. Schwartz-Salant and M. Stein, 119–46. Wilmette, Ill.: Chiron Publications.

Marcuse, H. 1962. *Eros and civilization: A philosophical inquiry into Freud.* New York: Vintage.

Marsden, G. 1997. *The outrageous idea of Christian scholarship.* New York: Oxford University Press.

Marshak, M. 1998. The intersubjective nature of analysis. In *Contemporary Jungian anaylsis: Post-Jungian perspectives from the society of analytic psy-chology.* Ed. I Alister and C. Hauke, 57–72. London: Routledge.

Martin, L., and J. Goss, eds. 1985. *Essays on the study of Jung and religion.* Lanham, Md.: University Press of America.

Marty, M. 1970. *Righteous empire: The Protestant experience in America.* New York: Dial Press.

——. 1987. *Religion and republic: The American circumstance.* Boston: Bea-con Press.

Marx, K., and F. Engels. 1978. *The Marx-Engels reader.* Ed. R. Tucker. New York: W. W. Norton.

Maslow, A. 1968. *Toward a psychology of being.* 2nd ed. Princeton, N.J.: Van Nostrand.

——. 1970. *Religions, values, and peak-experiences.* New York: Penguin Books.

Mattingly, P. 1975. *The classless profession: American schoolmen in the nineteenth century.* New York: New York University Press.

Mattoon, M. 1984. *Understanding dreams.* Dallas, Tx.: Spring Press.

———. 1985. *Jungian psychology in perspective.* New York: Free Press.

Mayes, C. 1998a. The Holmes reports: Perils and possibilities. *Teaching and Teacher Education: An International Journal of Educational Research and Studies* 14 (8): 775–92.

———. 1998b. The use of contemplative practices in teacher education. *Encounter: Education for Meaning and Social Justice* 11 (3): 17–31.

———. 1999. Reflecting on the archetypes of teaching. *Teaching Education* 10 (2): 3–16.

———. 2001a. A transpersonal developmental model for teacher reflectivity. *Journal of Curriculum Studies* 33 (4): 477–93.

———. 2001b. Cultivating spiritual reflectivity in teachers. *Teacher Education Quarterly* 28 (2): 5–22.

———. 2002a. Personal and archetypal aspects of transference and countertransference in the classroom. *Encounter: Education for Meaning and Social Justice* 15 (2): 34–49.

———. 2002b. The teacher as an archetype of spirit. *Journal of Curriculum Studies* 34 (6): 699–718.

———. 2003a. *Seven curricular landscapes: An approach to the holistic curriculum.* Lanham, Md.: University Press of America.

———. 2003b. Foundations of an archetypal pedagogy. *Psychological Perspectives: A Semiannual Journal of Jungian Thought* (C. G. Institute of Los Angeles) 46:104–16.

———. 2003c. Alchemy and the teacher. *Teacher Education Quarterly* 30 (3): 81–98.

———. 2005. *Teaching mysteries: Foundations of a spiritual pedagogy.* Lanham, Md.: University Press of America.

———. In press, b. Teaching and time: Foundations of a temporal pedagogy. *Teacher Education Quarterly.*

———. In press, c. The teacher as shaman. *Journal of Curriculum Studies.*

Mayes, C., and P. Blackwell-Mayes. 2002. Spiritual reflectivity among Mormon teachers and administrators in public schools. *International Journal of Leadership in Education* 5 (2): 129–48.

Mayes, C., and S. Ferrin. 2001. The beliefs of spiritually committed public school teachers regarding religious expression in the classroom. *Religion and Education* 28 (1): 75–94.

McLynn, F. 1997. *Carl Jung: A biography.* London: Black Swan.

Messerli, J. 1976. *Horace Mann: A biography*. Cambridge, Mass.: Harvard University Press.

Miller, J. 1988. *The Holistic Curriculum*. Toronto, Ontario: The Ontario Institute for Studies in Education.

Miller, J., and W. Seller. 1985. *Curriculum: Perspectives and practice*. New York: Longman.

Mitchell, R. 2003. Personal communication. October.

Nash, R. 1999. *Faith, hype and clarity: Teaching about religion in American schools and colleges*. New York: Teachers College Press.

National Commission on Excellence in Education. 1983. *A nation at risk*. Washington, D.C.: Government Printing office.

Neumann, E. 1954. *The origins and history of consciousness*. Vols. 1–2. New York: Harper Brothers.

——. 1969. *Depth psychology and a new ethic*. New York: P.G. Putnam and Sons.

Noll, R. 1994. *The Jung cult: Origins of a charismatic movement*. Princeton, N.J.: Princeton University Press.

Nord, W. 1994. Ten suggestions for teaching about religion. In *Finding common ground: A first amendment guide to religion and public education*. Ed. C. Haynes and O. Thomas. Nashville, Tenn.: Vanderbilt University, Freedom Forum First Amendment Center.

——. 1995. *Religion and American education: Rethinking a national dilemma*. Chapel Hill: University of North Carolina Press.

O'Reilley, M. 1998. *Radical presence: Teaching as a contemplative activity*. Portsmouth, N.H.: Boynton/Cook.

Odajnyk, V. 1976. *Jung and politics: The political and social ideas of C. G. Jung*. New York: Harper and Row.

——. 1993. *Gathering the light: A psychology of meditation*. Boston: Shambhala.

Ornstein, A., and F. Hunkins. 1988. *Curriculum: Foundations, principles, and issues*. Boston: Allyn and Bacon.

Orr, D. 1988. Transference and countertransference: A historical survey. In *Essential papers on counter-transference*. Ed. B. Wolstein, 91–110. New York: New York University Press.

Paden, W. 1985. Jung and the phenomenology of religion. In *Essays on the study of Jung and religion*. Ed. L. Martin and J. Goss, 45–69. Lanham, Md.: University Press of America.

Palmer, M. 1997. *Freud and Jung on religion*. London: Routledge.

Palmer, P. 1983. *To know as we are known: A spirituality of education*. San Francisco, California: Harper Collins.

———. 1998. *The courage to teach: Exploring the inner landscape of a teacher's life.* San Francisco: Jossey-Bass.

Papadopoulos, R. 1991. Jung and the concept of the other. In *Jung in modern perspective: The master and his legacy.* Ed. R. Papadopoulos and G. Saayman, (pp.). Lindfield, Australia: Unity Press.

Papadopoulos, R., and G. Saayman, eds. 1984. *Jung in modern perspective: The master and his legacy.* Lindfield, Australia: Unity Press.

Piaget, J., and B. Inhelder. 1969. *The psychology of the child.* New York: Basic Books.

Progoff, I. 1955. *Jung's psychology and its social meaning.* New York: Grove Press.

Rama, S., R. Ballentine, and S. Ajaya. 1976. *Yoga and psychotherapy: The evolution of consciousness.* New Honesdale, Pa.: Himalayan Institute.

Ravitch, D. 1983. *The troubled crusade: American education, 1945–1980.* New York: Basic Books.

———. 2000. *Left back: A century of failed school reforms.* New York: Simon and Schuster.

Reinsmith, W. 1992. *Archetypal forms in teaching: A continuum.* New York: Greenwood Press.

Richards, P., and A. Bergin. 1998. *A spiritual strategy for counseling and psychotherapy.* Washington, D.C.: American Psychological Association.

Riegel, K. 1979. *Foundations of dialectical psychology.* New York: Academic Press.

Riordan, C. 1997. *Equality and achievement: An introduction to the sociology of education.* New York: Longman.

Rizutto, A-M. 1979. *The birth of the living God: A psychoanalytic study.* Chicago: University of Chicago Press.

Rogoff, B. 1984. *Everyday cognition: Its development and social context.* Cambridge, Mass.: Harvard University Press.

Rummelhart, D. 1980. Schemata: The building blocks of cognition. In *Theoretical issues in reading comprehension.* Ed. R. Spiro, B. Bruce, and W. Brewer, 125–67. Hillside, N.J.: Lawrence Erlbaum.

Samuels, A. 1997. *Jung and the post-Jungians.* London: Routledge.

———. 2001. *Politics on the couch: Citizenship and the internal life.* London: Routledge.

Sartre, J. 1956. *Being and nothingness: An essay on phenomenological ontology.* New York: Philosophical Library.

Satir, V. 1967. *Conjoint family therapy: A guide to theory and technique.* Palo Alto, Calif.: Science and Behavior Books.

Schwartz-Salant, N. 1995. Archetypal factors underlying sexual acting-out in the transference/countertransference process. In *Transference/countertransference*. Ed. N. Schwartz-Salant and M. Stein, 1–30. Wilmette, Ill.: Chiron Publications.

Sheridan, M., C. Wilmer, and L. Atcheson. 1994. Inclusion of content on religion and spirituality in the social work curriculum: A study of faculty views. *Journal of Social Work Education* 30 (3): 363–76.

Sklar, K. 1973. *Catherine Beecher: A study in American domesticity*. New Haven, Conn.: Yale University Press.

Spiegelman, J. 1985. *Hinduism and Jungian psychology*. Tempe, Ariz.: New Falcon.

———. 1996. *Psychotherapy as a mutual process*. Tempe, Ariz.: New Falcon.

Spring, J. 1976. *Educating the worker-citizen*. New York: McGraw-Hill.

Staude, J-R. 1981. *The adult development of C. G. Jung*. Boston : Routledge and Kegan Paul.

Stein, M., ed. 1984. *Jungian analysis*. Boulder, Colo.: Shambhala.

Stein, M. 1995. "Power, shamanism, and maieutics in the countertransference." In N. Schwartz-Salant & M. Stein (Eds.). *Transference/countertransference* (pp. 67–88). Wilmette, Ill.: Chiron.

Steinberg, W. 1990. *Circle of care: Clinical issues in psychotherapy*. Toronto, Ont.: Inner City Books.

Stevens, A. 1999. *On Jung: An updated edition with a reply to Jung's critics*. 2nd ed. Princeton, N.J.: Princeton University Press.

Stevens, W. 1990. *The palm at the end of the mind: Selected poems and a play*. Ed. Holly Stevens. New York: Vintage.

Stokes, D. 1997. Called to teach: Exploring the worldview of called prospective teachers during their preservice teacher education experience. Unpublished PhD diss., University of Utah, Salt Lake City.

Stone, L. 1988. The transference-countertransference complex. In *Essential papers on counter-transference*. Ed. B. Wolstein, 270–81. New York: New York University Press.

Tillich, P. 1956/1987. *The essential Tillich: An anthology of the writings of Paul Tillich*. Ed. E. Church. New York: Macmillan.

———. 1957. *Dynamics of faith*. New York: Harper and Row.

———. 1959. *Theology of culture*. Ed. R. Kimball. New York: Oxford University Press.

———. 1976. *The shaking of the foundations*. New York: Scribners.

Tower, L. 1988. The meanings and uses of countertransference. In *Essential papers on counter-transference*. Ed. B. Wolstein, 131–57. New York: New York University Press.

Tremmel, R. 1993. Zen and the art of reflective practice in teacher education. *Harvard Educational Journal* 63 (4): 434–58.

Trostli, R. 1991. "Educating as an art: The Waldorf approach." In *New directions in education: Selections from* Holistic Education Review. Ed. R. Miller, 338–53. Brandon, Vt.: Holistic Education Press.

Tyack, D. 1974. *The one best system: A history of American urban education.* Cambridge, Mass.: Harvard University Press.

Ulanov, A. 1999. *Religion and the spiritual in Carl Jung.* New York: Paulist Press.

Valli, L. 1990. Moral approaches to reflective practice. In *Encouraging reflective practice in education: An analysis of issues and programs.* Ed. R. Clift, W. Houston, and M. Pugach, 39–56. New York: Teachers College Press.

Van Manen, M. 1982. Phenomenological pedagogy. *Curriculum Inquiry* 12 (3): 283–99.

———. 1990. Moral approaches to reflective practice. In *Encouraging reflective practice in education: An analysis of issues and programs.* Ed. R. Clift, W. Houston, and M. Pugach, 20–35. New York: Teachers College Press.

Vaughan, F. 1985. *The inward arc: Healing and wholeness in psychotherapy and spirituality.* Boston, Mass.: New Science Library.

Vedfelt, O. 2001. *The dimensions of dreams: From Freud and Jung to Boss, Perls, and R.E.M.—a comprehensive sourcebook.* New York: Fromm International.

Vivas, E., and M. Krieger, eds. 1953. *The problems of aesthetics.* New York: Reinhart.

Von Franz, M.-L. 1970/1987. *The interpretation of fairy tales.* Boston: Shambhala.

———. 1984. Meaning and order: Concerning meeting points and differences between depth psychology and physics. In *Jung in modern perspective: The master and his legacy.* Ed. R. Papadopoulos and G. Saayman, 268–86. Lindfield, Australia: Unity Press.

Von Franz, M.-L., and J. Hillman. 1971. *Lectures on Jung's typology.* Dallas, Tx.: Spring Publications.

Warshaw, T. 1986. Preparation for teaching about religions in public schools. *Religious Education* 81 (1): 79–92.

Wehr, G. 2002. *Jung and Steiner: The birth of a new psychology.* Great Barrington, Mass.: Anthroposophic Press.

Weisinger, H. 1974. The myth and ritual approach to Shakespearian tragedy. In *Twentieth century criticism: The major statements.* Ed. W. J. Handy and M. Westbrook, 290–302. New York: Macmillan.

Wexler, P. 1996. *Holy sparks: Social theory, education and religion.* New York: St. Martin's Press.

Wheelwright, P. 1974. Poetry, myth, and reality. In *Twentieth century criticism: The major statements.* Ed. W. J. Handy and M. Westbrook, 252–266. New York: Macmillan.

White, V. 1952/1982. *God and the unconscious.* Dallas, Tx.: Spring Publications.

Whitmore, D. 1986. *Psychosynthesis in education: A guide to the joy of learning.* Rochester, Vt.: Destiny Books.

Wickes, F. 1927/1966. *The inner world of childhood.* Englewood Cliffs, N.J.: Prentice Hall.

Wiedemann, F. 1995. Mother, father, teacher, sister: Transference/countertransference with women in the first stage of animus development. In *Transference/countertransference.* Ed. N. Schwartz-Salant and M. Stein, 175–90. Wilmette, Ill.: Chiron Publications.

Wilber, K. 1983. *A sociable God: A brief introduction to a transcendental sociology.* New York: McGraw-Hill.

———. 1996. *A brief history of everything.* Boston: Shambhala.

———. 2000. *Integral psychology.* Boston: Shambhala.

Winnicott, D. W. 1988. Counter-transference. In *Essential papers on countertransference.* Ed. B. Wolstein, 262–69. New York: New York University Press.

———. 1990. On transference. In *Essential papers on transference.* Ed. A. Esman, 246–51. New York: New York University Press.

———. 1992. *Psychoanalytic explorations.* Ed. C. Winnicott, R. Shepherd, and M. Davis. Cambridge, Mass.: Harvard University Press.

Wolstein, B. 1988. The pluralism of perspectives on countertransference. In *Essential papers on counter-transference.* Ed. B. Wolstein, 339–54. New York: New York University Press.

———. 1988. Observations of countertransference. In *Essential papers on counter-transference.* Ed. B. Wolstein, 225–261. New York: New York University Press.

Woodman, M. 1990. *The ravaged bridegroom: Masculinity in women.* Toronto, Ont.: Inner City Books.

———. 1995. Transference and countertransference in analysis dealing with eating disorders. In *Transference/countertransference.* Ed. N. Schwartz-Salant and M. Stein, 53–66. Wilmette, Ill.: Chiron Publications.

Wrightsman, L. 1994. *Adult personality development: Theories and concepts.* Thousand Oaks, Calif.: Sage.

Zinn, H. 1990. *A people's history of the United States.* New York: Harper Perennial.

INDEX

ABOUT THE AUTHOR

Clifford Mayes is associate professor of education, Brigham Young University, Provo, Utah. Professor Mayes holds a Ph.D. in Cultural Foundations of Education from the University of Utah and a Psy.D. in Educational Psychology from the Southern California University for Professional Studies. In addition to his teaching and research, he also maintains a Jungian-oriented counseling practice. He is the author of *Seven Curricular Landscapes: An Approach to the Holistic Curriculum* (University Press of America, 2004) and *Teaching Mysteries: Foundations of a Spiritual Pedagogy* (University Press of America, 2005).